*BOUDDI: "HEART-LIKE POUNDING OF WAVES ON THE BEACH."*

# SIGNPOSTS TO THE PAST

## STORIES OF PLACES AND STREETS OF BOUDDI PENINSULA

# BEVERLEY J. RUNCIE

BA, GRAD DIP ED, M LIB

**Rockpossum Publishing**

Written by Beverely J Runcie
© 2025 Myfanwy J Webb & Kalena V Webb

All rights reserved.

Cover design by Kalena V Webb
Designed and edited by Kalena V Webb
Edited by Myfanwy J Webb

ISBN-978-0-6452775-4-8

**Reproduction and Communication for educational purposes**

The Australian *Copyright Act 1968* (the Act) allows a maximum of one chapter or 10% of the pages of this publication, whichever is the greater, to be reproduced and/or communicated by any educational institution for its educational purposes provided that the educational institution (or the body that administers it) has given a renumeration notice to Copyright Agency Limited (CAL) under the Act.

**Reproduction and Communication for other purposes**

Except as permitted under the Act (for example a fair dealing for the purpoes of study, research, criticism or review) no part of the publication may be reproduced, stored in a retrieval system, communicated or transmitted in any form or by any means without prior written permission. All inquiries should be made to the publisher.

Rockpossum Publishing has no responsibility for the persistence or accuracy of URLS for external or third-party internet websites reffered to in this publication and does not guarantee that any content on such websites is, or will remain accurate or appropriate.

# SIGNPOSTS TO THE PAST

## AUTHOR

Beverley Joan Runcie, BA, GRAD DIP ED, M LIB

Prior to completing this book, Beverley Joan Runcie, 83 of Killcare, NSW, died in September 2022 after an unexpected illness. Her qualifications include; Bachelor of Arts (Sydney), Graduate Diploma of Education (Kuring-gai) and Master of Librarianship (NSW). She was Head of Division/ Assistant Principal Dept. of TAFE, Sydney Technical College 1980-90s.

Beverley taught disadvantaged schoolchildren in the East End, London, who thought she was a wonderful teacher. She later taught adults how to become librarians.

Beverley had a passion for ancient history and with her husband Donald, visited many ancient historical sites around the world. She also educated herself about Indigenous culture. Beverley was also highly knowledgeable and passionate about geography, geology and botany.

# CONTENTS

**I**
ACKNOWLEDGEMENTS

**III**
PREFACE

**1**
CHAPTER 1: INTRODUCTION

**2**
*1.1 GEOGRAPHICAL LIMITS OF BOUDDI PENINSULA*

**2**
*1.2 BRIEF HISTORY OF PLACE AND STREET NAMING IN AUSTRALIA*

**4-5**
*1.3 EARLY EUROPEAN SETTLEMENT AND INDIGENOUS NAMES*

**7**
CHAPTER 2: THE BOUDDI PENINSULA: A BRIEF HISTORY

**8-9**
*2.1 ABORIGINAL PEOPLE: THE FIRST PEOPLE ON BOUDDI PENINSULA*

**10-11**
*2.2 EARLY EUROPEAN SETTLEMENT ON THE BOUDDI PENINSULA*

**12-13**
*2.3 BOUDDI ABORGINAL NAMES*

**15-17**
CHAPTER 3: NEED FOR STANDARDISATION OF PLACE & STREET NAMES

**19 - 61**
CHAPTER 4: LISTING OF PLACE AND STREET NAMES A TO B

**63-139**
CHAPTER 5: LISTING OF PLACE AND STREET NAMES R TO Z

**141 - 189**
CHAPTER 6: LISTING OF PLACE AND STREET NAMES R TO Z

**191**
APPENDIX

**192-195**
*APPENDIX 1: MAPS OF ESTATE SUBDIVSION*

**196**
*APPENDIX 2: ROAD TYPES OF BOUDDI PENINSULA*

**196-197**
*APPENDIX 3: PLACE NAME TYPES OF BOUDDI PENINSULA*

**198-203**
*APPENDIX 4: MAPS OF BOUDDI PENINSULA*

**204-213**
REFERENCES

**214-216**
INDEX

# Acknowledgements

I wish to acknowledge the Traditional Custodians of this land. I pay respects to the Elders, past, present and future and recognise the continuing connection and contribution to this land.

Aboriginal and Torres Strait Islander readers please be advised that the following contains images, names, information, and other material that involve people who have passed away.

Many people have been involved in this project and I have been most grateful for their input and advice. Thank you to Dawn Springett, Helen Menzies for assistance with the setup of the book. For reading and commenting on the draft I thank Gwen Dundon, Geoff Potter, Phil Donnelly (including continued support) Robyn Warburton and John Runcie. Thank you to the following people who assisted with information, Deb Holloman, Helen Monks, David and Helen Dufty. Gary Nipperess, Cindy Dobbins, Kaye Shaw.

I apologise if I have omitted anyone. Be assured I have valued your help.

I take responsibility for any errors or omissions.

The above is transcribed from Beverley's handwritten notes after her passing which may have omissions of people and incorrect spelling of names.

## ABBREVIATIONS

**CC BY 2.0** = CREATIVE COMMONS BY ATTRIBUTION 2.0 GENERIC

**CC BY-SA 3.0** = ATTRIBUTION-SHAREALIKE 3.0 UNPORTED

**CC BY 4.0** = CREATIVE COMMONS ATTRIBUTION 4.0 INTERNATIONAL LICENCE

**NPWS** = NSW NATIONAL PARKS AND WILDLIFE SERVICE

*Putty Beach at Killcare, 2024.* Photo: Myfanwy J. Webb.

## EDITOR, PHOTOGRAPHY

**Dr Myfanwy Jane Webb, BSc, Hons, PhD**

When Mum was ill in hospital, not knowing if she could hear me, I told her I would finish her book for her. She has given my daughter and I the priceless experience of feeling like the three of us are working together on her book, after she has passed. Kalena and I would often say to each other "Yes, Nan would love this". Privileged to provide photographs, edit and add Indigenous content, I am very proud of Mum's significant work and my daughter's artistic talent and precision eye for detail.

My career as medical researcher, animal behaviourist and biologist has resulted in the publication of books, book chapters, academic papers and magazine articles. My photography includes selling images through I-Stock/Getty Images, publishing magazine articles with my accompanying photographs and creating calendars and diaries.

## EDITOR, BOOK DESIGNER

**Miss Kalena Violet Webb, BA, GRAD DIP**

I am so lucky to have given the opportunity to work on this book. Nan's love of history and geography have influenced me greatly. I am grateful to have grown up here and appreciate such a beautiful part of the world. I have fond memories of my brother Jeremy and I staying over at Nan and Pop's place at Killcare, exploring the bush behind their house where we would search for water dragon lizards and look down to Killcare Beach below.

I am a graduate in anthropology, Critical Indigenous Studies, and an artist. I have published illustrations in the University of Technology Sydney Animal Handling Guidebook, produced infographics for the Durumbura Dhurabang Stakeholder Biocultural Project and have been successful in designing an ecological pitch for the new housing development, "Midtown Macpark".

# Preface

Imagine if there were no place names or street names. Where would the postman deliver your mail? Would an ambulance be able to find you? How would you tell your friends or tradespeople how to find your home? Think of the confusion this would cause. Not only do we need place and street names, but we often regard them with affection. Most people know the place where they were born, and many know the place and street where they lived as children. Where do you live now and in which street? Have you ever wondered how these places and streets acquired their names? This book is different from traditional local history. It looks at the history of the place names and street names of the Bouddi Peninsula. That history begins with some of the place names given to the area by Indigenous Australian people before white settlement and subsequent place names given in the twentieth century. Street names were assigned only from the early twentieth century as in the early days all transport was by water and there were no formal roads on the Peninsula until the initial land holdings were subdivided. Only a few places named by the original Aboriginal people of the Bouddi area survive. Also, in the twentieth century some Bouddi streets were named using Aboriginal words which were not of this area.

Place names and street names all have a story to tell. For instance: Did you know a group of Aboriginal people saved a boy after witnessing a shipwreck off Box Head in 1809? Did you know the Rip Bridge was called 'the bridge to nowhere' when it began construction? Did you know Turo Park was named after Turo Downes an Aboriginal man who lived in the area for many years and was loved by all? Did you know at the end of Bombi Road South there was a RAAF Radar Station situated on the cliff top during World War II which monitored sea and air movements? Perhaps you may wonder why and when Killcare was given its singular name.

Looking at the history of the names can tell us much about the culture and society of the people who have lived there. Historians for the large part have neglected writing about place and street names and the history attached to them. I believe it is important to capture this history. I also believe it can provide a strong feeling of community connection for present readers, especially those with a Bouddi link.

What you will find under each place or street heading will be who named it, why it was named this, what the name means, when it was first used and some interesting history about it.

Beverley Runcie BA, Grad Dip Ed, Masters Lib

CHAPTER ONE

# 1
# INTRODUCTION

[ *Introduction*

# 1.1 - GEOGRAPHICAL LIMITS OF BOUDDI PENINSULA

The Bouddi Peninsula lies on the north side of the entrance to Broken Bay in New South Wales. It is approximately 100 kilometres by road and only 41 kilometres 'as the crow flies' from Sydney CBD. The Peninsula is largely a plateau rising to its highest point of 160 metres at Mt Bouddi within the Bouddi National Park. It has spectacular views over the Pacific Ocean to Manly, Palm Beach, Broken Bay, and Pittwater to the south and Brisbane Water to the north and west.

The Peninsula includes the small communities of Hardys Bay, Killcare, Killcare Heights, Pretty Beach and Wagstaffe. Most of the area, however, is taken up by the 1532-hectare Bouddi National Park which begins at south MacMasters Beach and stretches to Box Head, about 10 kilometres in distance. Being a peninsula, the area attracts no through traffic. This is one reason why it still has a village atmosphere, the population appreciating being surrounded by the Bouddi National Park, Brisbane Water, and the Pacific Ocean.

# 1.2 - BRIEF HISTORY OF PLACE AND STREET NAMING IN AUSTRALIA

## WHY IS NAMING IMPORTANT?

The study of place names which is called toponymy can tell us much about the history and the people of an area over time. The naming of places began with the need to communicate with each other, especially in rural areas. For example: 'We'll meet you at Rocky Creek', or 'Move the sheep over to One Tree Hill'. People have strong personal attachments to place names as they share memories with that place. Laura Kostanski put it neatly:

'The naming of places is… a core human activity. Places without names are merely spaces', and Ruth Wajnryb stated: 'I've come to see place names as a window of the world of the people who were here before us…This doesn't mean the stories have to be conclusively verified. There are over a dozen theories for example, about how Dee Why got its name!'

Some of the place and street names of the Bouddi Peninsula fall into this category and perhaps we may never know their true origin. People identify with place and along with their name and date of birth, place of birth will be an integral part of their identity all their life.

Odonymy is the study of street names and is a sub discipline of toponymy. Street names often reflect official views at the time of naming and can tell us something of the political, social, cultural, and historical events of the time. They can give us another window into local history. Apart from place names and street names we should also consider and include in any listing micro-toponyms which are names for a small part of a larger named entity. For example, in the Bouddi Peninsula, 'The Yum Yum Tree' and 'The Dog Track' are local but unofficial names. It is important to include them as they are a rich source of history of place.

Place and street names have always been part of an area's heritage. If the origins of these names are recorded it adds to an area's idiosyncratic history. Most of the place names and street names (Appendix 3) in the Bouddi Peninsula have only been allocated in the twentieth century; however, the origin of some are already lost. Why is Putty Beach called Putty? Why is Blythe Street called Blythe? The origins of some may never be found.

[PREVIOUS SPREADS]

*Sunset Box Head, 2024.* Photo: Myfanwy J. Webb.

*Bouddi Coastal Walk, 2024.* Photo: Myfanwy J. Webb.

*Little Tallow Beach, 2024.* Photo: Myfanwy J. Webb.

*Introduction*

[IMAGES] (ABOVE)

*Location of Bouddi Peninsula, 2025.* Photo: OpenStreetMap, CC BY 4.0.

[ *Introduction*

# "I LIKE THE NATIVE NAMES, AS PARRAMATTA, AND ILLAWARRA, AND WOOLLOOMOOLOO; NANDOWRA, WOOGARORA, BULKOMATTA..."

## 1.3 EARLY EUROPEAN SETTLEMENT AND INDIGENOUS NAMES

When Europeans first arrived in Australia and began naming places it was more correct to say that they were 'renaming' as the Indigenous Australian people had already named the most significant features of the landscape. So, Australia has two naming systems, an Indigenous system, and an introduced system.

Understandably, the early settlers were keen to assign European names to places. Captain James Cook named Botany Bay and Governor Arthur Phillip named Sydney (originally, he preferred New Albion, Albion being an ancient name for England, but Phillip changed it in honour of the British Home Secretary Lord Sydney). They were following customs of the day, naming places after natural features, or after people in power in England. English names were also chosen for nostalgic reasons, for example the naming of places after a hometown or the name of a previous house in England. To be fair, Governor Phillip was the first to approve and encourage the use of Indigenous names and was responsible for changing the name of Rose Hill to Parramatta which means 'place of eels'.

Explorers and surveyors and later settlers were the first Europeans to name geographical features, and these then appeared on maps. The naming of places remained very ad hoc in the early days of the settlement until it was found that there were many places being given the same name which caused confusion. In many of the early land grants, where it was required that the land that they were applying for be described, the grantees would often add in the Indigenous name used for the area. One of these was Patrick Mulhall who described his land at what is now Wagstaffe, 'Gorangorang' (Kourung Gourung) in 1841.

By 1828 the Governor had informed the Surveyor General Sir Thomas Mitchell that the same names should not be given to several places in different parts of the colony and that Indigenous names be adopted where possible. The Governor had the final say as to the adoption of all names. Surveyor-General Mitchell championed the use of Indigenous names, and he was responsible for much of the naming until his death in 1855. He saw a practical reason for this and wrote: 'The great convenience of using native names is obvious. For instance, so long as any of the Aborigines can be found in the neighbourhood…future travellers may verify my map. Whereas new names are of no use in this respect'. Mitchell's directive greatly influenced the surveyors who mapped the country as settlement spread.

It should be noted that the early recorders of Aboriginal place names and words, written down by non-Aboriginal people, were not linguists and very often not well educated. Often the written word as written by the early recorders bears little resemblance to the Aboriginal word and there is confusion over pronunciation.

John Dunmore Lang, a Scottish-born Australian Presbyterian minister, writer, historian, politician and activist, expressed his opinion by writing a poem 'Colonial Nomenclature' in 1824. Here is part of it:

# Introduction

*I like the native names, as Parramatta,*
*And Illawarra, and Woolloomooloo;*
*Nandowra, Woogarora, Bulkomatta,*
*Tomah, Toongabbie, Mittagong, Meroo;*
*Buckobble, Cumleroy, and Goolingatta,*
*The Warragumby, Bargo, Burradoo;*
*Cookbundoon, Carrabaiga, Wingecarribbee,*
*The Wollondilly, Yurumbon, Bungarribee.*
*I hate your Goulburn Downs and Goulburn Plains,*
*And Goulburn River and the Goulburn Range,*
*And Mount Goulburn and Goulburn Vale! One's brains*
*I hate your Goulburn Downs and Goulburn Plains,*
*And Goulburn River and the Goulburn Range,*
*And Mount Goulburn and Goulburn Vale! One's brains*
*Are turned with Goulburns! Vile scorbutic mange*
*For immortality! Had I the reins*
*Of Government a fortnight, I would change*
*These Downing Street appellatives, and give*
*The country names that should deserve to live.*

Not everyone was enamored with the use of Indigenous names; one newspaper correspondent calling them 'uncouth and horrible', and many wanted to retain links with Britain. Unfortunately, most Indigenous place names were ignored and lost in the early days of the colony and with that their spiritual and cultural meanings were also lost.

In the twentieth century poems about Australian place names have been featured by such poets as: A.D. Hope in 'Country Places', John Manifold in 'The Map' and Douglas Stewart in 'Place Names'. Even the song, 'I've been everywhere' written by Geoff Mack in 1959 and sung by Lucky Starr in 1962 became very popular. They all delighted in the sound of the Aboriginal names.

In the 1990s The Geographical Names Board of NSW initiated a program to reinstate Aboriginal place names and implement a dual naming system. It wasn't until 2003 that the Australian National Placenames Survey began to reinstate Aboriginal names in Port Jackson and Botany Bay. Other regions in the ACT and NSW were encouraged to adopt this policy.

This is still hotly debated, both the Guringai (from the south side of the Hawkesbury River) and the Darkinjung claiming custodial ownership. However, even the name Guringai is in dispute with the Guringai people from the greater Port Stephens, Barrington and Forster areas who claim the name as theirs. It is possible that neighbouring groups such as the Sydney Language, Garigal, Dharuk and Awabakal may also have had some influence on the language originally spoken.

The second group are Aboriginal names which were given much later by non-Aboriginal people and were not necessarily original to the Bouddi area. In the 20th century Aboriginal names from other parts of Australia began to be used for place names, street names and house names.

They were often chosen for the pleasant sound of the name. On the Bouddi Peninsula these later names were Araluen, Bulkara, Bullimah, Burran, Nukara, Oroo, Otella, Owanda, Taworri and perhaps Putty. Interestingly the Gosford Shire Council officers in the 1960s and 1970s used a copy of 'Australian Aboriginal words and place names and their meanings', compiled by Sydney J. Endacott to select street and reserve names. The cover subtitle of this publication is: 'A choice of 3,000 pleasant-sounding words from which to choose an appropriate Australian name' and the council officers ticked the names they chose in the book. Unfortunately, the names are not attributed to any individual Aboriginal cultural or language group and often the meanings of the words are unverifiable. They appear to have been a mixture of South Australian and Victorian Aboriginal terms.

*Killcare Beach.* Artist: Kate E. York.

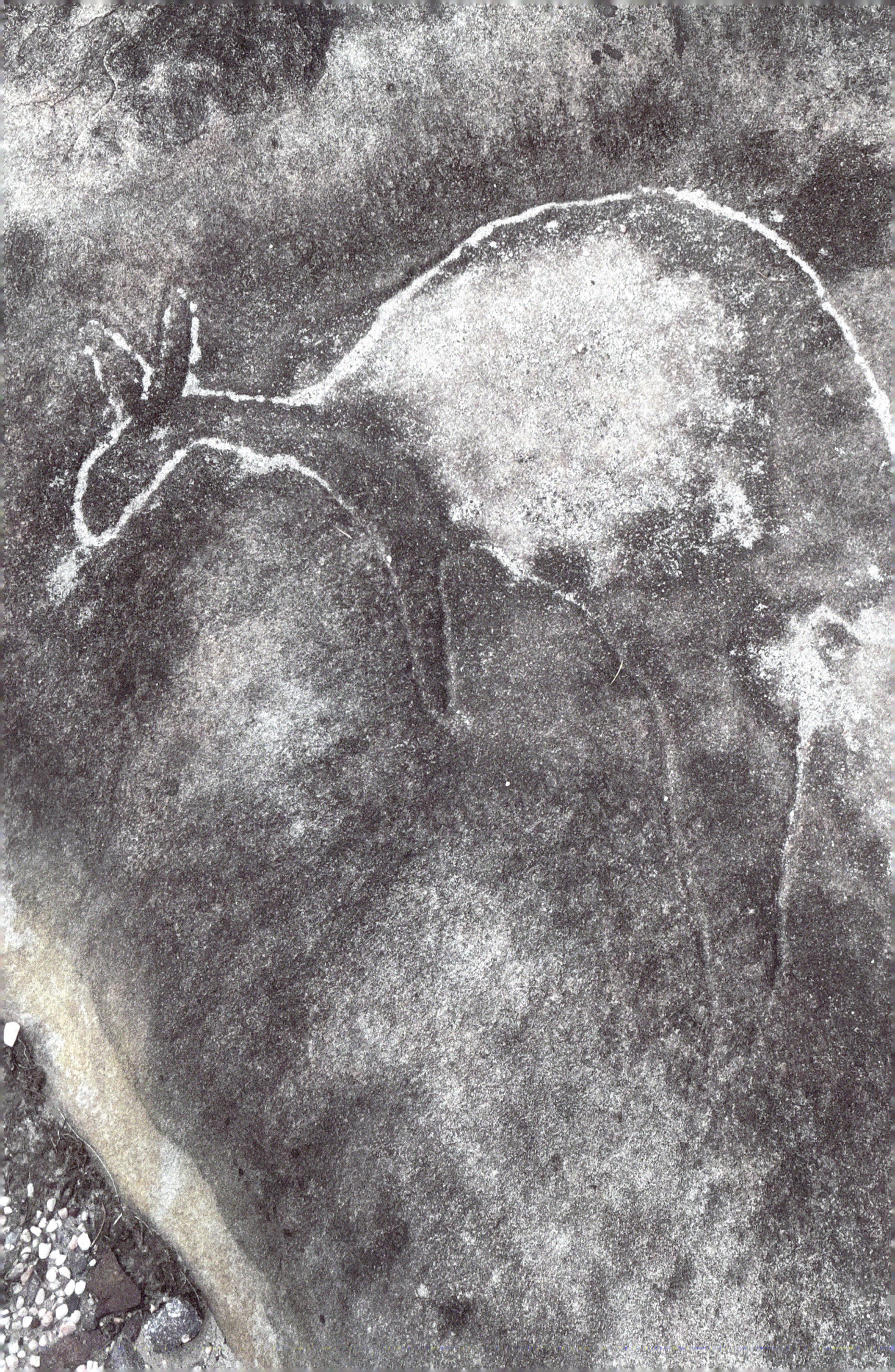

CHAPTER TWO

2

# THE BOUDDI PENINSULA:

# A BRIEF HISTORY

[ *The Bouddi Peninsula*

[PREVIOUS SPREAD]

*Kangaroo rock engraving, Bouddi National Park, 2024. Photo: Myfanwy J. Webb.*

*Aboriginal family in a canoe, 1920.* Modified from: Australian Missionary Anthropologists.

## 2.1 - ABORIGINAL PEOPLE: THE FIRST PEOPLE ON THE BOUDDI PENINSULA

The first settlers on the peninsula were Aboriginal people. Archaeological fieldwork in the nearby Mangrove Creek area has shown evidence of habitation going back 11,000 years. However, they were living around Bouddi probably much earlier when the Bouddi Peninsula was the Bouddi Plateau. The landscape about 18,000 years ago would have been quite different.

The coastline was about 20 kilometres east of what is now Broken Bay and there was a broad open plain up to the present cliff edge. Hawkesbury River consisted of small freshwater streams flowing over bedrock. By 7,000 years ago, warmer temperatures caused the large-scale melting of ice and the subsequent rise of the sea level. The water reached the present cliffs and spread up the river valleys forming the landscape we see today.

The Indigenous people who lived on the green wooded plains would have needed to move westward and to higher ground.[1] It is believed that Aboriginal people of the Sydney and Broken Bay area were living on the coast much earlier than we have proof for, however the rise of the sea has destroyed evidence of this. There are many signs still existing of the First People spread over the Bouddi Peninsula which give us some details of their life. There are rock engravings, cave art and middens along the seashore and in caves.

Which coastal Aboriginal cultural or language groups inhabited the land immediately north of the Hawkesbury River is debated. It is thought that Broken Bay is a place where different community group boundaries met with Brisbane Water, a part of the traditional lands of Darkinjung, Awakabal and Gurunggai Aboriginal people. Ever since the first fleet arrived there has been confusion surrounding these boundaries. Some or all of the cultural and language groups of the Eora, Garigal, Dharuk, Darkinjung, and the Awabakal from the north have had influence in the Brisbane Water area. The National Parks and Wildlife Service accepts that the Bouddi area is the traditional country of the Darkinjung Aboriginal people. According to the Darkinjung Local Aboriginal Land Council, the Darkinjung people's land extends 'from the Hawkesbury River in the south, Lake Macquarie in the north, the McDonald River and Wollombi up to Mt Yengo in the west and the Pacific Ocean in the East'.[2]

Relationships between the Indigenous people on both north and south sides of Broken Bay and the Hawkesbury (Deerubbin) River at the time of Sydney Cove settlement are known to be cooperative and unified. No doubt this was the case prior to 1770. In 1788, five weeks after settling, Governor Phillip set off with 40 men in a long boat to assess nearby countryside for settlement expansion.[3] The party negotiated the narrow entrance into Brisbane Water at Half Tide Rocks, and then almost immediately landed on a beach, most likely Lobster Beach. They found several bark huts with lobster carapaces lying about, and inside were several Aboriginal women, young and old. Terrified at first, the women relaxed after presents were offered. Further upstream they noticed introduced goods among the Aboriginal people such as trade beads and a European straw hat and people they had seen at Port Jackson were recognised.

*Aboriginal camp, 1905 (Port Macquarie).* Modified from: Thomas Dick.

In the year 1789, smallpox began to spread. By the time European settlers took up land in Brisbane Water in the 1820s the Aboriginal population was reduced considerably by smallpox and other introduced diseases such as influenza. Further decline continued as many Aboriginal people moved away from the settled areas when they were denied access to their traditional land by the new settlers. Unfortunately, it was inevitable that the Aboriginal communities dispersed and languages they spoke were largely lost.

It has been estimated that in 1788 at the time of the first European settlement there were more than 250 Aboriginal languages including 800 dialects spoken in Australia. In 2019 'only 13 traditional Indigenous languages are still acquired by children' and 'approximately another 100 or so are spoken to various degrees by older generations, with many of these languages at risk as Elders pass away.'[4] Although much of the traditional language has disappeared it remains important to retain what we can as it plays an important role in the sense of identity.

Unfortunately, it wasn't until the late 1800s before detailed anthropological research was undertaken. By this time the Aboriginal population was reduced to very small groups. This meant knowledge of cultural boundaries and language was very limited and often inaccurate.[5] The consequence for us considering language is that even the few original Aboriginal place names that we know of for the Bouddi Peninsula, we cannot always know their meaning for certain. The meaning of Aboriginal place names is closely linked with spiritual beliefs as spiritual belief and places are inextricably entwined. The importance of retaining Aboriginal names is emphasised by Dorothy Tunbridge when she said: 'After the passage of time, place names may be all that some Aboriginal communities have left of what was once their language'.[6]

*Margaret, Aboriginal girl, 1938 (Bomaderry).*
Modified from: Mitchell Library, State Library of NSW.

[ *The Bouddi Peninsula*

[IMAGE] (LEFT)

*Governor Phillip, 1937.*
Photo: Mitchell Library,
State Library of NSW.

## 2.2 – EARLY EUROPEAN SETTLEMENT ON THE BOUDDI PENINSULA

In March 1788 only five weeks after the arrival of the First Fleet in Port Jackson, Governor Arthur Phillip visited Broken Bay, Pittwater and Brisbane Water looking for good agricultural land and land suitable for settlements. However, his report was not encouraging as the land was mostly high and rocky and heavily timbered down to the water. Also, the entrance to Brisbane Water was narrow and once that was negotiated the shallows and sandy shoals together with the problems created by the ebb tide at The Rip made navigation of large vessels dangerous, if not impossible. With the discovery of the Hawkesbury/Nepean River system the new colony's attention was directed to the fresh water and fertile alluvial soil of the Richmond and Windsor areas. Settlers then began to use the Hawkesbury River to transport goods to and from Sydney.

However, no real interest was shown in Brisbane Water until the 1820s and initially the new settlers chose land near its entrance. James Webb appears to be the first to settle here in 1823, his land being on the waterfront on the western side of The Rip. By 1824 the first settler on the Bouddi Peninsula, James Mallen, was living at the western end of Hardys Bay. Patrick Mulhall, William Spears, Elizabeth Murray and William Ward were all landholders on the peninsula by 1840.

The early settlers were really subsistence farmers. They made a living by timber felling, shingle splitting, small scale cattle grazing and shell collecting for lime burning which was used in the production of mortar. Shipbuilding became an important industry for the best part of a century. Initially, there was no direct road from Sydney to Brisbane Water and very few roads in the area.

The terrain encompassing Brisbane Water is quite steep with isolated pockets of flat land available to settle on making it difficult to build roads. The residents relied on the water for transport, for shipping goods to and from Sydney and just for day-to-day living. Market Day in Gosford each Thursday was an important day for residents, and ferries were kept busy taking them and bringing them back with their supplies. It was very much a social occasion. With the arrival of the railway at Woy Woy in 1888 the Bouddi Peninsula became more readily accessible, particularly when the ferries began bringing people across from Woy Woy and Ettalong. Once the railway was opened there was a growing interest in the beauty of Brisbane Water.

In the early years of the twentieth century, land on the Peninsula began to be subdivided and advertised as a holiday destination. Holiday makers built small cottages known as 'weekenders' and would catch a ferry at Woy Woy for Wagstaffe and Killcare. T W Simpson opened a boarding house at Wagstaffe called Manly House (Wagstaffe Community Hall is now on that site) in 1907. He then operated the first ferry service to bring patrons and also prospective land purchasers from Woy Woy to Wagstaffe Point.[7]

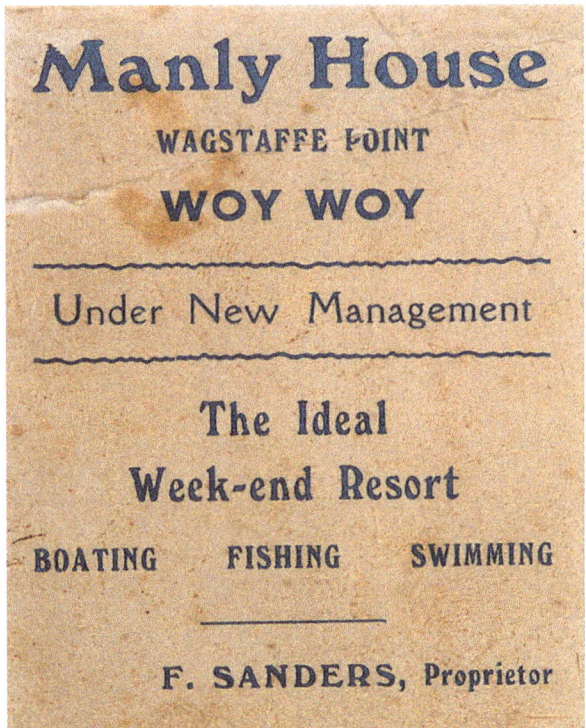

Manly House Resort, Wagstaffe Advertisement, date unknown. Photo: Bouddi Photos Past and Present, Flickr, CC BY 2.0.

Pretty Beach Road and small boys, date unknown. Photo: Bouddi Photos Past and Present, Flickr, CC BY 2.0.

Roads on the Peninsula were not formed until the mid-1900s. For example, The Scenic Road from Kincumber to Killcare was opened for motor traffic in December 1926 but remained a rough drive until the 1960s. The state of the roads in the area has always been an issue.

Although by the 1950s the roads between Killcare and Wagstaffe were sealed, other roads such as Venice and Como were needing attention.[8] Significantly, the major roads into the Peninsula, The Scenic Road from MacMasters Beach to Killcare, and Wards Hill Road from Empire Bay Drive had not been sealed.

During the 50s, 60s and 70s the Wagstaffe Pretty Beach Citizens (later Progress) Association was extremely active in informing the Gosford Shire Council about the poor state of the roads and requesting work be done to improve them. Even in the 1980s not every road was in good repair and the Progress Association continued to press Council for repairs.[9] It wasn't until the Rip Bridge was completed in 1974 that roads really began to improve. As late as the 1990s the Bouddi area was considered by Bruce Elder to be 'quiet and isolated'. To go to Bouddi is to travel back to a time when there were few people in the greater Sydney area'.[10]

A road expressway from Sydney, the electrification of the railway, the building of The Rip Bridge and the upgrading of Wards Hill Road and The Scenic Drive, all contributed to the opening up of the Bouddi Peninsula. The original weekenders are disappearing and large modern 21st century houses are replacing them. Bouddi is attracting 'sea changers' who are leaving the city and choosing a lifestyle of beach and bush within a caring community. Now the population consists of people who work locally as well as people who commute to the city, weekenders and retirees.

[ *The Bouddi Peninsula*

## 2.3 – BOUDDI ABORIGINAL NAMES

ALLAMBIE
ARALUEN
BOGEY HOLE
BOMBI
BOMBORA
BOUDDI
BULBARARING
BULKARA
BULLIMAH
BURRAN

GERRIN
KOURUNG GOURUNG
MOURAWARING
NUKARA
OROO
OTELLA
OWANDA
PUTTY (?)
TAWORRI

The names in red are Aboriginal words from the original people who lived in Bouddi Peninsula as noted by Felton Matthew in 1831. Those in black probably have no relationship to the Peninsula.

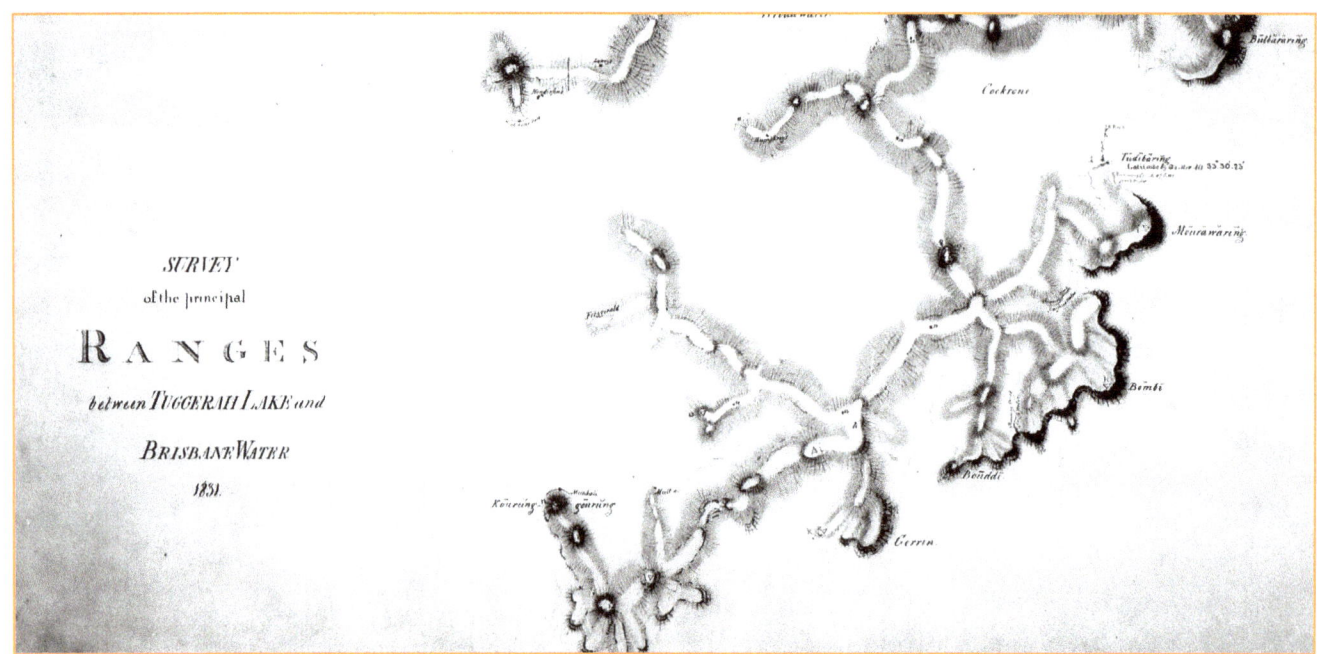

*Early map showing Indigenous place names by surveyor Felton Mathew, 1831.* Photo: New South Wales State Archives: NRS 13859, SA Map 594 (see also Appendix 4.7).

*A Brief History*

*North Arm of Broken Bay from Lion Island, 1789.* Artist: William Bradley, Courtesy of Mitchell Library, State Library of New South Wales.

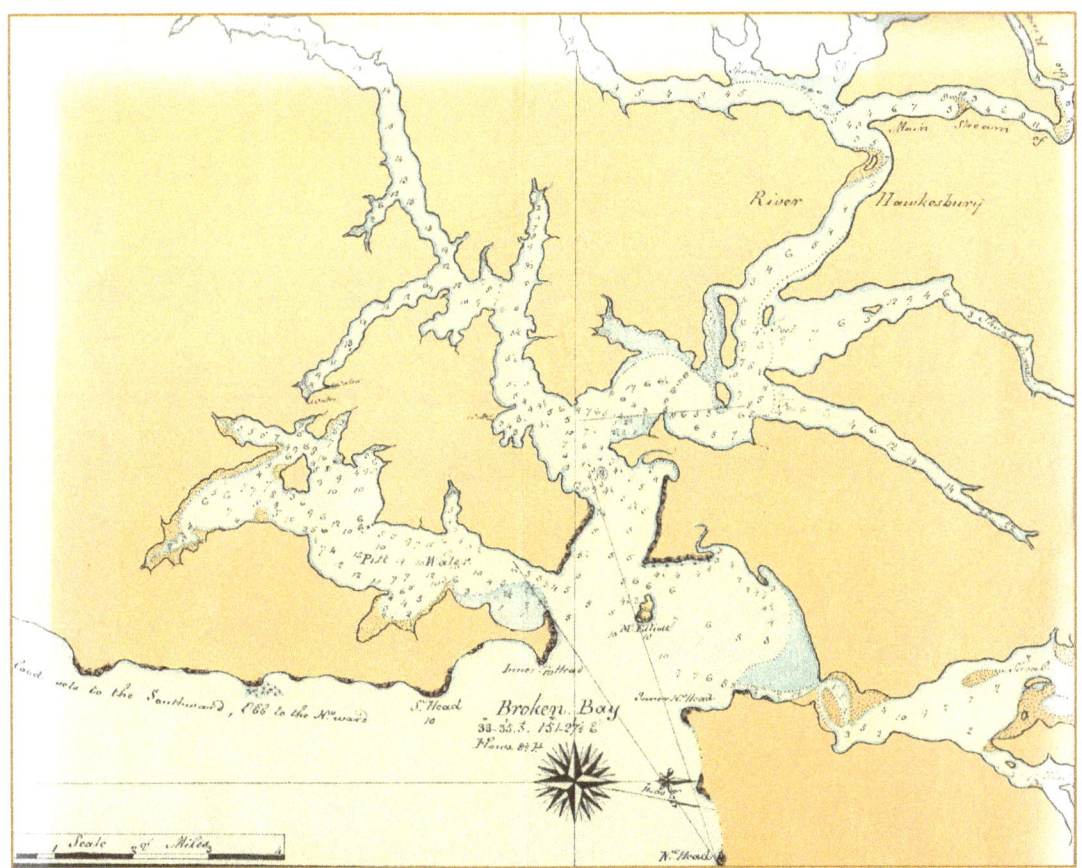

*Bradley's Chart of Broken Bay, 1792.* Photo: Mitchell Library, State Library of New South Wales.

CHAPTER THREE

# 3

# NEED FOR STANDARISATION OF PLACE & STREET NAMES

## Need for Standardisation of Place and Street Names

[PREVIOUS SPREAD]

*Killcare Heights Estate, 1928.* Photo: Bouddi Photos Past and Present, Flickr, CC BY 2.0.

As the population expanded and new names appeared, the need for some standardisation became necessary. World War II instigated a demand for topographic mapping and by the early 1950s the United Nations had set up a group of experts on geographic names. *The New South Wales Geographical Names Act, 1966* came into being and in the same year the Geographical Names Board of New South Wales was set up. All names must be assessed by the Board. It records the origin, history, meaning and pronunciation of each name if that information is available. It also records discontinued place names and includes the latitude and longitude. It is also involved in the naming of suburbs, localities and roads, working closely with councils. This information is available online at the Geographical Name Register of NSW.

In 1984 The Committee for Geographical Names of Australasia was formed to coordinate place naming activities across Australia and New Zealand. In 2015 the name was changed to the Permanent Committee of Place Names. It works with the United Nations Group of Experts on Geographical Names.

Such standardisation of both place and roads assists the community, government bodies and emergency services and can also have Indigenous reconciliation benefits. This means also that spelling is consistent, so 'Wagstaffe' which had often been spelled without the 'e' has had its 'e' restored and 'Killcare' which was for some years spelled with one 'l', leading some people to believe it was of Irish origin, now has the missing 'l' restored. Place names often have two parts, a generic and specific. For example: for Putty Beach, 'Putty' is the generic and 'Beach' is the specific.

The Geographical Names Board of NSW includes guidelines such as 'Names of Aboriginal origin or with a historical background are preferred' and 'The Possessive form should be avoided whenever possible'. For example: 'Hardys Bay' is written without the apostrophe. The Register is a work in progress and public input is welcome.

Road naming in New South Wales usually is initiated by developers opening new estates or by Local Government employees. The procedures of the *NSW Roads Regulation 2018* must be followed, and several government bodies must be notified of a proposal, including the Geographical Names Board of NSW.

The Board initiated an online road naming system in 2013 to improve the efficiency and precision of road naming.[11] Just like toponyms, odonyms also have two parts. For example: 'Araluen' is the generic and 'Drive' is the specific. Some countries do not have the same definition for all types of streets and roads and some do not distinguish between drives, avenues and streets etc. New South Wales does have firm definitions. For example: 'Drive' is a 'Wide thoroughfare allowing a steady flow of traffic without many cross-streets' and 'Street' is a 'Public roadway in a town, city or urban area, especially a paved thoroughfare with footpaths and buildings along one or both sides'[12] (See Appendix 2). The roads in the Bouddi Peninsula were named before these standards existed but any new roads would conform.

*Signpost Cluster, 2023.* Photo: Myfanwy J. Webb.

*Need for Standardisation of Place and Street Names*

# What is included for each entry in this book.

- What do we really want to know about a place or street name?
- Who named it?
- Why was it named this?
- What does the name mean?
- Where does it come from? i.e. which language or region?
- When was it first used?
- Is there any interesting history attached to it?
- How do we know these things? i.e. the source(s) of the information?

Each entry attempts to answer these questions.

*Looking towards Bouddi Peninsula from Ettalong, 2007.* Photo: Bouddi Photos Past and Present, Flickr, CC BY 2.0.

SIGNPOSTS TO THE PAST

CHAPTER FOUR

# 4

# LISTING OF PLACE & STREET NAMES

## A-B

[PREVIOUS SPREAD]

*Manly View Rd & Hats St signpost, 2024.*
Photo: Myfanwy J. Webb.

# ALBERT STREET, WAGSTAFFE

## BEGINNINGS

Indigenous people lived in this area well before white settlement. Evidence of this can be seen in Albert Street where the road, when it was widened, cut through a midden which is in front of a small cave or overhang.

*Albert Street cave and midden, 2020.* Photo: Beverley J. Runcie.

Albert Street first appeared on the subdivision 'Wagstaffe's Point Estate' in December 1906 which advertised portions of land for sale to the public (Appendix 1.8). It is not known for certain who Albert was. George Wagstaffe who purchased the land in 1890 had left for the Solomon Islands in January 1906 and Albert Anderson was appointed caretaker.[13] Perhaps when the subdivision was drawn up that year Albert Street was named after him.

Two years before in 1904, 'Wagstaffe's Subdivision' was first offered for sale with larger blocks of land and no streets marked. The auctioneer was Albert Ernest Middleton, but the land failed to sell, so it was further subdivided into smaller blocks and roads added. (Appendix 1.9) Could the original auctioneer have had a hand in naming the roads on the new subdivision of 1906 and named Albert Street after himself? Could the original auctioneer have had a hand in naming the roads on the new subdivision of 1906 and named Albert Street after himself?

David Shaw has recently reported that Albert Street was named after his grandfather Albert Joseph (1873-1947). His daughter Molly Janet was David's mother. For the first 20 years of Albert's career, he worked as a draftsman in the Survey Branch of the NSW Land Department, and it is in this capacity that he may have been involved with land at Wagstaffe.

In 1909 Albert bought '*The Observer*' newspaper in Tamworth and proceeded to build up the business becoming Managing Director of the Tamworth Newspaper Co. Pty. Ltd. Albert involved himself in journalistic affairs of NSW and made a great contribution to public life in the New England community. He earned himself a place in the 'Who's Who in Australia'.

Albert's grandson says he bought land at Wagstaffe on what later became known as The San Toy Estate and would visit him in his school holidays, arriving by ferry to Wagstaffe. The house was called '*Tipperary*'. Apparently, Albert was very friendly with Sir Keith Murdoch, also a journalist and newspaper man and who also bought land at Wagstaffe. They would meet at Wagstaffe when Murdoch came to Sydney. Perhaps we have now solved the problem of the naming Albert Street.[14]

## HISTORY

In 1909 Lots 72-74 on the western hill side of Albert Street were bought by Thomas Simpson who owned Manly House at Wagstaffe Wharf.[15] In 1918 these lots were subdivided into a new subdivision of 18 lots (now Nos.17-45) called the Hilltop Estate. It was advertised as 'The Dress Circle of Woy Woy' and offered terms of £5 deposit and £2 monthly at 5 percent interest per annum.[16] Frank Smith, who was a carpenter, built a house at No.39 in 1941[17] and became an important community supporter. He was very active in the Community Association and built the altar at St Peters, the Church in Wagstaffe Avenue. He also helped to build the Community Hall at Wagstaffe. His granddaughter Kaye and her husband Robert Francis rebuilt the house and live there permanently.[18]

In the early 1960s Albert Street was extended south as a fire trail to provide vehicle access to the Bouddi National Park for emergency services. It also provided pedestrian access from Wagstafffe to Box Head and from Hawke Head Drive to Lobster Beach. Unfortunately, the trail traversed private properties and over the years this created problems of security and liability for the landholders. A gate was erected at the end of Albert Street which closed the fire trail and a new access to the National Park was sought. For further information about this important community project, see the entries for LOBSTER BEACH TRACK and for FLANNEL FLOWER TRACK.

The community has always had issues with the state of the road. The Pretty Beach Wagstaff [sic] Citizens Association contacted the Gosford Shire Council in 1961 after the fire brigade attended a fire in Albert Street stating the road was so narrow the fire tender went off the road. The Association called for a widening of the road and requested it to be connected to Mulhall Street. In 1969 it still had not been tar-sealed and the Council placed it in the 'future program of works'. By 1977 it was in very poor condition with drains and gutters in a bad way.[19] Albert Street in 2021 was still quite narrow and was only sealed from Bulkara Street to Mulhall Street. The remainder remained unsealed.

# ALLAMBIE ROAD, KILLCARE

## BEGINNINGS

Allambie is from an Aboriginal word 'allambee' meaning 'to remain awhile'.[20] It is not a local word and was chosen by Gosford Shire officers for its pleasant sound. Similar definitions appear also by H M Cooper, allambi meaning a quiet place and James Baylis, allambee meaning to stay or dwell.[22]

## HISTORY

Although this road was gazetted in 1970 and was to run parallel to the surf beach between Anthony Crescent and Putty Beach Drive beginning in Taworri Road, it was never made into a public road.[23] It is now used as a fire break behind the houses on the south side of Anthony Crescent and has a locked gate. It is included here because it is shown on some maps, including the Gosford Electronic Map, and appears on some Global Positioning Systems (GPS) a navigational aid used in vehicles.

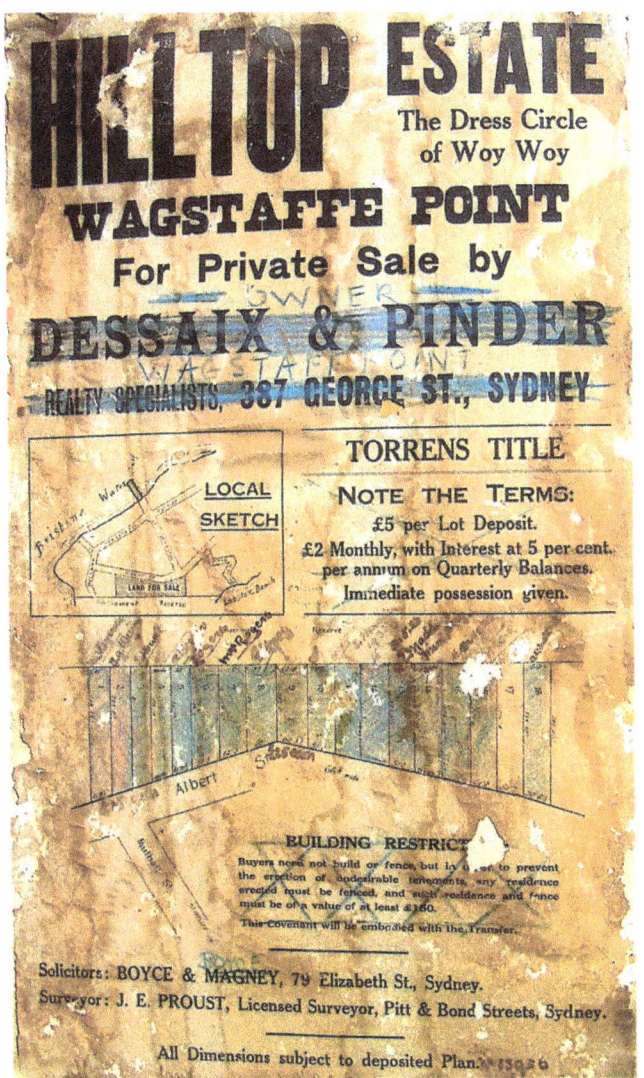

*Hilltop Estate Albert Avenue, 1918.* Photo: Bouddi Photos Past and Present, Flickr, CC BY 2.0.

[ *Listing of Place & Street Names: A to B*

# ALLEN STROM LOOKOUT,
## BOUDDI NATIONAL PARK

### BEGINNINGS

Allen Strom and his wife Beryl worked tirelessly for the community, the environment, and education. This lookout dedicated to Allen was one of his favourite places in Bouddi National Park. The Allen Strom lookout is within Bouddi National Park at the end of the Rocky Point Fire Trail which commences at the top of Wards Hill Road. It overlooks Hardys Bay and Wagstaffe and looks westwards across Brisbane Water to Ettalong and Brisbane Water National Park.

### HISTORY

The plaque at the lookout says:

*Allen Strom A.M. (1915-1997) made a lifelong contribution to the protection of Gosford City's environment. He had a broad vision for the area and a deep concern about the cumulative effect of adverse small decisions. His tenacious work for the environment helped to conserve the city's ecosystems and the splendid vista from this lookout.*

*Allen Strom Lookout Plaque, 2024.* Photo: Myfanwy J. Webb.

For more information about Allen Strom see the entry for STROM CENTRE.

*Listing of Place & Street Names: A to B*

*View of Hardys Bay from Allen Strom Lookout, 2000s.* Photo: Bouddi Photos Past and Present, Flickr, CC BY 2.0.

[ *Listing of Place & Street Names: A to B*

# ANTHONY CRESCENT, KILLCARE

## BEGINNINGS

Anthony Crescent is situated on the surf side of Killcare running parallel to and behind Putty Beach Drive.

The Crescent was named after Anthony Newhouse, the son of Arnold Newhouse (1927-2006) and Yvonne née Steinberg. Arnold was the developer of the Kilcare [sic] Beach Estate. He was an active pioneer in establishing the Australia-Israel Chamber of Commerce in 1970 to promote the export of Israeli goods to Australia.[24] In 1980 Arnold was awarded an MBE for service to the Jewish community.[25] Anthony followed his father in Real Estate.

## HISTORY

Anthony Crescent was first named on the Gosford City Council's DP235311 and shown but not named on a map of a subdivision 'Kilcare [sic] Beach' advertised in 'The Sun-Herald' January 8, 1967 by N & K Developments Pty. Ltd. (see Appendix 1.1). In fact, it appears to have been first offered for sale in 1964 when Homewise Ltd advertised land which seems to encompass land above the cliff in Killcare Heights as well as Anthony Crescent (Appendix 1.11). The artists of both advertisements obviously didn't appreciate that there was a cliff, and the roads could not be connected. Anthony Crescent was already kerbed, guttered and sealed when the subdivision first came onto the market. It also had electricity but no water or sewerage.

*View of Putty Beach from above Anthony Crescent, 2023.* Photo: Myfanwy J. Webb

*Listing of Place & Street Names: A to B*

*View from 8 Anthony Crescent, 1979.* Photo: Myfanwy J. Webb.

*8 Anthony Crescent building house, 1973.* Photo: Donald G. Runcie.

*View of Anthony Crescent.* Photo: Myfanwy J. Webb.

*Runcie Family 8 Anthony Crescent, 1979.* Photo: Myfanwy J. Webb.

*8 Anthony Cr before completion, 1973.* Photo: Donald G. Runcie.

[ *Listing of Place & Street Names: A to B*

*Early Araluen Drive, date unknown.* Photo: Bouddi Photos Past and Present, Flickr, CC BY 2.0.

*Araluen Drive where marina is today, date unknown.* Photo: Bouddi Photos Past and Present, Flickr, CC BY 2.0.

*First bridge built by Wally Worthington at corner of Araluen and Heath Rd, 1925.* Photo: Bouddi Photos Past and Present, Flickr, CC BY 2.0.

# ARALUEN DRIVE, KILLCARE & HARDYS BAY

## BEGINNINGS

Why the name Araluen was chosen for the road is uncertain but there are several possibilities:

Araluen is an Aboriginal word meaning 'plenty of water' and most commonly 'place of water lilies'. A.W. Reed says the name Araluen was first used for Araluen, a town near Braidwood in NSW and meant 'place of water lilies'. Apparently before gold mining began there were many lagoons in the valley and water lilies were common. Aboriginal groups would meet there as the bulbs were a staple part of their diet. Araluen Drive was probably named by Gosford Shire Council officers for its pleasant sound and is unlikely to be a local Aboriginal word.[26]

It could however be named after an early house built at 8 Araluen Drive named '*Araluen*' which would have been built when the road was called Government or Bay Road. However, when the house was named Araluen is not known.

Also, there may be a connection with the poet Henry Kendall, who lived in West Gosford with the Fagan family for a time and had a daughter he named Araluen. He wrote two poems entitled '*Araluen*', one to celebrate Araluen the village near Braidwood, NSW and later one to his daughter, Araluen, who died when very young. Charles Swancott says he was living in Gosford when he wrote the poem 'in memory of his daughter, which many critics consider is one of his best'.[27]

## HISTORY

Originally Araluen Drive was first shown as Government (Bay) Road [sic] in the 1916 subdivision, 'Killcare Estate' (Appendix 1.2). It only went as far as Stanley Street to the east and near the creek where Heath Road begins at the western end.

In 1964 Araluen Drive was officially declared as 'commencing at its intersection with Arthur Road [now Heath Road] and adjacent to the Pretty Beach Public School, thence going generally north-east, south and north-east, terminating at its intersection with Stanley Street, being a public road of approximately 1¼ miles in length and of variable width'.[28] This meant the road followed the water's edge for the whole length. In 1970 the name was extended from Stanley Street to the beginning of Hardys Bay Parade.[29] A further change occurred in 1978 when the section of Araluen Drive between Stanley Street and Noble Road was renamed as Noble Road.[30]

Bruce Dunlop reports that the section between the Hardys Bay Club and the point was known as The Reserve and was initially a grassed area.[31] It remained a grassy tract until the 1960s.[32] This name was still in use in 1954.[33]

A push began in 1965 to open Araluen Drive Extension, what we now call the 'Dog Track' to traffic. This section of the road begins near Pretty Beach Public School and follows the water's edge around to the point. The Hardys Bay Killcare Progress Association wanted it made for one-way traffic and Heath Road one way in the opposite direction. This was the consequence of the poor condition of Heath Road at the time. Action was still being sought during the 70s and 80s until in 1989 Council ruled that the extension would not be opened for traffic and an upgrade of Heath Road would commence. The 'Dog Track' would instead have a slip rail barrier constructed at either end. Correspondence continued until Council put an end to the matter in 1994.[34] The community is now very happy with keeping the extension as a walking track.

In 1973 the Council had been filling and widening along the waterfront at Hardys Bay.[35] By 2007, realising there would be an increase in the traffic around the retail precinct at Araluen Drive and Killcare Road, the local community led by Killcare Wagstaffe Trust put to Council a plan for parking and paths. The plan was drawn by David Bowe, a local architect and addressed Araluen Drive west of Killcare Road to the creek. Council was encouraging. However, ten years later little had been done to alleviate a growing problem. In June 2017 a new 'Hardys Bay Foreshore Renewal Proposal' was developed by residents and community minded landscape architects with an emphasis on providing 'the community with an open and inviting foreshore place'.[36] Little has been done in Araluen Drive to improve parking along the foreshore. However, Central Coast Council planned to undertake some road works in 2020, delayed unfortunately by the COVID-19 pandemic.[37]

Once the first houses were built around Hardys Bay after 1916 a few shops appeared near the two wharves, one at the western end of the now Araluen Drive and one at the bottom of Killcare Road.

The Hardys Bay Cash Store was the first shop on the western side of Hardys Bay and was close to the point in Araluen Drive. Later the Nocks opened their General Store further down (No.160), an imposing two-storey building and built a private wharf. Mr Nock was given permission to open a Post Office at his store in 1921.[38] At the time there was no formed road, and this section of Araluen Drive was called The Reserve. A few doors away on the corner of Otella Avenue was a butcher shop (No.156).[39] Eric Pearsall who lived at No.140 for many years is remembered by a seat opposite the house. A plaque says:

*Eric Pearsall*

*1914-2008*

*Over 50 years in Hardys Bay*

*Eric loved the Bay and was loved by everyone.*

The Hardys Bay Community Hall (No.114), originally called Booth's Hall, as it was built by Joe Booth, and later Hardys Bay Hall was built along this stretch. It was a focal point for the community and holiday makers especially for dances. After World War II it was taken over by the Hardys Bay Sub-Branch of the **Returned & Services League of Australia (RSL)** and dances still continued. The hall first built in 1923 suffered some misfortunes. It was blown down in a gale and rebuilt in 1926 and in 1957 it was gutted by fire and again rebuilt. In 1983 the inaugural service of the Hardys Bay Community Church was held there and by 1988 the Church had bought the building from the RSL. The RSL relocated to new premises in Araluen Drive in 1982 and finally the Subbranch amalgamated with the Woy Woy Ettalong Subbranch in 1990.[40] Hardys Bay Club although not now an RSL Club in 2021, continues to operate as a community club and retains the War Memorial in its grounds where a ceremony is still performed each Anzac Day.

Tucked into the corner where the Hardys Bay Club is now, Ray Martin owned a dairy farm at the beginning of World War II and his cows would graze on the Reserve. Sadly, Ray went to war in 1942 and died as a prisoner of war while working on the Thai Burma Railway.[41] This land is in fact where the first settler on the Bouddi Peninsula, James Mallen already had 25 horned

*Anderson family at Killcare Wharf with Araluen Drive in background, 1938-9.* Photo: Bouddi Photos Past and Present, Flickr, CC BY 2.0.

*Old Butcher Shop, Hardys Bay, date unknown.* Photo: Bouddi Photos Past and Present, Flickr, CC BY 2.0.

*Seal, Hardys Bay, 1913.* Photo: Bouddi Photos Past and Present, Flickr, CC BY 2.0.

cattle in January 1824 when he applied for temporary occupation of the land.[42]

In these early days the Killcare end of Araluen Drive also had some local businesses. The first shop was on the waterfront in the 1920s at No.50 when the road was then called Bay or Government Road. It was a general store and later a fruit and vegetable shop. The shop was finally demolished, and four cabins built. In the 1960s two shops were built on the site, a take-away food store and a butcher. Neville Hazzard also had a real estate agency next door (No.52) in the 1950s and 1960s. In due course these buildings were demolished and the villas which are there now were erected.[43] C B Ford Real Estate was at No.48 Araluen Drive and Ford was advertising in the Erina Shire Holiday and Touring Guide by 1928.[44]

On the corner of Araluen Drive and Killcare Road is a shop known as 'The Old Killcare Store' (No.54) which was built in the 1930s. Over the years it has changed hands many times, mainly remaining as a mixed business and now is a café/restaurant called Hardys Bistro. During the 1960s, before the Rip Bridge was built Ron Radford who had a pharmacy at 302 Ocean View Road, Ettalong, would deliver medicines etc. across the water via his amphibious car to the store.

On the opposite corner was another general store (No.56) which began before 1919 selling from a shed on the land. The later building was finally demolished and a liquor store with a small general store was built there. This building has had another upgrade and now has accommodation above and a small landscape and garden business called Elyse in Wonderland has been added. Next door at No.58 is a wood fired pizza shop, 'The View', which was originally built as a post office. At No.60 there is 'Anchor on Hardys Bay' restaurant.

A little further east in Araluen Drive, past the Killcare Wharf is the Killcare Marina. It was built in the 1960s and now provides maintenance, storage and hires vessels. The current marina replaced the first one which was gutted by fire in 1995.[45]

On the corner of Owanda Crescent is an electricity sub-station. Just opposite the park at the end of Stanley Street on the waterfront is a stone wall partly hidden by mangroves. It is believed to be the foundations of William Ward's shed or boathouse and is listed as an historic site by the Central Coast Council. See the entry for WARDS WALL for information about the controversy regarding its origins. Ward settled here possibly as early as 1825.[46]

*Killcare Store, 2025.* Photo: Myfanwy J. Webb.

*Sir Arthur Rickard oil painting, 1931.*

Artist: Sir John Longstaff, Courtesy of Art in Australia.

## ARTHUR ROAD, HARDYS BAY & PRETTY BEACH

### BEGINNINGS

Arthur Road (now called Heath Road) first appears on a subdivision map 'Pretty Beach Extension Estate' in 1912 (Appendix 1.7). The land was offered for sale by Arthur Rickard & Co Ltd and Arthur Road appears to be named after himself, Arthur Senior, i.e. Sir Arthur Rickard (1868-1948).

Sir Arthur Rickard was a real estate developer and was important in the land development of the Bouddi Peninsula. Between 1910 and 1920 he opened up four large tracts of land suitable for housing. They were Pretty Beach Estate in 1910 (Appendix 1.6), Pretty Beach Extension in 1912 (Appendix 1.7), Killcare Estate in 1916 (Appendix 1.2) and Killcare Extension Estate in 1920 (Appendix 1.3).

Sir Arthur began his career in Melbourne as a mercantile broker and agent and about 1899 went into the wholesale grocery business. This didn't last long however as the imported foodstuff were often infested with weevils. In 1904 he registered Arthur Rickard Co. Ltd, a real estate firm, and developed an inventive advertising technique with illustrated advertisements urging people to buy not rent. Sir Arthur was probably the first person to advertise land and houses for sale in this modern way. He was extremely successful, opening new housing estates over a large area extending to Wyong, the Blue Mountains and Port Hacking. He even persuaded the railways department to build stations at Warrimoo and Bullaburra to service his Estates. Arthur was the foundation president of the Millions Club established to encourage British migration and he had many and varied business interests which led to him being appointed Knight of the British Empire (KBE) in 1920. Those who visit Taronga Zoo in Sydney may be interested to know that Sir Arthur donated the floral clock to the Zoo in 1928. Unfortunately, the Depression of 1929 saw land sales disappear and many could not pay their mortgage instalments and returned their land, which meant the company had to pay rates on land no one wanted to buy. As a result of this Arthur Rickard & Co Ltd went into liquidation in 1930. However, he remains 'the outstanding land developer of his era, his extroverted personality evident through most of his advertisements'. [47]

Alternatively, Arthur Road could have been named after Sir Arthur Rickard's son by his first wife Annie. His full name was Arthur Lancelot Rickard (1895-1949) and he served as an officer in the A.I.F. in World War I and World War II. In World War I he was awarded the Military Cross and in World War II was awarded the Distinguished Service Order. He was also mentioned in dispatches on numerous occasions in both WWI and

## "THE OUTSTANDING LAND DEVELOPER OF HIS ERA, HIS EXTROVERTED PERSONALITY EVIDENT THROUGH MOST OF HIS ADVERTISEMENTS".

WWII. Between the wars he became a director and sales manager in his father's company. He was known for 'his intelligence, wit and gentleness'. After the Second World War he formed a small property development company but suffered from ill health and died in 1949.[48]

### HISTORY

Arthur Road which is now called Heath Road first appears as mentioned on the 'Pretty Beach Extension Estate', a subdivision made in 1912. Originally, only the western section of the road from where Pretty Beach School is now, to the end of the point was named Arthur Road. The remainder on the east side was called Heath Road in the original subdivision (Appendix 1.7).

It was still being called Arthur Road in 1954.[49] The name change to Heath Road was gazetted in 1970.[50]

See also the entry for HEATH ROAD

## BABS ROAD, KILLCARE HEIGHTS

### BEGINNINGS

Babs Road was named after Babette Pauline White (1919-2005), elder daughter of Sir Ernest Keith White. Her mother was Lady Pauline White, née Mason.

Babette was born in Gosford, NSW and married Lieutenant John Lawrence Downing of the US Navy, in Philadelphia, Pennsylvania in 1943.[51] She met her husband when his American squadron visited Sydney

*Babette (Babs) White in wheelbarrow with sister Jacqueline, date unknown.* Photo: Tyrrell Family.

and had then corresponded.[52] Just before their marriage John had a lucky escape after his ship the Chicago was sunk and he was in the water for two hours before being rescued.[53]

Babette continued to live in the United States and had three children, Anne, Baden and Craig and was a keen tennis player. She died in Columbia, South Carolina aged 86 and her husband died less than a year later in 2006.[54]

### HISTORY

Babette's father Sir Ernest Keith White named Babs Road after his elder daughter when he purchased and subdivided land he called 'The Killcare Heights Estate' in 1928 (Appendix 1.4).

See also the entries for BADEN STREET, JACQUELINE AVENUE and PAULINE AVENUE.

[ *Listing of Place & Street Names: A to B*

# BADEN STREET,
## KILLCARE HEIGHTS

### BEGINNINGS

Baden Street was named after Baden Keith White (1923-1944), an only son of Sir Ernest Keith White and his mother Lady Pauline White, née Mason.

Baden was a Flying Officer in the No.108 squadron Royal Australian Air Force in World War II and died in a flight over the Mediterranean in 1944. He was on a night flying test flight in a Beaufighter aircraft, which included firing the guns. He fired four short bursts into the sea and when commencing a climbing turn the wing tip appeared to strike the water and subsequently crashed. Both the Pilot Officer and Baden were killed, and no trace of their bodies was found. This occurred about 1½ miles SE of Filfola (Filfla), a Maltese islet.[55] Baden enlisted at the age of 18 and died when he was 20. He is listed on the Malta Memorial in Malta.[56] He was

*Baden Street, Smithy Street and Babs Road Signpost, 2024.* Photo: Myfanwy J. Webb.

*White family from left Babs, Ernest, Jacqueline, Pauline, Baden, 1941.* Photo: Tyrrell Family.

sorely missed by his family and Baden Road in Neutral Bay at Kurraba Point was named after Baden White by his father, as was the family home *Baden House* (now demolished) on that site.[57]

### HISTORY

Baden Street was named by Baden's father Sir Eric Keith White who purchased and subdivided the land called the 'Killcare Heights Estate' in 1928. The name first appeared on this subdivision (Appendix 1.4).

A children's playground was proposed for Baden Street in 1983, installed by Council in 1984 and included swings, a slippery dip and a small roundabout. It was built at the end of the street, which is not a through road, but by the late 1990s it was demolished.[58] This was probably because of the high cost of maintenance, and its isolation and proximity to the bush was believed to be a safety risk for the children.

See also the entries for BABS ROAD, JACQUELINE AVENUE and PAULINE AVENUE.

# THE BAR, WAGSTAFFE

## BEGINNINGS

The Bar is an extensive sand bar at the entrance to Brisbane Water. Its official name is 'Wagstaffe Bar' and the Geographical Names Board of NSW list 'Wagstaff Bar' and 'The Bar' as previous names.[59] Some locals still call it 'The Bar'. It is also called 'Ettalong Bar'.

## HISTORY

This sand bar initially impeded any settlement until the early 1820s and has always been and still is an obstacle for large vessels.

For further information see the entry for WAGSTAFFE BAR.

*Note Simpson's ferry 'Irene' with its signage 'Woy Woy to the Bar' at Wagstaffe Wharf, 1920s.* Photo: Courtesy of Central Coast Council.

# BAY ROAD, KILLCARE

## BEGINNINGS

This is an early descriptive name for Araluen Drive which skirts the Hardys Bay waterfront.

## HISTORY

On the 'Killcare Estate' subdivision in 1916 it appears as 'Govt (Bay) Rd' (Appendix 1.2). The name 'Bay Road' was still in use in the 1950s[60] and in 1964 it was officially named Araluen Drive.[61]

*First store on Bay/Government Road (later Araluen Drive), 1920s.* Photo: Bouddi Photos Past and Present, Flickr, CC BY 2.0.

[ *Listing of Place & Street Names: A to B*

*'Martinsyde' Tea Rooms & Dairy, 1926.* Photo: Bouddi Photos Past and Present, Flickr, CC BY 2.0.

# BEACH DRIVE, KILLCARE

## BEGINNINGS

This is a descriptive name as Beach Drive leads from The Scenic Road to Killcare Beach. At the beach end is the Bogey Hole or rockpool and the Killcare Surf Life Saving Club.

## HISTORY

When the land was first subdivided in 1930 as the 'Martins Killcare Beach Estate', the road was included as part of Grandview Crescent. However, that road did not extend as far as the Surf Club until later (Appendix 1.5).

As early as 1919 Alexander Martin, the original purchaser of the land asked the Council for a road to his property.[62] His house 'Martinsyde' was situated near where the Killcare Surf Lifesaving Club is today at No.80 Beach Drive and he and his wife ran a dairy farm and later popular Tea Rooms.[63] In 1927 Alexander Martin approached the Council again and generously proposed a 'road through his property to give access to the southern end of Killcare Beach'.[64]

Finally, in 1934 Alexander Martin and Erina Shire Council reached an agreement for the resumption by the Council of some of his land to enable Beach Drive to be continued for another 200 yards. This gave the public access right down to the beach and was finally officially named in 1937.[65]

In 1962 the name of the part of the road which runs from The Scenic Drive down to the foreshores of Putty Beach was officially changed from Grandview Crescent to Beach Drive.[66]

The Killcare Surf Club at the end of Beach Drive was formed in 1929 and has had three club houses. The

*Listing of Place & Street Names: A to B*

*'Martinsyde', 1922.* Photo: Bouddi Photos Past and Present, Flickr, CC BY 2.0.

*Fire at Beach Drive, 1946.* Photo: Bouddi Photos Past and Present, Flickr, CC BY 2.0.

first was built in 1934, the second in 1971 and the third was opened in 2009.[67] Lifesavers can now see surfers in trouble from a watch tower and with the Bogey Hole (rockpool) nearby, this end of the beach continues to be a focus for beachgoers. For more information about the Bogey Hole see the entry for BOGEY HOLE. There is also a kiosk and restaurant in the Surf Club, and it has facilities for large gatherings such as weddings, art displays etc.

In 1973 Beach Drive was bituminised and land for more car parking was set aside adjacent to the beach.[68]

*Beach Drive Houses overlooking Putty Beach, 1990.* Photo: Bouddi Photos Past and Present, Flickr, CC BY 2.0.

[ *Listing of Place & Street Names: A to B*

*John Menton's grave, 2024.*
Photo: Myfanwy J. Webb.

# BLYTH STREET,
## KILLCARE HEIGHTS

### BEGINNINGS

The origin of the name 'Blythe' is unknown. Arthur Rickard & Co was the developer responsible for the subdivision. Unlike nearby Stanley Street and Noble Road which were named after relatives of Sir Arthur Rickard, no family link has been found with the name 'Blythe'. Blythe is used as a surname and is also a first name for both boys and girls, so it may have been named after a person. Alternatively, the word comes from the Middle English and Old English 'blithe' meaning joyous, cheerful, so perhaps it was named with this spirit in mind.

### HISTORY

Blythe Street first appears on the 'Killcare Estate' subdivision in 1916 (Appendix 1.2).

There is an early grave with a headstone in Blythe Street just around the corner from Stanley Street. It is that of a baby and reads:

*Sacred to the memory of John Menton born the 1st of July 1837 and departed this life the 15th of October 1837.*

It is believed that he drowned with two women family members, but no deaths have been officially recorded. Apparently, the women were buried nearby. Beryl Strom said, 'the only clue [to the Menton family] is about the same time there was a street in East Gosford named Menton, now changed to Minton'. There was an ex-convict John Minton living in the Brisbane Water area at the same time as the death of the baby so perhaps he was the father.[69] The headstone was cracked by a fire in the early 1960s and Council fixed this and put a fence around it in 1980. Vandals damaged it in 1992 and Council then repaired it again.[70] By 2020 it was over-grown and community volunteers have worked to restore it and the reserve around it.

James Burns Fraser, after whom Fraser Road was named lived in No.28 Blythe Street and it is still owned by the Fraser family. James had bought the land and house from his friend Bill Meyers and retired there in 1946.

Mick Myer built and lived in a house in Blythe Street in 1919. Mick was a builder and helped build Grandview Crescent and clear rocks from the Bogey Hole. He also ran a dairy and after his death in 1939 his son Bert Myer who lived at No.18 took over running the farm. Bert with his wife Jean became important and active members of the community until he died aged 99.[71]

# BOGEY (BOGIE) HOLE, KILLCARE

## BEGINNINGS

The swimming or bathing pool on the western side of Killcare Beach near the Surf Club is known as the Bogey Hole.

Bogey is from an Aboriginal word 'bogee' meaning 'to swim' or 'bathe' which William Dawes recorded in his notebook between 1790 and 1792.[72] It is believed to be a Dharuk word. The first recording of it is in 1788 when Colby said on coming out of the water 'Bogie d'oway' which meant, 'I have bathed, or I have been bathing'.[73] Colby (Colebee) was a Cadigal Aboriginal man who came from what is now the eastern suburbs area of Sydney. He and another Aboriginal person Bennelong were abducted in 1789 by Governor Arthur Philip who wanted to learn about their language and customs.[74] Other spellings of bogey are bugi, bogie, bogi, bogee, bogu, bo-ga & bo-gay.

## HISTORY

The earliest known purpose-built ocean bogey hole in Australia is in Newcastle when in 1819 Major James Morriset had convicts cut one out of the rock platform for him to bathe in.[75] It is still in public use today, after being closed temporarily while the cliff above it was stabilised in 2016.

Originally the Bogey Hole at Killcare Beach was a small natural tidal rock pool and was in use from the early days of settlement.

It occasionally became silted up with sand (it still does) and in 1928 'a short rock wall' was recommended to prevent this happening.[76] Also in 1938 the Surf Life Saving Club expressed a need for enlarging the Bogey Hole.[77] Nicholas George (Mick) Myer who moved to Killcare in 1919 and his son Edmund (Ted) helped remove rocks from the Bogey Hole using wooden poles as a gantry.[78]

In 1984 the NSW Department of Works 'proposed to run a pipeline into the natural rock pool at the Surf

*Aboriginal men spearing fish, date unknown.* Modified from: Mitchell Library, State Library of NSW.

*Mick & son Ted Myer removing rocks for Bogey Hole, 1928.* Photo: Bouddi Photos Past and Present, Flickr, CC BY 2.0.

*Bogey Hole, 1915.* Modified from: Wilmot Butler Collection, Courtesy of Central Coast Council.

[ *Listing of Place & Street Names: A to B*

*Bogey Hole postcard, date unknown.* Photo: Bouddi Photos Past and Present, Flickr, CC BY 2.0.

*Bogey Hole, 2024.* Photo: Myfanwy J. Webb.

*Listing of Place & Street Names: A to B*

Club end of Putty Beach'. The Progress Association argued that 'This pool is known locally as the Bogey Hole and it is the only safe area for small children to sea bathe and it is heavily used throughout the year'. The community was listened to and fortunately the pipe was located further up the beach.[79]

After a heavy storm when the sand is washed from the flat sandstone rocks around the Bogey Hole, ancient ripple marks can be seen. These ripple marks are from the ancient river that brought the grains of sand from rocks formed between 500 and 700 million years ago. The rock pool today remains popular and is still a tidal pool with a ring of rocks protecting it from the surf.

*Myfanwy and BlueBell at Bogey Hole, 1980s.* Photo: Beverley J. Runcie.

# BOMBI MOOR,
## BOUDDI NATIONAL PARK

### BEGINNINGS

Bombi Moor is within the Bouddi National Park and lies between Little Beach and Caves Bay. Along with nearby Mourawaring Moor it 'contains the largest relatively undisturbed samples of low coastal heath on perched sand dunes on the Central Coast'. The sand dunes are either the remnants of an ancient beach which existed when the coastline was some distance out to sea and subsequent erosion has left them high on the top of the cliffs[80] or maybe the result of a tsunami formed after a tectonic event in the Tasman Sea, lifting sand out and up from beyond the continental shelf. For information about the name Bombi see the entry for BOMBI POINT.

### HISTORY

During the 1950s and 1960s about 50 hectares of land just west of the Moor was mined for silica sand for the manufacture of optical glass and later for fill for St Huberts Island. When mining was completed in 1978 this area was added to Bouddi National Park.[81] The moorland behind Bombi Point has dense heathland which provides spectacular wildflower displays in spring. For further information about the soil and vegetation of Bombi Moor see the 'Bouddi Peninsula Study'.[82]

*Killcare Beach ripple marks after storm, 1974.* Photo: Beverley J. Runcie.

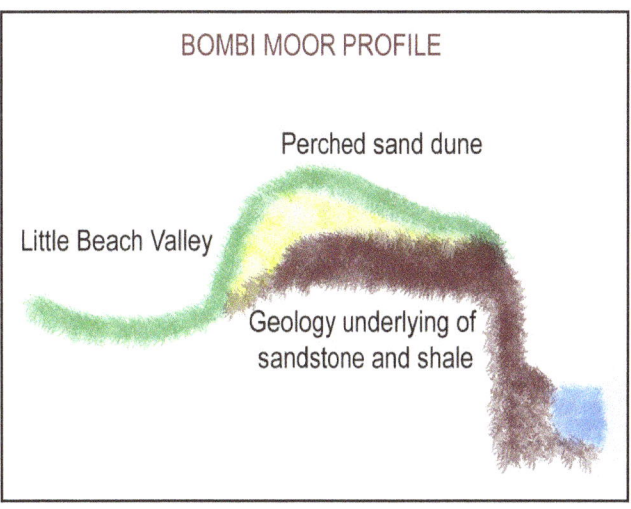

*Bombi Moor profile, 2025.* Illustration: Myfanwy J. Webb.

SIGNPOSTS TO THE PAST

[ *Listing of Place & Street Names: A to B*

# BOMBI POINT,
## BOUDDI NATIONAL PARK

### BEGINNINGS

The name 'Bombi' appears on an 1831 map by surveyor Felton Mathew so it is a local Aboriginal word.[83]

'Bombi' is said to mean 'water swirling about rocks'. This meaning is listed by F.C. Bennett in 'The Story of the Aboriginal People of the Central Coast of New South Wales' which was first published in 1968 but unfortunately he does not give a source.[84] The term 'Bombo' is listed as meaning 'thunder' by F.D. McCarthy and the similar name 'Bondi' or 'Boondi' is also listed which means 'water breaking over rocks' and is close to Bennett's definition.[85] Jeremy Steele suggests the word may be from 'Boom-bee', or 'Bwo-me' which translate to 'breath' or 'blow' and mentions 'Boam Billi' the name for Shark Island in Sydney Harbour where wind blowing would likely be a dominant feature. Bombi Point would also be likely to be a place of blowing wind. Steele wrote a thesis about the Aboriginal language of Sydney in 2005.[86]

### HISTORY

This point is the most southerly of the three points of 'Cape Three Points' in Bouddi National Park and is just northeast of Caves Bay. Captain James Cook named 'Cape Three Points' as he sailed northwards from Botany Bay in May 1770 without naming the individual points.[87]

It is now officially named 'Third Point' and Bombi is listed as a previous name although it still appears on some current maps as Bombi Point.[88]

# BOMBI ROAD NORTH,
## MACMASTERS BEACH

### BEGINNINGS

For information about the name 'Bombi' see the entry for BOMBI POINT.

*Bombi Rd north and south, 2020.* Modified from: Localsearch.

### HISTORY

Bombi Road North is on the edge of Bouddi National Park.

Initially Bombi Road was not divided into north and south. Apparently in the 1930s, The Scenic Road 'climbed out of the Little Beach area via today's Bombi Road'.[89]

Because of the steep terrain Bombi Road North and South now do not meet. Bombi Road North meets The Scenic Road just south of Grahame Drive. There are two properties along Bombi Road North.

*Bombi Rd South signpost, 2024.* Photo: Myfanwy J. Webb.

# BOMBI ROAD SOUTH, MACMASTERS BEACH

## BEGINNINGS

This road leads off The Scenic Road to high ground behind Bombi Point. There are quite a few properties on Bombi Road South. For information about the name 'Bombi' see the entry for BOMBI POINT.

## HISTORY

Because of the height of the land, which affords an excellent view of the coast, this area was chosen during World War II for the site of the Bombi Radar Station.

The radar unit was known as No.19 Radar Station Royal Australian Air Force and became operational in April 1942. Its role was to monitor enemy air and sea movements and threats to the Australian coast. The unit was finally disbanded in September 1946. Few remains survive; the largest is a sandbagged machine gun post which is slowly disintegrating. Most of this land which was requisitioned by the Defence Forces from private ownership was returned and there are now houses along Bombi Road South.[90]

Bombi Road South is also the site of the Bouddi Digital TV Broadcast tower which services the Bouddi area and areas surrounding Brisbane Water.

*Bombi Rd transmission tower, 2024.* Photo: Myfanwy J. Webb.

*Land mullet (Egernia major), 2019.* Photo: Myfanwy J. Webb.

*Overgrown gun emplacement, 2024.* Photo: Myfanwy J. Webb.

[ *Listing of Place & Street Names: A to B*

# BOMBORA,

## BEGINNINGS

A bombora is an isolated shallow area in the sea some distance offshore where waves break over a submerged rock, shelf or reef. The bombora is not easily seen.

The word is believed to come from a Dharuk Aboriginal word 'bumbora' and first used for the bombora in Sydney Harbour at Dobroyd Point. That bombora is now officially named Gowlland Bombora after Commander John Gowlland who drowned there when his boat capsized in 1874.[91] The Dharawal people from the south coast used the word 'bumbura'. Bombora is one of the few Aboriginal words which have passed into Australian English. It is commonly abbreviated to 'bommie' or 'bommy'.[92]

The word bombora has been listed by F.C. Bennett in 1968 as an Aboriginal word meaning 'water swirling around sunken rocks' which is as good a description as any.[93]

## HISTORY

There are two bomboras off the Bouddi Peninsula. The larger is off the east end of Maitland Bay and is called the Maitland Bombora or East Bombora. This is registered with the Geographical Names Board of NSW as Maitland Bumbora with Maitland Bombora as a variant.[94] The smaller bombora is off the east end of Putty Beach or West Bombora to distinguish it from the Maitland Bombora. A map from 1852 when Captain J Lort Stokes surveyed the coast indicates the bomboras as East Reef and West Reef. One hundred years later the Royal Australian Navy's hydrographic survey map of Broken Bay also names them East Reef and West Reef.[95]

Over the years there have been vessels wrecked on both bomboras. In the 19th century at least two ships were lost on the Maitland bombora: *Rebecca* in 1878 and *Heath* in 1889. Both were trading between Sydney and Newcastle.[96] It appears that the *Maitland* in 1898 avoided the bombora but was lifted high by an enormous wave and crashed onto the rocks of the rock platform where it broke in two.[97] A family of four drowned in 1973 when their cruiser *Attunga* capsized after smashing into Maitland Bay bombora in heavy seas. The *Attunga* was a Halversen hire craft and should not have ventured outside Broken Bay.[98]

As early as 1809 the *Argument* came to grief on the West (Putty) bombora (at the time called Short Reef) and lost all on board and a cargo of wheat destined for Sydney. The Captain appeared to mistake the reef for the entrance to Broken Bay when seeking shelter.[99] Sandi Leo remembered seeing more than one ship sink off the Putty Beach bombora from her home in Many View Road.[100] In 1990 a seven metre yacht, '*Island Girl*' after leaving Pittwater for Queensland hit the Putty Beach bombora and overturned in high seas where it broke up and the owner was drowned.[101]

*Maitland Bay bombora, 2016.* Photo: Myfanwy J. Webb.

# BOUDDI,

## BEGINNINGS

Bouddi is a suburb on the Bouddi Peninsula and is wholly within the northern section of Bouddi National Park.

The name Bouddi (pronounced boodee) first appears on an 1831 map by surveyor Felton Mathew marking the most prominent feature of what is now in Bouddi National Park, the eastern headland of Maitland Bay.[102] Notably Mathew was working under Thomas Mitchell the Surveyor General of NSW at the time. Mitchell was keen that local Aboriginal names be given to places newly surveyed, and it seems Mathew had followed his direction. Bouddi was a local Aboriginal name.

Felton Mathew also indicated on his map the pronunciation of Bouddi with diacritical marks placing a macron (a line above the vowel) over the u to sound as in 'mood' and a breve (bottom half of a circle) over the i to sound as in 'rick'. This means Bouddi was pronounced Boodee. Kevin Duncan of the Darkinjung Aboriginal Land Council confirms this is the pronunciation of the Darkinjung People.[103]

There has been debate for many years as to the meaning of Bouddi although all agree it is an Aboriginal word. Here are some of the meanings offered:

'The heart' is the most popular. This meaning comes from a list of Aboriginal words in John Hunter's Journal of 1793 where the word 'but but' or 'boot boot' means 'the heart'.[104] Philip Gidley King around 1786-90 recorded that 'bud bud' meant 'the sound of a heart beating'.[105] Barry Corr has said 'Aboriginal languages are highly metaphorical…a made object has the same name as what it was made from, or incorporates it. Thus, the sound of breaking waves on an incoming tide may well share the onomatopoeic sound of a beating heart'.[106]

The word 'Bondi' or 'Boondi' a word similar to 'Bouddi' is also said to mean 'the noise made by the sea breaking'. This was mentioned by surveyor James Larmer in 1832.[107] George Thornton, who spent time with the local Aboriginal people, wrote in 1896 that 'the place called 'Bondi' should be 'Boondi' meaning 'the noise made by the sea waves breaking on the beach there'.[108] W. Bishop who compiled a list of Aboriginal words in 1928 using the State Library of NSW records and other sources listed 'Boondi' as meaning 'Big nulla-nulla; knee' and 'Boondee' as a 'Heavy-headed club'.[109]

Jeremy Steele suggests the word 'puti' may be close to 'Bouddi' and is the word for 'oil' as in 'anointing with oil' noted by the Rev. Lancelot Threlkeld who was a missionary with the Lake Macquarie Awabakal people in the early 19th century. This word is from his translation of the Gospel according to Luke from the Bible.[110]

There is a place named Putty near Windsor, NSW and it could be that the name for Bouddi is derived from the same Aboriginal word. For a discussion about that see the entry for PUTTY BEACH

Maybe F.C. Bennett is close to the mark when he states, '[Bouddi] is an Aboriginal word. It is the same word as is used in the Port Stephens/Forster area as BOOTI and this latter version is probably closer to the original pronunciation. Both sounds are derived from the Aboriginal word for the heart–Boot. Aboriginal words are sometimes repeated for emphasis, and this would indicate the sound of the heart beating or the heart-like pounding of the waves on the beach'.[111]

Bouddi was gazetted as a suburb in 1996.[112]

*Bouddi Point at left side, 2024.* Photo: Myfanwy J. Webb.

[ *Listing of Place & Street Names: A to B*

# BOUDDI COASTAL WALK,
## MACMASTERS, KILLCARE

### BEGINNINGS

Some decades ago, the path from Putty Beach northwards was once a narrow dirt and rocky track with clay sections that became slippery after rain and was dangerously close to the cliffs. The catalyst for upgrading this track was when Donald Runcie, Beverley Runcie's husband, sprained his ankle while walking to Bullimah Beach. A rescue helicopter winched him aboard and flew him to Royal North Shore Hospital in Sydney. Soon after, National Parks and Wildlife Service built the wooden boardwalk with railings for that section of the Bouddi Coastal Walk.

In 2020 the NSW Government set aside $1.4 million over 4 years for upgrading the 8-kilometre Bouddi Coastal Walk which extends from Putty Beach to MacMasters Beach. This spectacular walk is 8.5km one-way and takes between 3hrs 30mins to 4 hrs 40mins with a rating of Grade 3.

This upgrade, completed in 2023, has included five new lookouts with viewing platforms. These are named using Indigenous words for significant features of each individual site. The use of quarried sandstone with the same geological origins (Hawkesbury Sandstone) as the coastline plateau, embeds the artifical track with the natural landcape and protects the land from the impact of visiting human feet.

For information about the name Bouddi see the entry for BOUDDI and BOUDDI NATIONAL PARK.

*Bullimah rock platform, 2018.* Photo: Myfanwy J. Webb.

*Bouddi Coastal Walk, Putty Beach, 2025.* Photo: Kalena V. Webb.

## DADAR LOOKOUT

Dadar is an Indigenous term for the soft springy native grass known as Kangaroo grass (*Themeda australis*). This tussocky grass has sensitive foilage and is part of the endangered ecological community of Themeda Grasslands.

*Dadar Lookout and kangaroo grass, 2025.* Photo: Myfanwy J. Webb.

*Listing of Place & Street Names: A to B*

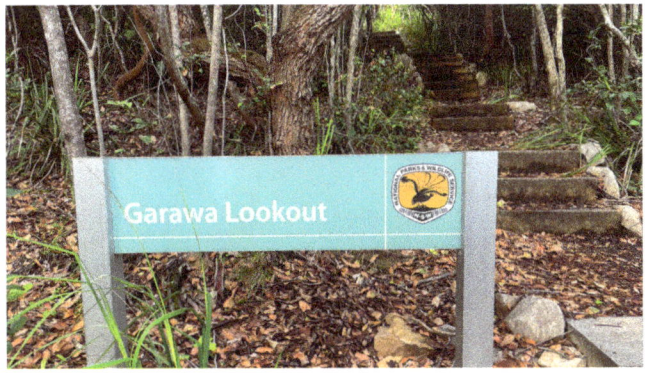

*Garawa Lookout, 2025.* Photo: Myfanwy J. Webb.

*Marang Lookout, 2025.* Photo: Myfanwy J. Webb.

*Mullian Lookout, 2025.* Photo: Myfanwy J. Webb.

*Toorongong Lookout, 2025.* Photo: Myfanwy J. Webb.

## GARAWA LOOKOUT

Garawa Lookout is positioned above Little Beach, towards the northerly end of the Bouddi Coastal Walk.

Garawa is an Indigenous word that means ocean. The South Pacific Ocean at this point along the coast forms a natural wedge into the land. It is here that the water flows down from the heath lands into the tall Eucalypt forest, through the sands of the beach to finally merge with the ocean.

## MARANG LOOKOUT

This lookout offers an expansive view of the namesake and heart of the region, Bouddi Point.

Marang is an Indigenous name for sandy beach. When walking upon the beach towards Bouddi, you might hear the deep whooshing sound of a heart beating, as waves rush up and over the sand and then slip back out to the depths again. The low cliff walls enhance this acoustic resonance of energy from sea to land.

## MULLIAN LOOKOUT

This lookout offers a view to the Northern Beaches and beyond to Boora Point, Malabar (Eastern Suburbs), Sydney, a distance of 50km away.

Mullian is an Indigenous name for the White-bellied Sea-eagle (*Haliaeetus leucogaster*). If you see the bonded pair that have their territory along this part of the coastline, you can identify the female as she is the larger of the mated pair.

## TOORONGONG LOOKOUT

This lookout is positioned at the migration turning point for whale species to slightly alter their direction during their movement along the coast. You can view their route to the south from this vantage, towards the headlands of Sydney, visible in the distance. Toorongong is an Indigenous word for whale.

[ *Listing of Place & Street Names: A to B*

# BOUDDI FARM,
## KILLCARE HEIGHTS

### BEGINNINGS

For information about the name Bouddi see the entry for BOUDDI.

### HISTORY

Situated at 251 The Scenic Road, Bouddi Farm was the home of Australian artist Russell Drysdale (1912-1981) and his wife Maisie. The property adjoining the Bouddi National Park was bought by the Drysdales in 1964. Drysdale commissioned architect Guilford Bell to design the house, which was in three pavilions, one each for sleeping, living and working although a separate studio was built a little later. The house, finished in 1966, faced north with extensive views over bushland and Brisbane Water and it was here that Drysdale and his wife entertained family and friends, many of them local.

Drysdale was knighted in 1969. He lived and painted at Bouddi Farm until his death in 1981. Maisie Drysdale remained at Bouddi Farm until she died in 2001 and the property was sold the following year. For further information about Drysdale's life at Bouddi Farm see the following references.[113]

*'Man and Death Adder' by Artist Russell Drysdale.* Photo: Bouddi Photos Past and Present, Flickr, CC BY 2.0.

# BOUDDI GRAND DEEP,
## BOUDDI NATIONAL PARK

### BEGINNINGS

For information about the name Bouddi see the entry for BOUDDI. The Bouddi Grand Deep is a natural amphitheatre in Bouddi National Park. It sits behind Maitland Bay and rises steeply to The Scenic Road.

### HISTORY

The Bouddi Grand Deep contains a variety of plant and animal communities and is important as it is largely undisturbed.

It has closed forest areas where the canopy is dense, and the understory remains moist. As a result, it produces rainforest and deep sheltered moist gullies. This encourages cabbage tree palms, lillypillies, turpentines and coachwood with an understory of small trees, shrubs, lianas, ferns, herbs and epiphytes. Some birds found in this remnant rainforest are the green catbird, brown pigeon, wonga pigeon and the satin and regent bowerbird.

The Bouddi Grand Deep also has open forest areas

*Russell Drysdale at Bouddi Farm.* Photo: Bouddi Photos Past and Present, Flickr, CC BY 2.0.

## Listing of Place & Street Names: A to B

with a semi closed canopy cover and a moist and dense understory. For further details see the 'Bouddi Peninsula Study: Coastwatch'.[114]

On the track down to Maitland Bay, John Wall who purchased the land in 1945 and built the first house at what is now the Maitland Bay Centre, carved a sign into a rock beside some steps which said 'GOOD WATER IN FERNS' with an arrow pointing into the Grand Deep. This would have helped early bushwalkers as there was no water available at Maitland Bay. Sadly, as buildings multiplied along Scenic Drive it was feared the water would be polluted and the sign was chipped out some time after 2010. The sign is still decipherable, although covered with lichen, on the rock which is about 20 metres past the bridge on the Maitland Bay track.

# BOUDDI LOOKOUT,

## BEGINNINGS

For information about the name Bouddi see the entry for BOUDDI.

Bouddi Lookout, also called Mt Bouddi Lookout and Mt Bouddi Outlook, is about one kilometre from Dingeldei Picnic Area on the track leading down to Maitland Bay.

## HISTORY

It is an informal lookout on a rocky platform without railings. From there is a view out to the Pacific Ocean. The Bouddi Lookout was officially named in 1977.

[IMAGE] (LEFT)

*Cabbage Tree Palm (Livistona australis), 2020.* Photo: Myfanwy J. Webb.

[IMAGE] (BELOW)

*Bullimah Lookout and Bullimah Spur, 2016.* Photo: Myfanwy J. Webb.

[ *Listing of Place & Street Names: A to B*

# BOUDDI NATIONAL PARK,

## BEGINNINGS

For information about the name Bouddi see the entry for BOUDDI.

Bouddi National Park is a particularly beautiful area. It sits between the Pacific Ocean and the bay waters of Brisbane Water.

It offers a variety of vegetation including heathland, dry sclerophyll forests and pockets of rainforest. The many bush tracks entice the bushwalker to discover both bush and beaches. The Park also includes important evidence of the first Aboriginal inhabitants including rock engravings, paintings and middens.

## HISTORY

Marie Byles, a Sydney solicitor and conservationist (see the entry for MARIE BYLES LOOKOUT) was instrumental in the formation of the Park. In 1922 she visited the area with some friends and saw its potential for use as a perpetual public parkland.

The name Bouddi Natural Park was chosen by the park trustees at a meeting in 1936 because 'Bouddi' was the original Aboriginal name of the most prominent headland of the area and 'Natural' being the way the trustees hoped to keep the area although the name changed twice after this. Initially the park comprised of the strip of land along the coast, originally a coal reserve, from MacMasters Beach to Putty Beach. It was declared as a State Park in 1935 and had an area of 650 acres (263 hectares). Despite sand mining on Putty Beach and Tallow Beach and the west of Bombi Moor, these areas were later included in the Park.

There are three camping and picnic areas in the park at Little Beach, Tallow Beach and Putty Beach. The Putty Beach area was redesigned and renovated and the road realigned and sealed in 2012.

Note that the National Parks and Wildlife Service which manages the National Park uses the word 'Trail' when it has vehicle access, and the word 'Track' is usually confined to walking tracks.

The Park was renamed Bouddi State Park in 1967 and at that time totaled 530 hectares. In 1974 it became Bouddi National Park and it continues to grow with land acquired by Gosford City Council [now Central Coast Council] and under the Coastal Open Space System (COSS). It is now over 1500 hectares and was officially declared a Reserve in 1976.[118] Housing and private land has remained in discreet areas and is virtually surrounded by the Park.[119]

In 2020 the NSW Government set aside $1.4 million over 4 years for upgrading the 8-kilometre Bouddi Coastal Walk which extends from Putty Beach to MacMasters Beach.[120]

*Listing of Place & Street Names: A to B*

Aboriginal men on cliff top, 1905. Modified from: Dick Thomas (Port Macquarie).

BBQ in Bouddi National Park, 1980. Photo: Myfanwy J. Webb.

Bouddi National Park north west outlook, 2023. Photo: Myfanwy J. Webb.

[ *Listing of Place & Street Names: A to B*

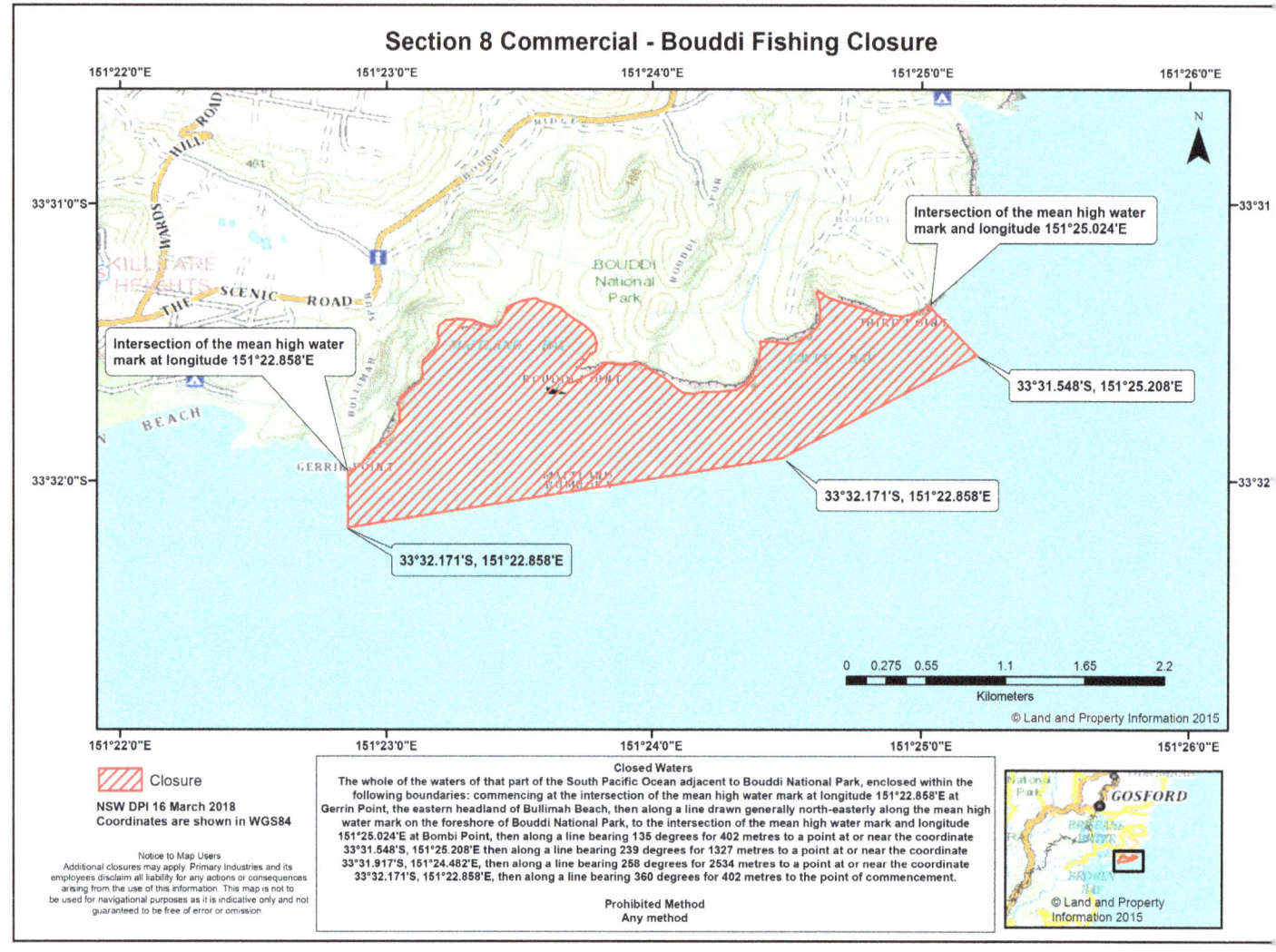

*Bouddi National Park Marine Extension, 2015.* Photo: New South Wales Land and Property Information.

# BOUDDI NATIONAL PARK MARINE EXTENSION

## BEGINNINGS

Bouddi Marine Extension is a marine reserve off the coast of Bouddi National Park. It extends from Gerrin Point to Third (Bombi) Point and so includes Maitland Bay and Caves Bay. Covering an area of over 287 hectares it includes the seabed as well as the waters above it.

For information about the name Bouddi see the entry for BOUDDI.

## HISTORY

Bouddi Marine Extension was officially reserved as a marine sanctuary zone in 1971 and fishing prohibition commenced in 1973. It was one of the earliest marine protected areas in the state. The boundary of the marine extension can be seen on 1:25,000 Topographic map 'Broken Bay' 9130-I-N published by Land & Property Information, NSW. Detailed GPS coordinates can be found on the NSW Department of Primary Industries NSW website.

Fishing, taking worms, shellfish and crustaceans of all kinds is prohibited in this zone which helps protect marine life. The marine extension is managed co-operatively between NSW Fisheries, Waterways Authority of NSW and National Parks and Wildlife Service. Research has shown an increase in the numbers and diversity of marine life in the marine extension.[121]

# BOUDDI PENINSULA

## BEGINNINGS

The Bouddi Peninsula encompasses the suburbs of Killcare, Killcare Heights, Hardys Bay, Pretty Beach and Wagstaffe as well at Bouddi and Box Head. It is a plateau with Mt Bouddi as its highest point at 166 metres and falling to about 100 metres behind Lobster Beach.

For information about the name Bouddi see the entry for BOUDDI.

## HISTORY

The Bouddi National Park now forms a large part of the Bouddi Peninsula, extending from MacMasters Beach to Rileys Bay including the ridge above Daleys Point and to Box Head, the northern headland of Broken Bay.

Bouddi Peninsula was officially designated as a Peninsula in 1972, although it should be noted that officially the northern boundary begins at Erina Creek and Wamberal.[122]

*Bush Fire smoke over Bouddi Peninsula.* Photo: Bouddi Photos Past and Present, Flickr, CC BY 2.0.

*Satellite photo of Bouddi Peninsula.* Photo: Bouddi Photos Past and Present, Flickr, CC BY 2.0.

*Bouddi National Park Marine Extension, 2025.* Photo: Myfanwy J. Webb.

## BOUDDI POINT,
### BOUDDI NATIONAL PARK

Bouddi Point was named by the local Aboriginal people and was noted by surveyor Felton Mathew in 1831 on a map of the area. It is now a prominent feature of the Bouddi National Park being the eastern headland of Maitland Bay and was officially named in 1977.

For information about the name Bouddi see the entry for BOUDDI.

*Maitland Bay and Bouddi Point, 2016.* Photo: Myfanwy J. Webb.

## BOX HEAD,
### BOUDDI NATIONAL PARK

### BEGINNINGS

Box Head is the northern headland of the entrance to Broken Bay. The name Box Head has also been assigned as a suburb name although the area remains in the south end of Bouddi National Park and there is no settlement there.

The origin of the name is unknown. However, viewing the headland from the water, it looks box shaped. Could it have been named Box Head because it looks like a box from the waters of Broken Bay?

### HISTORY

Lieutenant William Bradley assisted John Hunter in surveying the waterways of the area in 1789 and produced a chart of Broken Bay where he named Box Head, 'Inner North Head'.[124] However, this name wasn't adopted.

The name Box Head has been in use since at least 1809 as it is mentioned in the *Sydney Gazette* when the sloop '*Hazard*... which got ashore at Box Head, has been got off, with the loss of her whole freight of wheat. The captain drowned and the only other crew, a boy was saved by the humane exertions of several natives, who had been spectators of the disaster.' The Hazard lost 400 bushels of wheat and another vessel the Argument was wrecked nearby in the same squall with its cargo of wheat.[124] The loss of the wheat which was being transported from the Hawkesbury to Port Jackson would have been a cause of great concern to the growing colony.

The name also appears as 'Box Head' on an 1831 map by surveyor Felton Mathew.[126] By 1837 it appears in Government documents.[127] 'A map of the County of Cumberland in the Colony of New South Wales', published in 1840 and compiled by the surveyor W.H. Wells, shows the name 'Box Head' and under it is written 'North Head'.[128]

When Australia began to think about war in 1939, the Coastal Scenic Road League stated that, 'Box Head was the Gibraltar of Broken Bay and the Hawkesbury, and its level plateau would make a fine landing ground for aeroplanes'[129]. Unsurprisingly this suggestion was not acted upon.

It has also been referred to as Hawk or Hawke Head. Interestingly the road leading to the headland is named Hawke Head Drive not Box Head Drive. See also the entry for HAWK(E) HEAD.

A large area of Box Head had been reserved for 'Public Purposes' in 1876 and was included in the Bouddi National Park in 1972. It was officially named Box Head in 1977 by the Geographical Names Board, the previous name noted as 'Box or Hawke Head'. Box Head as a suburb was officially named in 1996.[130]

*Listing of Place & Street Names: A to B*

*Myfanwy J. Webb at Box Head after bushfire, 1981.*
Photo: Beverley J. Runcie.

*Box Head, 2017.*
Photo: Peter D. Runcie.

[ *Listing of Place & Street Names: A to B*

# BRISBANE WATER,

## BEGINNINGS

Brisbane Water is the northeast arm of Broken Bay and was originally referred to as the 'North East Arm'. The first mention of the use of the name Brisbane Water is in a memorial James Webb, the first settler sent to the Colonial Secretary asking for a grant of land in August 1824. He said that as a boat wright he had been able 'to realize a little capital in cattle and effects, with which he has seated himself on the west bank of the North East Arm of Broken Bay (now known by the name of "Brisbane Water.")'[131] After it was surveyed in 1825 it was formally renamed to honour Governor Sir Thomas MacDougall Brisbane who was Governor of New South Wales between 1821 and 1825.

*Brisbane Water before construction of the Rip Bridge, 1920s.* Photo: Bouddi Photos Past and Present, Flickr, CC BY 2.0.

## HISTORY

Brisbane Water was first explored by Governor Phillip as early as March 1788, but was dismissed as a suitable location for a settlement. He found that the entrance was narrow and proved difficult for vessels. Once the entrance was negotiated there were sand bars, much shallow water and 'The Rip' with its strong tidal pull. The land was high and rocky and heavily timbered down to the water and there were only small pockets of flat land suitable for farming. These factors meant settlement did not get going until the 1820s. Once the discovery of the rich alluvial soil plains of Richmond and Windsor was made, attention was directed there.

The first land grant in Brisbane Water was given in 1811 to William Nash for land near Rileys Bay. [132] However he did not settle, and the first settler was James Webb who took up land opposite near Blackwall Mountain and The Rip in 1823.

The early settlers relied on water transport as there was no road to the district. In fact, there were very few roads around Brisbane Water itself and it was not until the Hawkesbury Bridge and railway was completed in 1889 that the population began to increase. The first reasonably direct road access from Sydney to Gosford which included the Peats Ferry crossing of the Hawkesbury was established in 1930.

Early settlers in Brisbane Water were subsistence farmers making a living running a few cattle, timber cutting, shingle splitting, shell collecting (for mortar) and later shipping and shipbuilding.[133] Fishing was popular in the early days, but Brisbane Water was soon overfished and was permanently closed to commercial fishing in 1911.[134] Licenses for oyster leases also became necessary.

# BROKEN BAY,

## BEGINNINGS

The naming of Broken Bay is attributed to Captain James Cook. He wrote in his journal that the ship '*Endeavour*' on 7 May 1770 passed 'At sunset … some broken land that appeared to form a bay … This bay I named 'Broken Bay'.[135] However he passed 'our' Broken Bay at night and Matthew Flinders travelling north in 1802 checked Cook's latitude readings and believed Cook saw instead the entrance to Narrabeen Lake to the south.[136] Trevor Lipscombe examines this in an article entitled 'Broken Bay – two bays or one?' from Placenames Australia.[137]

*Listing of Place & Street Names: A to B*

*Early view of Broken Bay before 1927.* Photo: William Henry Broadhurst, 1855-1927, Courtesy of State Library of New South Wales.

## HISTORY

The name Broken Bay has been used from the first days of the settlement as Lieutenant William Bradley states in his journal that on 2nd February 1788 Governor Phillip and a party of men left Port Jackson 'for the purpose of examining Broken Bay, victualled for 7 days'. On a return journey in August 1789 to survey the area, Bradley clearly marks the name 'Broken Bay' on his map.[138] It is appropriately named as it has many bays, coves and creeks.

Broken Bay is a drowned valley estuary of the Hawkesbury River and has three main branches: Pittwater, Cowan Creek and Brisbane Water. Governor Phillip first realised the bay was an estuary in June 1789 when he explored further upstream and named the Hawkesbury River, finally reaching the fertile alluvial plains around Windsor. The entrance to Broken Bay lies between Box Head to the north which is part of Bouddi Peninsula and Barrenjoey Head to the south.

In the early days Broken Bay was used as a refuge for small coastal vessels and for regular shipping between Windsor and Sydney via the Hawkesbury River. Not all vessels which sought shelter from stormy weather however were successful. As early as April 1803 the *Sydney Gazette* records the loss of the sloop *Hope* in Broken Bay with its cargo of maize, potatoes and melons. Less than a month later, another sloop, *John* was wrecked in the bay in bad weather and lost a cargo of wheat, maize, potatoes and pumpkins. The loss of food would have been keenly felt in the emerging colony. Many more shipwrecks occurred over the years which followed.[139] Today the bay is mainly used for recreation. As late as 1865 it was considered a 'wild but delightful spot' and 'scarcely any of the citizens of Sydney are aware of the magnificent harbour of refuge that lies within so short a distance of their own commanding anchorage'.[140] Much of the land surrounding Broken Bay is preserved as national park land and includes Brisbane Water National Park, Ku-ring-gai Chase National Park (including Barrenjoey Headland) and of course Bouddi National Park.

*View to high bluff, Bulbararing (First Point) from MacMasters Beach, 2024.* Photo: Myfanwy J. Webb.

*Listing of Place & Street Names: A to B*

# BULBARARING, COPACABANA

## BEGINNINGS

Bulbararing Point, just south of Avoca Beach, is not in the Bouddi Peninsula but is included here because of its link with Bouddi. Bulbararing is an Aboriginal word which F. C. Bennett believed meant 'a high rocky headland' but that meaning has not yet been verified.[141]

## HISTORY

This is the most northerly of the three points of 'Cape Three Points'. Captain James Cook named 'Cape Three Points' as he sailed northwards in May 1770. He wrote 'Some pretty high land which projected out in three bluff points and occasioned my calling it Cape Three Points' without naming the individual points.[142]

'Bulbararing' appears on an 1831 map by surveyor Felton Mathew [143] (see Appendix 4.7) and would have been a local Aboriginal name. Many current maps use that name, but it is now officially named 'First Point' and Bulbararing is listed as a previous name.[144] Tudibaring Headland, also on the early surveyed map means 'where waves pound like a heart beating' and is located 450 metres north of MacMasters ocean pool. Current maps inaccurately name Bulbararing as Tudibaring Headland.

# BULKARA STREET, WAGSTAFFE

## BEGINNINGS

Bulkara Street is at the end of Wagstaffe Avenue leading to houses near Kourong Gourong Point and Wagstaffe Point.

Bulkara is probably an Aboriginal word but as this street was not named until 1906 it is possibly not a word used by the original Aboriginal people for this area. The meaning of Bulkara is probably from the word 'bulkirra' an Aboriginal word of the Awabakal people living around Lake Macquarie and Newcastle area. It means 'any mountain' (from the word 'bulka'), or 'the back of a man or beast' used metaphorically and was recorded by Rev. L.E. Threlkeld in 1834.[145] McCarthy listed the meaning of 'bulkara' as 'mountain'.[146] The Sydney Aboriginal people used the name 'bulga' which means hill and these meanings appear appropriate for this street as there is certainly a hill behind Bulkara Street.[147]

There is also an Aboriginal verb 'bulka' to kill or strike, a word from the Kurnu people in Western NSW.[148]

## HISTORY

Bulkara Street first appears on 'Wagstaffe's Point Estate' subdivision in 1906 (Appendix 1.8). It remained unformed until the early 1960s when the Citizen's Association asked the Gosford Council to form the road to give access to ratepayers' property.[149] The San Toy Estate fronted onto Bulkara Street. For more information about the San Toy Estate see the entry for SAN TOY ESTATE.

In 1969 Bulkara Street had still not been tar-sealed but Council placed it 'in the future program of works'.[150]

*San Toy Estate, 1960s.* Photo: Bouddi Photos Past and Present, Flickr, CC BY 2.0.

*Plaque at entrance of San Toy, 2000s.* Photo: Bouddi Photos Past and Present, Flickr, CC BY 2.0.

SIGNPOSTS TO THE PAST

[ *Listing of Place & Street Names: A to B*

# BULLIMAH BEACH,
## BOUDDI NATIONAL PARK

### BEGINNINGS

Bullimah Beach is a small ocean beach in Bouddi National Park situated between Putty Beach and Maitland Bay and accessed by an easy board walk above the cliffs.

Bullima (Bullimah) is an Aboriginal word meaning Spirit Land and similarly Sky-Camp or Heaven.[151] F. C. Bennett lists the meaning of Bullimar as 'Yours' but does not indicate his source.[152] It may not be a local Aboriginal name.

### HISTORY

Charles D'Arcy Roberts (1909-1943) was a solicitor, very active in the National Parks Association and a founding trustee of Bouddi Natural Park. He died in World War II while a prisoner of war of the Japanese on the Burma Railway in 1943. For more about Charles see 'Two-minute postcards: the story of a lost soldier' and an excellent video filmed in Bouddi on YouTube.[153]

Marie Byles and colleagues 'arranged that the tiniest beach should be named for him, Bullimah, the Home of the Great Spirit'.[154] A plaque at Bullimah Outlook at the end of the Bullimah Spur Track overlooking the beach was erected to honour Charles and in 1948 his parents were among those who came to the commemoration ceremony.[155]

*Charles D'Arcy Roberts, age 31, 1940.* Photo: War Service Records.

*Listing of Place & Street Names: A to B*

*Bullimah Beach, 2023.* Photo: Myfanwy J. Webb.

[ *Listing of Place & Street Names: A to B*

# BULLIMAH LOOKOUT,
## BOUDDI NATIONAL PARK

### BEGINNINGS

This lookout is in the Bouddi National Park and is at the end of the Bullimah Spur and affords a great view over Bullimah Beach and south to Barrenjoey Headland to Manly. Looking to the west the view takes in Putty Beach, Broken Bay, Pittwater, Lion Island and the entrance to the Hawkesbury River. The name was officially assigned in 1977.[156]

For information about the name Bullimah see the entry for BULLIMAH BEACH.

*Bullimah Outlook plaque, 2023.* Photo: Myfanwy J. Webb.

*Donald G. Runcie taking photographs at Bullimah Outlook, 2023.* Photo: Beverley J. Runcie.

# BURRAN ROAD, WAGSTAFFE

## BEGINNINGS

Burran is probably an Aboriginal word but not necessarily a local Aboriginal word as the road was not named until the twentieth century. Why it was called Burran is unknown. Here are a few possibilities:

Burran is an Aboriginal word meaning 'burnt grass'.[157] The following meaning could be linked. Burran is a period in the Dharawal calendar between January and March when it is very hot and dry.

Baylis lists 'burran' as meaning 'native cat' and Jakelin Troy mentions three similar words to Burran in her work 'The Sydney Language': burra is the Aboriginal word for sky, burra burra are Aboriginal words meaning 'eel' and buran buran is the Aboriginal name for stringybark (*Eucalyptus obliqua*). Grace Karskens lists buran spoken by the Dharruk and Darkinjung Aboriginal people as meaning narrow leafed stringybark (*Eucalyptus sparsifolia*) and uses the word burra for the fishhooks the women of Sydney made from turban shells.[159]

*Track to Lobster Beach, south of non-existent Burran Road, 2025.*
Photo: Myfanwy J. Webb.

## HISTORY

This was a short road starting in Albert Street and going up the hill to the ridge above Lobster Beach. It first appeared on the Wagstaffe Point subdivision map in December 1906 (Appendix 1.8). However, the road no longer exists. There may have been a track where Burran Road was because as late as 1939 some owners were listed as owning blocks of land in Burran Road.[160] Later most of the road reserve of Burran Road was closed and incorporated into the Bouddi National Park. The remainder is owned by Council and is unformed and not maintained and is now effectively a 'paper road'.[161] However, it can still be seen on some maps and is retained on some Council maps (see Appendix 4.5).

CHAPTER FIVE

# 5

# LISTING OF PLACE & STREET NAMES

## C-P

*Listing of Place & Street Names: C to P*

# CAPE THREE POINTS

## BEGINNINGS

Cape Three Points is a cape on the Tasman Sea which comprises First (Bulbararing), Second (Mourawaring) and Third (Bombi) Points and is just north of the entrance to Broken Bay (Appendix 4.7). The names in brackets are the original Aboriginal names. First Point is just south of Avoca Beach and Second and Third Points are within the Bouddi National Park.

## HISTORY

Captain James Cook named 'Cape Three Points' as he sailed northwards in 1770; however, he did not name the individual points. He wrote in his log on 7th May, 'Some pretty high land which projected out in three bluff points and occasioned my calling it Cape Three Points'.[162]

For more information about the individual points see the entries under their English names and their Aboriginal names.

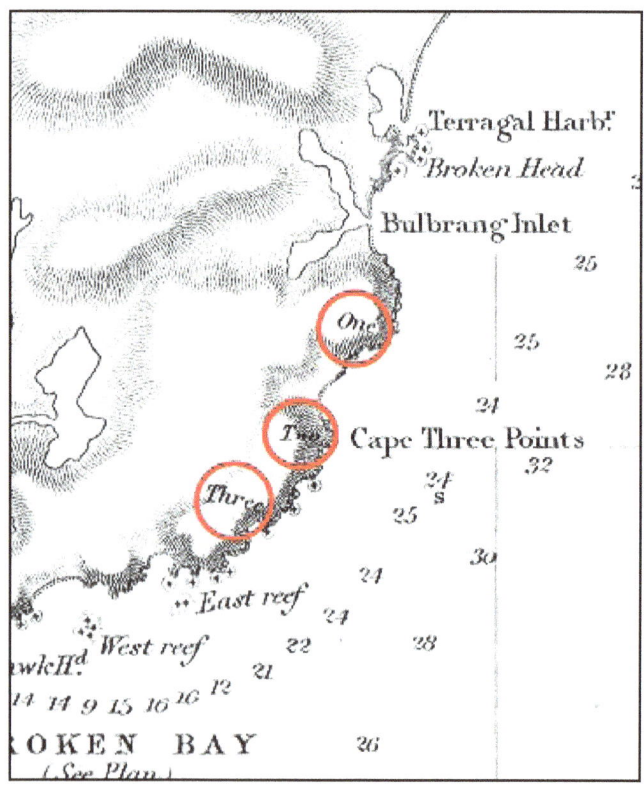

*John Lort Stokes' Chart showing three points, 1851.* Modified from: Trove.

[PREVIOUS SPREAD]

*Putty Beach at Night, 2024.* Photo: Myfanwy J. Webb.

*Bulbararing Headland, Copacabana 2025.* Photo: Myfanwy J. Webb.

# CAVES BAY & CAVES CREEK,
## BOUDDI NATIONAL PARK

### BEGINNINGS

Caves Bay is between Maitland Bay and Little Beach and is in Bouddi National Park. This is a descriptive name as there are numerous caves which are not far from the walking track crossing Cave Creek.

### HISTORY

There were signs in the caves of Aboriginal occupation and of fishermen who sheltered here in earlier times.[163] The Surveyor Felton Mathew in 1831 wrote on a map alongside what we now call Caves Creek the words 'Running Creek Fresh Water'; an important fact to note when exploring new territory.[164]

Caves Bay was previously called 'The Caves' and was officially assigned the name Caves Bay in 1977.[165] As it's in the Bouddi National Park Marine Extension, fishing/collecting of marine life on the foreshore and seabed are prohibited. Modern maps name wrong bay.

*Marine Extension sign, 2025. Photo: Myfanwy J. Webb.*

## COMO PARADE,
PRETTY BEACH

### BEGINNINGS

The origin of the name is unknown. However, because there is also Venice Road nearby and named at the same time, it is probable that Como was named after the town on Lake Como in Italy. Both Como and Venice conjure up visions of luxury holidays near the water and probably was an advertising ploy to attract buyers to the land.

Years later in 1936 a documentary film by Claude Flemming and sponsored by Woy Woy Shire Council was released entitled Woy Woy: *The Venice of Australia* which can be viewed on YouTube.[166]

### HISTORY

Como Parade first appeared on the 'Pretty Beach Estate' subdivision map in 1910 (Appendix 1.6). The road originally joined with Venice Road and was the earliest road from Hardys Bay to Wagstaffe. Pretty Beach Road was formed much later. Now Como Parade is a 'no through road'. There is no official link but there is an open area where people cross from Como to where High View Road meets Venice Road.

Jack Smith lived at 17 Como Parade with his sister Marjorie. Jack had a market garden in Venice Road and Marjorie taught the piano.[167]

Like Venice Road, Como Parade had not been sealed by 1967 and the Council said it was listed for 'future consideration'. Then in 1969 Council placed it in the 'future program of works'. By 1976 repairs had been made to Como Parade.[168] Forty years on in 2021 it is still very narrow and uncurbed, however the surface has been upgraded.

*Bill Dodd & Beryl at 'Cromer', corner of Como Pde, date unknown. Photo: Bouddi Photos Past and Present, Flickr, CC BY 2.0.*

*Como Parade corner present day, 2025. Photo: Myfanwy J. Webb.*

[ *Listing of Place & Street Names: C to P*

[IMAGE] (LEFT)

*William Michael Daley, 1870 - 1944.* Photo: © State of New South Wales through the Parliament of New South Wales.

# DALEYS POINT

## BEGINNINGS

While Daleys Point is not strictly in Bouddi Peninsula it is included here because of its position at the eastern end of the Rip Bridge allowing access to the Peninsula via Empire Bay Drive and Wards Hill Road and because it abuts Bouddi National Park. The suburb Daleys Point was named after William Michael Daley who purchased the land which had originally been granted to William Fitzgerald. The geographical point was initially called Fitzgerald's Point but was assigned the name Daleys Point in 1974 [169].

## HISTORY

Daleys Point has a registered place of significance to Aboriginal people and is listed on the Australian Heritage Database and the register of the National Estate. This site is an important ceremonial area with extensive rock engravings, grinding grooves and middens dated to 6000 to 5500 years ago. In 1974, the Department of Main Roads altered their proposed ridge road from the Rip Bridge to below the ridgeline thus preserving the important site.

William Fitzgerald was the first farmer on this northeastern side of The Rip. He arrived as a convict in 1824 with his brother Stephen also a convict. A few weeks after landing William received a Free Pardon.

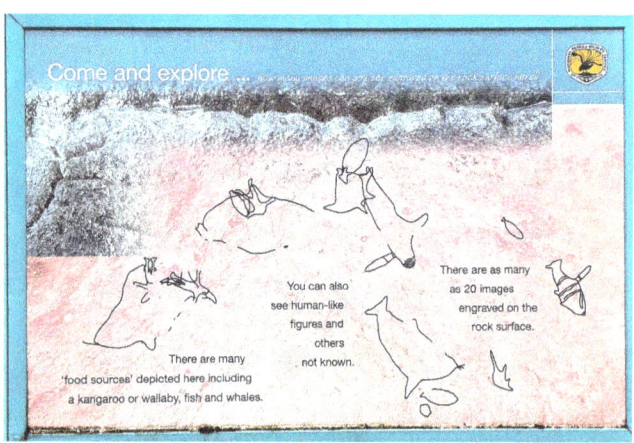

*Daleys Point sign, 2025.* Photo: Myfanwy J. Webb.

*Rock engraving at Daleys Point, 2025.* Photo: Myfanwy J. Webb.

He took up 100 acres at what is now known as Daleys Point and deferred a free trip home as he wanted to wait until Stephen was free to leave with him. He must have worked hard as by 1828 he had cleared 30 acres, cultivated 25 and had 60 cattle. His brother was assigned to him as was another convict.[170] However, Fitzgerald must have tired of farm life and in 1832 he became the licensee of a licensed house (pub) in Parramatta Road, Sydney called the *Spinning Wheel*.[171]

In 1887 Fitzgeralds Point is described as a 'favourite picnic ground… where the grass grows to the water's edge and there is plenty of shelter from the sun, and from the hill at the back we have the grandest view of nature, in all its beauty, that I ever beheld.'[172]

James Ryan initially bought Fitzgerald's land and William Michael Daley purchased it with a mortgage in 1896.

In April 1907 the 100 acres went to auction with Raine & Horne Auctioneers (Appendix 1.10). Most blocks were over one acre and were advertised as 'An excellent place for a seaside residence, for a week-end "crib" or "bolt hole"'. Four adjoining blocks facing Cockle Creek were reserved from the sale as this was where William Daley had a house with stables on Lot 8 and orchards planted on the others. Daley planted oranges, mandarins and lemons and summer fruits. The orchards were looked after by caretakers Mr and Mrs Bennett, followed by the Ives family who were connected by marriage to the Daleys.[173] All blocks did not sell and over the years land came up for sale with another auction held in November 1915 advertising 'Daleys' Point, Woy Woy, absolute Water Frontages right on the Rip'[174] (Appendix 1.12).

The land was only accessed by water, so land was slow to sell and the Tourist Guide of 1928 encouraged visitors stating: "There is no settlement but it is intended to put a waterfront road, from Empire Bay to Killcare through the estate".[175]

William Michael Daley (1870-1944) was born in Sydney and studied at the University of Sydney, becoming a solicitor. He was elected to the New South Wales Legislative Assembly as the Labor member for Sydney-Gipps transferring to Darling Harbour electorate in 1904. He married Daisy Emily Ives in 1903 and they had two children, Catherine and Stephen. Leaving politics he continued practicing as a solicitor until 1927.[176] William appears to have used his land at Daleys Point as a country retreat.

In appreciation of William Daley's work in parliament to have the Fisheries Act of 1903 passed, the residents of Brisbane Water presented him with an Illuminated Address (See below). It is beautifully decorated and includes a painting of Daley's house and two fishermen in a boat in front of his land. The Fisheries Act set out minimum weights and sizes of caught fish and crustaceans and anyone selling oysters was required to have a licence costing £1 [$2].[177]

The suburb Daleys Point was officially assigned in 1991.[178]

*Certificate, William Michael Daley Esq, 1903.* Photo: Courtesy of Central Coast Council.

# DAPHNES CAMP,
## BOUDDI NATIONAL PARK

### BEGINNINGS

Daphnes Camp is a flat area just behind Maitland Bay Beach and is within Bouddi National Park. It was named after Mary Olive Daphne McKern (née Ball) (1907-1971) who was honorary secretary to the Bouddi Natural Park Trust and a committed conservationist. She was involved with the Bouddi National Park from 1936 until her death in 1971.[179]

### HISTORY

This is the place where Marie Byles and the early volunteers camped while they worked on making walking trails in the 1930s and 40s.

*Goanna (Varanus), 2023.* Photo: Myfanwy J. Webb.

*Runcies, Barnes & Yorks at Daphnes Camp, Bouddi National Park, 1986.*

[BACKGROUND IMAGE] (LEFT & RIGHT)

*Ferns in Bouddi, 2024.* Photo: Myfanwy J. Webb.

*Opening Dingeldei Picnic Shelter, 1962.* Photo: Bouddi Photos Past and Present, Flickr, CC BY 2.0.

# DINGELDEI PICNIC SHELTER,
## BOUDDI NATIONAL PARK

### BEGINNINGS

This covered shelter shed is in the Mount Bouddi Picnic area at the end of Mount Bouddi Road in the Bouddi National Park. Sometimes the picnic area itself is called the Dingeldei Picnic Area.

Adolph William (Bill) Dingeldei (1897-1960) was a member of the Caloola Bushwalkers' Club and a trustee of Bouddi Natural Park Trust. He was a tireless worker in the National Park especially improving the tracks system and died suddenly in 1960.

### HISTORY

The Dingeldei Memorial Shelter in Bouddi National Park named after Bill Dingeldei was opened on 10 November 1962 in his memory. It was built entirely by subscription and voluntary labour and about 300 people attended the opening.[180] There are two plaques to commemorate the event; one is an official plaque revealed at the opening of the shelter and the other one was placed inside the shelter in 2002 by some of those who helped to build it.

The Mount Bouddi Track begins here and heads out to Bouddi Lookout and down to the coast to meet the Bouddi Coastal Walk just near Maitland Bay. For more information about this picnic area see the entry for MOUNT BOUDDI PICNIC SHELTER.

SIGNPOSTS TO THE PAST

[ *Listing of Place & Street Names: C to P*

# THE DOG TRACK,
## PRETTY BEACH

### BEGINNINGS

This walking track is an extension of Araluen Drive (which was gazetted in 1964)[181] in Hardys Bay beginning at the point and following the water's edge to the barrier at Pretty Beach. It is known by locals as The Dog Track and is where dogs can be walked. The Dog Track is an unofficial name and there is no sign.

### HISTORY

In 1965 to avoid traffic congestion on Heath Road it had been suggested this track should be turned into a one-way road with the traffic in Heath Road going the other way. This proposition was opposed strongly by many, and the plan was not taken up by Gosford City Council.[182]

Discussions with community associations and Council continued until the 1990s. It was finally agreed to put slip rail gates at each end of the extension with locks and make it available for walkers, cyclists and emergency vehicles.

Since 1999 a Bushcare group of volunteers regularly meet to eradicate weeds from the track and encourage native plant regrowth. In 2004 the Dog Track was declared an area for dogs to exercise off the leash.

It remains a pleasant walking track along the waterfront where people can walk their dogs. Two benches were placed along the track in 2016 for rest and contemplation and the plaques on each commemorate the following two local identities who worked to improve the Bouddi area.

Gwen Perrie (Gwendoline Greenhalgh) grew up in Wagstaffe during World War II and attended Pretty Beach School. She met her husband Max Perrie at Pretty Beach as his parents owned 2 cottages in Pretty Beach Road. In 1980 after living in Sydney for some time they moved back to the area. Unfortunately, Max became quite ill for many years and after his death Gwen became involved in local issues. She worked with Fay Gunther to upgrade the Wagstaffe Community Hall. Gwen continued working with Fay to improve facilities in the area and pursued funding from Federal, State and Local government to enable local projects to proceed. Gwen's happy smile and her considerable contribution will not be forgotten.[184]

*The Dog Track, 2024.* Photo: Myfanwy J. Webb.

*Dedicated to the Memory of*
*Gwen Perrie*
*1936-2013*
*In recognition of outstanding service to our community*

*Gwen Perrie & Fay Gunther, 1999.* Photo: Bouddi Photos Past and Present, Flickr, CC BY 2.0.

Richard Harper was an important member of our community who volunteered his time and skills working on Council committees and on the Wagstaffe to Killcare Community Association Committee to improve conditions in the area. He used his engineering skills in practical tasks as well as his lobbying skills. Richard was also known for his courteous and helpful manner and was sadly missed.[185]

*Dedicated to the Memory of*
*Richard Harper*
*1939-2016*
*In recognition of outstanding service to our community*

*Richard Harper.* Photo: Bouddi Photos Past and Present, Flickr, CC BY 2.0.

# ETTALONG CHANNEL

See the entry for WAGSTAFFE BAR.

# FIRST POINT,
## COPACABANA

First Point is the most northerly of the three points of 'Cape Three Points'.[186] First Point was originally known as 'Bulbararing', a local Aboriginal name which appears on an 1831 map by surveyor Felton Mathew (Appendix 4.7).[187] It is now officially named 'First Point'. Bulbararing is listed as a previous name[188] and Tudibaring named here on current maps is erroneous. See also BULBARARING POINT.

# FISHERMANS BAY,
## DALEYS POINT

### BEGINNINGS

Fishermans Bay is a bay just south of Daleys Point and about one kilometre north west of Rocky Point. Originally it was called Fisherman's Bight and a newspaper article in 1887 declared

> ...this is one of the best fishing grounds in the colony. Here schnappers, flathead, bream, whiting, soles, flounder, perch, salmon and numerous other fish that take the bait may be had, even sharks, fiddlers, stinging ray, etc.[189]

In the advertisement for 'Daleys Point Estate' in 1907 it was still referred to as Fisherman's Bight.[190]

### HISTORY

It was officially named Fishermans Bay in 1977 and it is reasonable to assume the name reflects its popularity as a favourite bay for fishing. It is very close to The Rip and the deep calmer waters of the Bay offer an excellent fishing location.

*Mullet (Mugil cephalus), 2017.* Photo: Myfanwy J. Webb.

SIGNPOSTS TO THE PAST

*Crowea flowering along track, 2025.* Photo: Myfanwy J. Webb.

*Palm Beach Ferry, 2025.* Photo: Myfanwy J. Webb.

# FLANNEL FLOWER TRACK,
## BOUDDI NATIONAL PARK

### BEGINNINGS

The Flannel Flower Track is within the western part of Bouddi National Park and branches off at the end of Hawke Head Drive to meet the Lobster Beach Track. It now offers a public walking track from Wagstaffe to Box Head, Tallow Beach and Killcare.

The Flannel Flower Track abounds with wildflowers in spring (especially flannel flowers) and passes through a magnificent stand of red gums (*Angophora costata*) and spotted gum (*Eucalyptus maculata*). It leads to a lookout with views to the west over Ettalong and Umina Beach to Brisbane Water National Park.

### HISTORY

The track originally began as a fire trail from Albert Street and had become an informal walking trail, however, it crossed or bordered several private properties. In 2003 property owners concerned about public liability with walkers on their land generously decided to grant public access across their property and transfer responsibility to the National Park.

Local organisations and the community raised money to assist the National Parks & Wildlife Service to pay for legal costs. It was a slow process, but persistence paid off and in January 2009 public access was legally granted.[192]

For further information see the entry for LOBSTER BEACH TRACK.

*Ancient red gum (Angophora costata), known to Indigenous people as a nurturing 'Granny Tree' with twisted limbs for holding, 2025.* Photo: Myfanwy J. Webb.

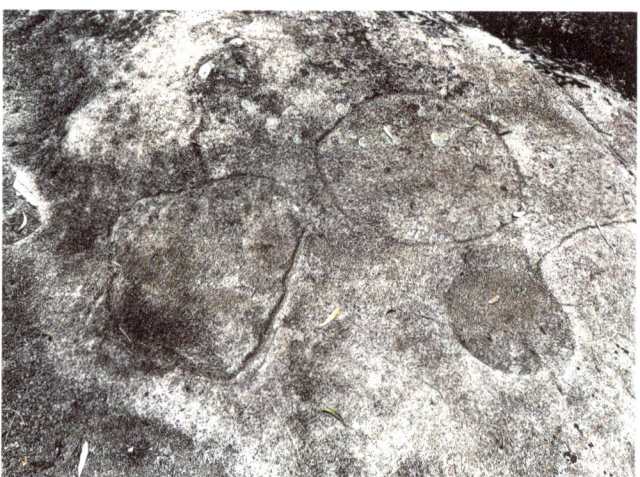
*Indigenous rock engravings, 2025.* Photo: Myfanwy J. Webb.

Flannel Flower, (*Actinotus helianthi*), 2023. Photo: Myfanwy J. Webb.

# FLETCHERS GLEN RESERVE,
## BOUDDI NATIONAL PARK

## BEGINNINGS

This is a small but important rainforest reserve tucked into the eastern corner of Killcare between Wards Hill Road and Fraser Road and has been part of Bouddi National Park since 2004.

Fletchers Glen Reserve was named after George Fletcher (1879-1936) who was the Health & Building Inspector for Erina Shire Council and later Gosford Municipality. In 1921 approximately 18 acres of land was resumed by the Council and was gazetted as a sanitary depot. George opposed the Council's move to use the area for this purpose and was successful.[193]

As late as 1964, a Gosford Shire Council map still showed Fletchers Glen Reserve marked as 'Sanitary Depot'. George who had served in the Boer War was also a noted Gosford historian and had a great sense of humour often writing for the Gosford Times about the hilarious 'Knockalong Club' under the nom-de-plume 'Perong'. George joined the Council in 1908 and worked there until he died suddenly in December 1936.[194]

## HISTORY

Originally Fletchers Glen was known as 'Fords Gully' or 'Fordys Gully' after the early landowners the Ford family who ran a dairy farm nearby.

Pamela Mainsbridge remembered family picnics there. Her mother would spread out the picnic food on picnic tables and the children would always climb up the waterfalls.[195] Bert Myer said the falls at the top of the Glen were called 'Sylvan Falls'.[196]

Bruce Dunlop remembered: 'The route to Maitland Bay was through the Fairy Glen, in the corner of Fraser Road and the hill to join a track descending into Maitland Bay'.[197]

Originally the lower area was cleared land for grazing and was a popular picnic area with picnic tables. Once the cattle went, weeds took over and a local land care group worked hard in the 1990s to eliminate them. Now the Glen supports a variety of native vegetation and fauna. There is a descriptive sign inside the forest reserve.

[IMAGES] *Fletchers Glen, National Park & Information signs, & Bush Turkey (Alectura lathami), 2025.* Photos: Myfanwy J. Webb.

*George Fletcher & family, 1929.* Photo: Courtesy of Central Coast Council.

# FLETCHERS GLEN ROAD,
## BOUDDI NATIONAL PARK

## BEGINNINGS

Fletchers Glen Road begins off Wards Hill Road just south of the Rocky Point Trail within the Bouddi National Park and runs westwards towards Rocky Point and Allen Strom Lookout. Fletchers Glen Road was named after George Fletcher who was responsible for saving Fletchers Glen from becoming a sewerage depot.

For more about George Fletcher see the entry for FLETCHERS GLEN RESERVE.

## HISTORY

The proposed road was first named and gazetted in 1970 and was planned to be about 200 metres long.[198] It can still be found on some maps, but the road was never developed, remaining a 'paper road' and is now gazetted as Bouddi National Park.

A National Park map shows Fletchers Glen Road commencing further south than the beginning of the Rocky Point Trail and that Trail crosses over it. At the end of Fletchers Glen Road is another 'paper' road winding downhill to meet Fraser Road.[199] This is believed to be the first route that William Ward and subsequently the early settlers used, to reach what is now known as Killcare Heights.

[ *Listing of Place & Street Names: C to P*

# FLORA AVENUE,
## HARDYS BAY

### BEGINNINGS

Flora Avenue is located at the western end of Nukara Avenue.

The origin of the name Flora is unknown. Possibilities: Flora is Latin name for the Roman goddess of flowers and spring. Perhaps it celebrates the spectacular native flora of the area. Flora is also a girl's first name so this street could be named after someone specific, perhaps a relative of the developer or whoever named the street.

### HISTORY

Flora Avenue was named before 1928 because there is an auction listing in the 'Sun' newspaper in October 1928 advertising a block of land for sale at Woy Woy, Hardie's [sic] Bay in Flora Avenue.[200]

# FRASER ROAD,
## KILLCARE

### BEGINNINGS

Originally named Government Road in the 'Killcare Extension Estate' subdivision of 1920 (Appendix 1.3) and was changed sometime in the 1960s to Fraser Road to honour (posthumously) James Burns Fraser of Blythe Street for his interest and work in the community. Fraser Road begins at one end of Noble Road and swings around to the east in a loop under the hill ending at the junction of Blythe Street and Stanley Street. See also the entry for GOVERNMENT ROAD.

### HISTORY

James Burns Fraser (1878-1963) was born

*Listing of Place & Street Names: C to P*

*View of Hardys Bay from above Fraser Rd, date unknown.* Photo: Bouddi Photos Past and Present, Flickr, CC BY 2.0.

in Scotland and migrated to Australia with his parents when he was about 8 years old. He worked on a farm, as a stoker on local coastal ships and then as a bread carter.

He married Sarah Rachel Wilson (1881-1966) and they had four children, Jane, Florence, Mary and James Wilson. Wilson. After serving in World War I, James set up a basket making business in Sydney in the 1920s and worked with Bill Meyer whose father Bill Meyer Senior had land at Killcare.

*James Burns Fraser, wife Sarah Rachel Fraser née Wilson and children from left Jane, Florence, Mary Maude and James Wilson Fraser (aged 6), 1913.* Photo: Bouddi Photos Past and Present, Flickr, CC BY 2.0.

James Burns Fraser bought one of Bill's blocks in Blythe Street with a house on it (No, 28) and in 1946 retired to it with his wife Sarah. After some improvements to the house, it has remained in the Fraser family.

Jim involved himself in community affairs. He helped to establish the local Returned Servicemen's League sub-branch's club liquor license, raised money for the local Fire Brigade, helped set up the local branch of the Australian Labor Party, is given credit for having the sea wall built along Hardys Bay and was also a correspondent for the local newspaper *The Gosford Star* submitting stories of local interest.[201]

Although James Burns Fraser died in 1963 the Fraser family continues to live in the area and to participate in local affairs.

# GERRIN POINT, BOUDDI NATIONAL PARK

## BEGINNINGS

The name 'Gerrin' first appears on an 1831 map by surveyor Felton Mathew [202] (Appenndix 4.7) and is a local Aboriginal word which F C Bennett said means 'danger' although he did not give the source of this information.[203]

Jakelin Troy in 'The Sydney Language' lists variations of the word djirrun, jerrun and jerron meaning 'fear, afraid, frightened', and jee-run as 'coward' and 'run away'.[204] Jeremy Steele has listed words kirrin, gee-reen, gerring from the Awabakal language meaning 'light', 'pain', and 'quick'.[205] While we may not know the original meaning for gerrin most of these meanings indicate caution should be taken at that place. Indeed, the beach known as Bullimah Beach shelves steeply and is not suitable for swimming and waves breaking over the rocks at the Point can also be dangerous.

## HISTORY

Gerrin Point is between Bullimah Beach and Maitland Bay in Bouddi National Park and marks the most westerly point of the Bouddi National Park Marine Extension. No fishing or collecting of marine life is permitted in the marine extension. The name Gerrin Point was officially assigned in March 1977.[206]

# GOVERNMENT ROAD, KILLCARE

## BEGINNINGS

This name first appeared on the 'Killcare Estate' subdivision in 1916 (Appendix 1.2). Government Road began at the top of Killcare Road and ran west (now Nukara Avenue) (Appendix 1.3) until it reached where Flora Ave is today. The road then turned east and followed the waterfront as far as Stanley Street and this was named Government (Bay) Road. This section is now named

*Listing of Place & Street Names: C to P*

[BACKGROUND SPREAD]
(LEFT)

*Little Tallow, 2024.*

Photo: Myfanwy J. Webb.

*View from Gerrin Point Lookout, 2024.* Photo: Myfanwy J. Webb.

# "DJIRRUN, JERRUN AND JERRON, MEANING 'FEAR, AFRAID, FRIGHTENED" 'COWARD' AND 'RUN AWAY'."

*Early Broadhurst photo, Government/Bay Road (Araluen) with Killcare Road reaching the hilltop, date unknown.* Photo: Bouddi Photos Past and Present, Flickr, CC BY 2.0.

Araluen Drive (see Appendix 4.5).

In the early days it was common practice to initially name an important public road 'Government Road'. This identified the road for administrative purposes and was a temporary name until an official name was given. Later, as the area became more populated a more individual name was chosen. The name Government Road was still in use during the 1950s.[207] Probably the locals still called it Bay Road until this time.

## HISTORY

On the 'Killcare Extension Estate' subdivision in 1920, Government Road extended from Noble Road to the left up the hill towards Wards Hill Road. Part of the road then turned right at Noble Road in a loop and finished at the corner of Blythe Street and Stanley Street (Appendix 1.3). This section became known as Fraser Road in the 1960s.[208]

The Ford family was well known in the area from the early days. John Thomas Middleton Ford known as Jack (1902-1968) with his wife Hilda (née Marshall) had a dairy farm in Government Road (originally at No.18 and now renumbered at No.32 Fraser Road). They were to have nine children and continued to farm until the 1950s.

For further information see the entry for FRASER ROAD.

*The building of Grandview Crescent, date unknown.*
Photo: Bouddi Photos Past and Present, Flickr, CC BY 2.0.

# GRANDBEACH LANE, KILLCARE

## BEGINNINGS

This is a composite name formed from Grandview Crescent and Beach Drive.

## HISTORY

This lane was previously a sanitary service lane, a 'dunny' lane between Grandview Crescent & Beach Drive. It was named in the early 2000s to provide access to a new home which was built at the back of a block at No.2 Beach Drive.

# GRANDVIEW CRESCENT, KILLCARE

## BEGINNINGS

Grandview Crescent is a descriptive name as the houses on the high side of the road especially, have grand views over Putty Beach.

## HISTORY

The name first appears on the Martins Killcare Beach Estate in 1930 (Appendix 1.5). Alexander Martin was the first owner of this land and ran a dairy farm and tea rooms as well called 'Martinsyde Tea Rooms'.[210]

The Crescent originally included what is now Beach Drive and extended from The Scenic Drive down to where it meets the present Grandview Crescent.

Before the 'Martins Killcare Beach Estate' was advertised for sale the road needed to be cut out of the hill and then levelled. Locals Nicholas George (Mick) Myer with his son Edmund (Ted) helped build the original 'back road' now known as Grandview Crescent.[211]

SIGNPOSTS TO THE PAST

# HALF TIDE ROCKS, WAGSTAFFE

## BEGINNINGS

These rocks are at Wagstaffe Point at the entrance to Brisbane Water within the Bouddi National Park and make navigation of vessels difficult.

Half tide is the state of the tide when it is halfway between high water and low water. Presumably the rocks are not visible until half tide. In fact, one map shows in brackets after the name Half Tide Rocks, 'covered at High Tide'.[212] The channels were dangerous at low tide so vessels had to wait for the rise of the tide to cross Half Tide Rocks. As sand channels move, the rocks had to be carefully negotiated making it tricky not just for sailing ships but also for steamships.[213]

## HISTORY

In 1876 the ketch *Brothers*, was wrecked on Half Tide Rocks amid strong winds and high seas. Captain Shields was able to get ashore over the rocks injuring his hands and his only crew man was blown overboard.[214]

There were plans in 1885 to blow up Half Tide Rocks to make it easier for steam vessels to enter Brisbane Water. The Government even 'granted £1000 for the removal of the half-tide rocks, so that this charming spot will soon be available for large steamers'.[215] This apparently did not go ahead and even after it was suggested again in 1922 after three accidents in six months at the entrance, the proposal was knocked back.[216]

It is believed by some that 'on the basis of their geological structure and shape, at least some of the underwater rocks at Half Tide Rocks have been placed there, with a view to forcing the water to flow into a narrower but deeper channel around its western end.'[217]

In 2014 residents were concerned that waves up to 1.5 metres high were breaking over the rocks and damaging jetties, sea walls and flooding waterfrontages at Wagstaffe Point. Locals believed it was probably due to the 2010 dredging off Lobster Beach which dumped sand to the south and southwestern part of the shoal. This sand shoal then deflected the waves which normally come in from the sea towards Ettalong Beach and reached Half Tide Rocks instead.[218]

There has been a rough track to Half Tide Rocks from Bulkara Street for many years but it has deteriorated. The National Parks and Wildlife Service has committed to upgrade its section of the track but because it crosses other tenure, commencing the work has been delayed. The Wagstaffe to Killcare Community Association put aside reserves to co-fund the work and was advised in November 2021 that the National Parks would shortly commence design works and seek tenders for construction. The COVID-19 epidemic appears to have delayed these plans.[219]

Half Tide Rocks was officially named in 1974[220] See also the entry for WAGSTAFFE BAR.

*Half Tide Rocks with Palm Beach Ferry, 1913.* Photo: Bouddi Photos Past and Present, Flickr, CC BY 2.0.

*Half Tide Rocks, 2024.* Photo: Myfanwy J. Webb.

# HARDYS BAY,

## BEGINNINGS

Hardys Bay is both the name of a suburb and of the bay which were named after Robert (Harry) Hardy (died 1914) who with his wife Mary was an early settler.

## HISTORY

The bay was originally called Ward's Bay after William Ward who settled there by about 1825.[221] Robert Hardy himself used the name Ward's Bay at an inquest in 1868.[222] By at least 1879 however it became known as Hardy's Bay.[223] It appears as Hardy's Bay on the 'Killcare Extension Estate' subdivision map in 1920 (Appendix 1.3).

Robert Hardy, who was known locally as 'Harry', bought land at the western end of the bay in 1865. It was originally owned by James Mallen who was the first settler in the Bouddi area and who took up land in 1825. Hardy retained a portion of his land until his death in late 1914 or early 1915.[224]

By all accounts Harry was a colourful character and Charles Swancott relates some amusing anecdotes of his life. He was a mariner and farmer and known for having a vineyard and selling wine to the locals. He was also known to be miserly and built a wharf which had a decking made of discarded packing cases.[225] The early settlers of Hardys Bay were subsistence farmers but when the land developers began to divide up the land for housing in 1912 to 1920 the emphasis shifted to attracting people to a holiday resort. Accommodation houses and holiday cottages began to spring up and gradually farming virtually disappeared.

In 1912 Arthur Rickard acquired land from William Spears and subdivided it, offering it for sale as the 'Pretty Beach Extension Estate' (see Appendix 1.7). It included Heath Road as far as the Dog Track and the Reserve, now Araluen Drive, both at the western end of Hardys Bay. There was a wharf and jetty and the promise of a twice daily ferry service from Woy Woy. Blocks of land were for sale at £25 and larger blocks for sale at £5 per acre.[226] By 1915 Sir Arthur had built what he called a 'Sea Park' to entice buyers for this land. The sea park included a wooden fence across the corner of the bay where Araluen Drive meets Heath Road. The fence of about 50 to 60 metres was built with a series of poles set in the sand with flat timber planks on top and was a deterrent for sharks. Don Anderson remembered playing there when he was young. He and his mates had fun seeing how far they could walk along the top planks before falling into the water. In this enclosure which was covered with water at high tide were swings and a see

*Hardys Bay Swimming Enclosure, date unknown.* Photo: Bouddi Photos Past and Present, Flickr, CC BY 2.0.

*Boys at Hardys Bay, 1976.* Photo: Donald G. Runcie.

*Hardys Bay at low tide, 2025.* Photo: Myfanwy J. Webb.

saw.[227] Rickard must have found the sea park successful as in 1919 he built another one in Sydney Harbour in Sirius Cove near the zoo when he advertised a land sale of the Sirius Beach Estate, Mosman.[228]

# HARDYS BAY PARADE, KILLCARE

## BEGINNINGS

Hardys Bay Parade is named after Robert (Harry) Hardy an early settler. This road follows Hardys Bay around the waterfront from Noble Road to its end near Rileys Bay.

## HISTORY

The name Hardys Bay Parade first appears on 'Killcare Extension Estate' subdivision in 1920 (Appendix 1.3).

Cathy Ford (née Woulfe) says that it was known earlier as 'Marine Drive'.[231]

In 2002 the first section of Hardys Bay Parade was raised to avoid flooding at high tide and was also widened.[232]

For information about Robert (Harry) Hardy see the entry for HARDYS BAY.

# HATS STREET, KILLCARE HEIGHTS

## BEGINNINGS

Hats Street first appeared on the map when Ernest Keith White (later Sir) the owner and developer of the subdsion 'Killcare Heights Estate' named it in 1928 (Appendix 1.4).

[ *Listing of Place & Street Names: C to P*

## HISTORY

Old time resident, Helen Warliker, believed it was named after the profession of Ernest White's wife, Pauline, who was a milliner.

White family descendants have stated this was nearly correct. Apparently while her husband was at war during World War I, Pauline created hats which she sold to the Sydney department store, David Jones. Pauline did not have formal training in millinery but she was very creative and a fine seamstress with a passion for hats. The money she saved helped her husband set up his business when he returned from the war.[233]

See also the entry for PAULINE AVENUE.

# HAWK(E)S HEAD, BOUDDI NATIONAL PARK

## BEGINNINGS

Hawke Head is an early name for Box Head and for many years the names were used concurrently. The origin of the name Hawke is unknown.

It was thought by some to be named after Edward, Lord Hawke, (1705-1781) who was First Lord of the Admiralty when Captain Cook passed here in 1770. However, Cook passed the Bouddi Peninsula at night and so didn't see the entrance to Broken Bay. By the time the first fleet arrived in 1788, Lord Hawke had died. Cook did in fact name a Cape Hawke just south of Forster and so this is probably where the confusion lies.[234] Even so Hawke Head could still have been named after Lord Hawke.

Perhaps it is it an abbreviated form of 'Hawkesbury' as it is at the entrance to Hawkesbury River. Governor Arthur Phillip named the river in 1789 to honour Charles Jenkinson, 1st Earl of Liverpool and 1st Baron Hawkesbury, Lord Hawkesbury. Lord Hawkesbury was a British statesman.[235]

As Hawke Head is also found spelt without the 'e' after Hawk, perhaps it was named after the White-Bellied Sea Eagle (*Haliaeetus leucogaster*) which still frequents the headland. Another name for this eagle is White-Bellied Fish-Hawk.

## HISTORY

This headland at the northern entrance to Broken Bay was first named Inner North Head by William Bradley in 1789 and was known as Box Head as early as 1809.[236]

However, later it also became known as Hawk or Hawke Head. It appears as Hawk Head on a survey plan in 1877 by James Barnett for the location of Barrenjoey Lighthouse.[237] By 1929 Erina Shire Council was still undecided and called it 'Box or Hawk Head'.[238] Some maps show both names.

It was officially named Box Head in 1977.[239] See also the entry for BOX HEAD.

*Eagle over Bouddi. (White-bellied sea eagle. Haliaeetus leucogaster over Putty Beach) 2014.* Artist: Kate E. York.

*Listing of Place & Street Names: C to P*

*Sunrise at Hawke Head Drive, 2022.* Photo: Myfanwy J. Webb.

# HAWKE HEAD DRIVE, HARDYS BAY & BOUDDI NATIONAL PARK

## BEGINNINGS

Hawke Head Drive begins at Nukara Avenue and then runs along the ridge towards Box or Hawke Head. It was named when Box Head was more commonly known as Hawke Head. Now that Box Head is the official name it is a curious name to those not knowing the history.

For more information about the name Hawk/e see the entry for HAWK(E) HEAD.

## HISTORY

In 1928 Councillor Tom Humphries led a group of Council members to the Bouddi area and they discussed resumptions of land, one being 'in connection with the road up to the plateau on the way to Box Head, from which such glorious views are obtained, and on which it is said a fine golf links will be established by a Sydney co.'[240] The golf links of course did not happen and the area has been included in the Bouddi National Park.

In the early 1960s a rough road was built to access Tallow Beach. It was built by sand miners who extracted rutile and zircon from the beach, and it became known as Hawke Head Drive.[241] The road remains unsealed apart from the beginning of it which serves some houses. This section was sealed in late 2019 after much community lobbying.[242]

Hawke Head Drive ends at a locked gate on top of the ridge above Tallow Beach. A track begins here which leads to the Box Head Track and the Flannel Flower Track as well as a track down to Tallow Beach.

Hawke Head Drive was officially named in 1970.[243]

SIGNPOSTS TO THE PAST

[ *Listing of Place & Street Names: C to P*

*First Hawkesbury River Bridge & Paddle Steamer 'General Gordon', date unknown.* Photo: Central Coast Council Library Service.

*Hawkesbury River Railway Bridges, looking north from Long Island, 2005.* Photo: Daramulan at the English Wikipedia, CC BY-SA 3.0.

# HAWKESBURY RIVER,

## BEGINNINGS

The Hawkesbury River enters Broken Bay before it reaches the sea between Barrenjoey Headland and Box Head. It is part of the Nepean/Hawkesbury River system.

The Aboriginal word for this river was 'Deerubbin' said to mean 'wide deep water'.[244] David Collins mentions the name 'Dee-rab-bun' in his 'Account of the English Colony in New South Wales' in August 1795.[245] Jim Smith mentions while it may be a Dharug word for part of the Hawkesbury River 'it may have been their word for rivers in general'. He also states: 'The Gundungurra, of the Blue Mountains and Burragorang Valley, used the same word (dyirraban) for one of the yam species found in riverside habitats'. Grace Karskens confirms that yams along the Hawkesbury-Nepean River were so important to the Gundungurra people that they named the river Dyirraban meaning Yam River.[246]

Governor Phillip named it Hawkesbury River in 1789 to honour Charles Jenkinson (1727-1808), 1st Earl of Liverpool and 1st Baron Hawkesbury. Lord Hawkesbury was a British statesman.[247]

*Aboriginal men with a fire in a canoe, 1905.* Modified from: Dick Thomas (Port Macquarie)

river gave fresh water to the settlers and as well offered transport for goods to the market in Port Jackson.[248]

In 2017 Professor Grace Karskens came across a list in the State Library of NSW entitled 'Native Names of Places on the Hawkesbury' written by the Rev. John McGarvie in 1829. As she researches the area with a team which includes Indigenous members, she consistently uses the spelling 'Dyarubbin' for the name of the Hawkesbury River.[249]

In 1969 the name Hawkesbury River was officially assigned and Deerubbun given as a previous name.[250]

## HISTORY

In March 1788 Governor Phillip after exploring Broken Bay, Brisbane Water, Pittwater and Cowan Creek reached Mullet Island, now called Dangar Island. He was determined to see if there was a river which could support settlers and provide food for the colony. It took numerous trips until July 1789 before Richmond Hill was reached, which Phillip had encountered on a previous overland trip and realised that the Hawkesbury and the Nepean River were the one river. It was decided to keep the original names and used the Grose River as the junction. These exploratory trips up the Hawkesbury River were significant. While most of the river had high cliffs there were a few tributaries suitable for small farms and close to what is now Windsor, low alluvial flats opened out, suitable for agriculture. While huge floods were a problem in these early days the

*Governor Phillip, 1787.* Photo: Mitchell Library, State Library of NSW.

[ *Listing of Place & Street Names: C to P*

# HEATH ROAD,
## HARDYS BAY & PRETTY BEACH

### BEGINNINGS

In earlier times Heath Road was called unofficially 'Back Road' and Araluen Drive below it was called 'Front Road'.²⁵¹

The founder of the company Arthur Rickard & Co. which put forward the original subdivision was Sir Arthur Rickard (1868-1948). His father was William Heath Rickard whose mother's maiden name was Hannah Heath and Arthur's brother was named Richard Heath Rickard. 'Heath' was therefore the maiden name of the paternal grandmother of Sir Arthur Rickard and the middle name of his brother Reverend Richard Heath Rickard.

For information about Arthur Rickard Snr and Jnr see the entry for ARTHUR STREET.

*Rev. Richard Heath Rickard (1858-1938).* Photo: Bouddi Photos Past and Present, Flickr, CC BY 2.0.

### HISTORY

Heath Road first appears on the subdivision map of the 'Pretty Beach Extension Estate' in 1912 (Appendix 1.7).

The western side was named Arthur Street on this subdivision and in 1970 the name 'Arthur' was dropped and the whole road was called Heath Road.²⁵²

When the 'Pretty Beach Extension Estate' came up for sale in 1912, it comprised part of the original grants made to two early settlers, William Spears at Pretty Beach and James Mallen at Hardys Bay; both had grants issued in the 1830s.²⁵³

As vehicular traffic increased on Heath Road there began a push to have it made a one-way road along with the opening of the Araluen Drive Extension (now informally called the 'Dog Track') a one way road in the other direction. The condition of Heath Road was very poor; it was very narrow, had a dangerous bend and there was concern about the safety of vehicles and pedestrians. There was ongoing discourse for many years between local community associations and Gosford City Council.

Discussions began in 1965 and continued until 1994 when the Council finally decided to keep the extension closed and allow Heath Road to continue with a two-way traffic flow. Gosford City Council embarked on a major upgrade of Heath Road during the 1990s. This involved drainage, kerb and guttering, easing of the hairpin bend and the building of retaining walls where needed. The cost for this in 1998 when the work was nearly completed was almost two million dollars.²⁵⁴

During the 1940s and 50s there was a factory at 94 Heath Road which made jeans and working clothes for the King Gee brand.²⁵⁵ In 2010 the Pretty Beach Community Preschool moved into a new state-of-the-art building at 150 Heath Road behind the Pretty Beach School. It was previously called Walsingham Preschool and had rented Catholic Church premises at 6 High View Road from 1968 until its relocation.²⁵⁶

[BACKGROUND IMAGE] (LEFT & RIGHT)

*Blackwall Mountain from Pretty Beach, 2000s.* Photo: Bouddi Photos Past and Present, Flickr, CC BY 2.0.

*Listing of Place & Street Names: C to P*

*Looking from Heath Road across Hardys Bay, date unknown.* Photo: Bouddi Photos Past and Present, Flickr, CC BY 2.0.

*25 Heath Road 'Douglas', 1940.* Photo: Bouddi Photos Past and Present, Flickr, CC BY 2.0.

[ *Listing of Place & Street Names: C to P*

# HIGH VIEW ROAD, PRETTY BEACH

## BEGINNINGS

High View Road is a descriptive name as the road rises uphill and affords excellent and extensive views over Wagstaffe, Pretty Beach and across to Booker Bay, Blackwall Mountain, Rileys Bay and the Rip Bridge.

## HISTORY

This name High View Road first appears on the 'Pretty Beach Estate' subdivision map in 1910 (Appendix 1.6).

It remained unsealed for most of the twentieth century but by 1969 Council had put it in the 'future program of works' for sealing. By the 1970s the road was in poor condition and in 1976 tradesmen were refusing to enter. The Pretty Beach Wagstaff [sic] Citizens/Progress Association decided to send a deputation to Council about it and several other streets. It also sent constant letters to put pressure on Council which finally resulted in action.[257]

An argument brewed in 1985 when owners of No.66 High View Road sought to demolish their weatherboard cottage built in 1918 to build a new brick veneer home. The cottage known as *Weona* had been listed in the Council's Gosford/Wyong History and Heritage

*Pretty Beach Cottage 'Weona', 2009.* Photo: Bouddi Photos Past and Present, Flickr, CC BY 2.0.

publication which had not been published when the owner bought the property.[258] Interestingly, the original cottage is still standing in 2025.

In the early days the closest Catholic Church was at South Kincumber, or at Woy Woy and parishioners from Wagstaffe and nearby would travel there by water. It wasn't until 1981 that a new church, Church of the Holy Family, was built in High View Road at Nos.6-8.[259] It finally closed down in 2006 due to lack of parishioners.[260] Walsingham Community Preschool rented the premises from the local parish from 1989 and remained there for twenty years after which it relocated to Heath Road.[261]

Tucked away in the bush at No.83 High View Road is Pretty Beach House, a luxury resort hotel which includes a main house with dining, lounge etc. and

*Wagstaffe Avenue meets High View Road, date unknown.* Photo: Bouddi Photos Past and Present, Flickr, CC BY 2.0.

*High View Road after storm, 2015.* Photo: Bouddi Photos Past and Present, Flickr, CC BY 2.0.

four, separate, one bedroom pavilions. It is on the edge of Bouddi National Park and has both bush and water views over the bay.

# IRON LADDER BEACH, BOUDDI NATIONAL PARK

## BEGINNINGS

Iron Ladder Beach was named by locals years ago because an iron ladder about 3½ metres long was erected above the beach for fisherman to reach a ledge so they could fish over a deep hole.

## HISTORY

This small beach, covered by most high tides, is located between Box Head and Little Box Head and is within the Bouddi National Park. It is only accessible by boat or by walking through the bush along a rough track. After many years the iron ladder rusted away and was replaced by a wooden ladder which fishermen took up each time and hid in the bushes. Over the years it too disappeared. It has been suggested that the National Parks Parks officers removed it as it could prove dangerous to the public as it did not comply with Occupation, Health and Safety standards.

The iron ladder was gone by 1921 when Mr W Kirton reported fishing there. He said, 'Generally, it is reached via Pretty Beach, and it involves a stiff walk with a climb at the end. The Iron Ladder has disappeared, but it is easy to get down with a twisted wire, and then you can fish from a rock about 10ft [3mtrs] above the water over a bottom clean and sandy in front of the rock, and broken with reefs below on either side. I got a good mixed lot of fish, including some large black bream and a seven-pound groper on the rod'.[262]

Nearby under where the creek flows over a rock there are indentations carved into the rock and the date 5/2/55 although the history attached to this hasn't been discovered.

Iron Ladder Beach was officially named in 1977.[263]

*Iron Ladder Beach, 1987.* Photo: Donald G. Runcie.

[ *Listing of Place & Street Names: C to P*

*Jacqueline White & Walter Tyrrell on their wedding day, 1946.*
Photo: Tyrrell Family.

## JACQUELINE AVENUE, KILLCARE HEIGHTS

### BEGINNINGS

Jacqueline Avenue was named after Jacqueline Adele (Dell) White (1921-1997), younger daughter of Sir Ernest Keith White who owned and subdivided the land called the 'Killcare Heights Estate' in 1928 (Appendix 1.4). Her mother was Lady Pauline White, née Mason.

### HISTORY

On the plan of the 'Killcare Heights Estate' the name of the street was originally written as Jacqueline Street but was later changed to Jacqueline Avenue.

During World War II Jacqueline White joined the Women's Auxiliary Air Force (Royal Australian Air Force) and in 1946 she married Walter Astley Tyrrell in Durban, South Africa.[264] Walter joined the Australian Military Forces at the outbreak of World War II and was awarded an MBE for 'Bravery and Devotion in Greece and Crete' for actions undertaken in 1941. Walter spent the years 1941 to 1945 as Prisoner of War in Germany.[265] During that time he and his mates talked about adventures they would have when they were released, and Walter realised one of his dreams by going to South Africa. Jacqueline had met him at an 'end of the war' party and sailed to South Africa to be with him. On returning to Australia in 1948, Walter went into business with his father-in-law, Ernest Keith White.

Jacqueline and Walter had two daughters Penelope Anne (an architectural drafter) and Pauline Jane (a freelance editor), and twin boys Timothy (a solicitor) and Jeremy (an architect). Jacqueline was a very creative person, an amazing gardener and was dedicated to her children. She is buried at Wamberal Cemetery, Central Coast of NSW.[266]

See also the entries for BABS ROAD, BADEN STREET and PAULINE AVENUE.

## JOY STREET, KILLCARE

### BEGINNINGS

Who Joy was is unknown.

### HISTORY

This was a proposed road which appears on some early street directories and still appears on some maps. It was named at the end of Anthony Crescent where there is a turning circle, but the name wasn't used when the subdivision was put on the market and remains part of Anthony Crescent.

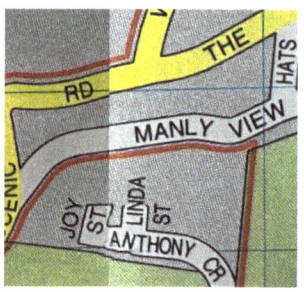

*Joy St on map, 1998.* Modified from: Universal Press.

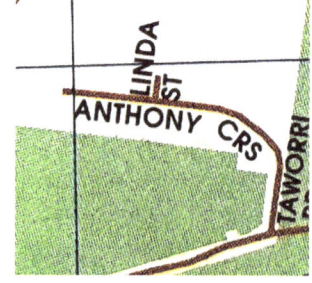

*Joy St absent on map, 2020.* Modified from: Localsearch.

*Listing of Place & Street Names: C to P*

# "'KILLCARE' IS A PUN AS IN 'TO RELAX' OR 'TO KILL CARE'"

## KILLCARE,

### BEGINNINGS

Killcare is a suburb encompassing both ocean side and bay side.

The name 'Killcare' is a pun as in 'to relax' or 'to kill care' or as some wags say, 'Come to Killcare to kill care'. Such whimsical naming of places and houses was popular in the first half of the twentieth century especially for houses as street numbering at that time wasn't compulsory. Local houses began to be built and often were named with such names as '*Av-a-rest*', '*Duz Us*' and '*Weona*' to emphasise the holiday atmosphere. '*Snoon*' was the unofficial name of 8 Anthony Crescent.

Arthur Rickard subdivided land which he called the Pretty Beach Extension in 1912. In September 1914 he advertised four new cottages for sale on the Pretty Beach Extension.[267] One of them was called '*Killcare*' a waterfront reserve house (Lot 75 now No.130) on what is now Araluen Drive overlooking Hardys Bay. This

*Downtown Killcare, date unknown.* Photo: Bouddi Photos Past and Present, Flickr, CC BY 2.0.

is the first time the name Killcare has appeared in the newspapers.

Only a few weeks later in October 1914 the *Sunday Times* mentions this: 'Messrs Rickard and Co. Ltd., are opening up a new subdivision at Woy Woy, which is named the Killcare Estate, and those who have spent a holiday at Woy Woy will realise the appropriateness of the new name'.[268] Woy Woy is mentioned as the Bouddi area was mainly accessed by ferry from Woy Woy and that name was well known by holiday makers who arrived by train.

The 'Killcare Estate' was not offered to the public

[ *Listing of Place & Street Names: C to P*

until two years later in 1916. It appears likely Rickard chose the name as he believed the carefree nature of it would influence buyers to invest in land to build holiday homes. Maybe he took the name from the house called '*Killcare*' and used it for the name of the subdivision. It also may have started the trend for these types of house names on the Bouddi Peninsula.

## HISTORY

Killcare Estate was the name of the subdivision advertised for sale in 1916 (Appendix 1.2).

The land was originally owned by Richard Fitzgerald a former convict who was promised the land in 1823 but which came into his possession in 1837. Fitzgerald went on to be a large property holder and become a 'millionaire' in our terms. He does not appear to have ever lived on his Killcare land.[269]

Over the years the spelling of the area changed to 'Kilcare' and many thought it was of Irish derivation. A local launch *Regent Bird* changed its name to *Kilcare Star* around 1948 and as it plied its way around Brisbane Water, people would have assumed that this spelling was correct.[270] Both spellings appeared on different council signs and became confusing. In 1972 the spelling was officially recorded as Killcare, so reverting to the original.[271]

Killcare was officially gazetted as a suburb in 1972 and 1991.[272] Local residents often affectionately call it Killy and a local charity which helps anyone in the area when they are experiencing difficulties is called 'Killy Cares'.

## KILLCARE BEACH, KILLCARE

### BEGINNINGS

The name Killcare Beach is locally associated with the western end of Putty Beach where the Killcare Surf Club and the Bogey Hole are situated. The Geographical Names Board of NSW does not recognise 'Killcare

*Group on Putty Beach, date unknown.* Photo: Courtesy of Central Coast Council.

*Putty Beach.* Photo: Bouddi Photos Past and Present, Flickr, CC BY 2.0.

*Aboriginal man on beach making boomerang, 1905.* Photo: Dick Thomas (Port Macquarie).

*Killcare postcard.* Photo: Bouddi Photos Past and Present, Flickr, CC BY 2.0.

*Terri Mares longboard surfer on Killcare Beach. Photo: The Sun.*

[ *Listing of Place & Street Names: C to P*

Beach' as an official name but as a variant and officially the entire beach is called Putty Beach.²⁷³ The western end is Council owned and the eastern end of Putty Beach is in Bouddi National Park. The division is near where Taworri Road meets Putty Beach Drive.

### HISTORY

During the late 1950s and early 1960s the beach was mined for rutile and the very high sand dunes which could be seen so prominently from Palm Beach were removed along with original native vegetation behind them. Unfortunately, after mining ceased, the South African plant 'bitou bush' (*Chrysanthemoides monilifera*) was planted to stabilise the remaining sand and has now become a pest which overtakes native bush and in turn destroys native wildlife habitat. It is difficult to eradicate as the seeds are spread by birds.²⁷⁴

In 2018 marine grade fitness equipment was financed and installed near the Killcare Surf Club especially welcomed by locals including seniors.²⁷⁵

See also the entry for PUTTY BEACH. For information about the name Killcare see the entry for KILLCARE.

*Bogey Hole & Killcare surf beach, date unknown.* Photo: Bouddi Photos Past and Present, Flickr, CC BY 2.0.

*Sandhills Putty Beach, date unknown.* Photo: Bouddi Photos Past and Present, Flickr, CC BY 2.0.

## KILLCARE HEIGHTS,

### BEGINNINGS

This is the name of a suburb on an elevated part of Killcare. Unofficially it was called Killcare Heights after the 'Killcare Heights Estate' was opened up in 1928 by Sir Ernest Keith White (Appendix 1.4). The initial auction sale was postponed on 7th April due to rain and the auction was held on 21 April 1928 instead. It was advertised as having '294 Choice Lots commanding Glorious views of Broken Bay, Lion Island, Barrenjoey and the Coast Line with Manly in the distance'. The price of blocks ranged from £20 to £50 with a deposit of £3, no interest and the balance spread over five years.²⁷⁶

*Fish spotting from Putty Beach, 1930.* Photo: Bouddi Photos Past and Present, Flickr, CC BY 2.0.

*Killcare with tents of Aboriginal camp, 1913.* Photo: Courtesy of Central Coast Council.

*Listing of Place & Street Names: C to P*

## HISTORY

Housing blocks in the Killcare Heights Estate did not sell quickly after they first came onto the market. In October 1928 none had sold and were advertised again. Inticements included an increase in land values after completion of the new Northern Road and a planned punt service from Ettalong to Wagstaffe (which never eventuated). The 1930s Depression and World War II followed halting land sales.

In 1948, 283 building lots were advertised as a 'delightful holiday resort', having frontages of 50 to 200ft frontages and from £10 to £60. Another attempt to sell land was made in 1964 when blocks now went onto the market from £145 a block with only a £10 deposit. It appears from the advertisement that the land offered by Homewise, was on either side of Manly View Road and included Anthony Crescent underneath the cliff (Appendix 1.11). N & K Developments Pty Ltd took over the sales in 1965 and made a push to sell the land as 'Kilcare Beach' Estate (see Appendix 1.1).

The name Killcare Heights was officially assigned in 1991. For more information about the Killcare Heights Estate see the entry for PAULINE AVENUE For information about the name Killcare see the entry for KILLCARE.

*Killcare Heights, left to right; Scenic Road, Pauline Ave, Manly View Road, Babs Road, Baden Street, Smithy Street, Jacqueline Ave, MacDonald Street, date unknown.* Photo: Bouddi Photos Past and Present, Flickr, CC BY 2.0.

*Killcare Heights Lookout now 'Marie Byles Lookout' postcard.* Photo: Bouddi Photos Past and Present, Flickr, CC BY 2.0.

[ *Listing of Place & Street Names: C to P*

# KILLCARE ROAD,
## KILLCARE

### BEGINNINGS

Killcare Road runs from the wharf in Hardys Bay up the hill towards the surf beach to The Scenic Drive.

### HISTORY

The name first appears on the 'Killcare Estate' subdivision map in 1916 (Appendix 1.2). Initially, Killcare Road crossed over Scenic Road and went no further than the bend, where the last house is. This section later was named Putty Beach Drive.

A photograph taken in 1908 shows the road as a very rough track and it looks impassable to any traffic other than pedestrians. Pam Mainsbridge remembers it was a red clay road (perhaps laterite from Killcare Heights) originally.[282]

*Killcare Road, 2025.* Photo: Myfanwy J. Webb.

*Early Killcare Road with red muddy gravel, date unknown.* Photo: Bouddi Photos Past and Present, Flickr, CC BY 2.0.

Thomas and Martha Jane (Doll) Fraser owned much of the land from Killcare Road across to Martha Jane Avenue and built the family home at the top of Killcare Road, at No.27. When this was demolished in 1973 the land sold for $30,000 and a private road was formed. Blocks were then subdivided along the road, each block selling for for$13,000. Subsequent houses built have the postal address of Killcare Road.[283] In April 2021, one of the houses along this part of the road sold for $1,500,000.

The first business in Killcare Road was the McCall brothers whose real estate business was at No.4. It was originally the garage of the house above it and is now Belle Property Real Estate.[284] Opposite at No.1 is a group of shops which includes Ray White Real Estate, Alira Hair and Moochinside which is a gift shop and stocks home decorating items, fashion and jewellery. Next door is The Fat Goose which is a café, delicatessen, bakery and patisserie.

For information about the name Killcare see the entry for KILLCARE.

*Killcare Road, date unknown.* Photo: Bouddi Photos Past and Present, Flickr, CC BY 2.0.

Listing of Place & Street Names: C to P

# KOURUNG GOURUNG POINT,
## WAGSTAFFE

### BEGINNINGS

'Kourung Gourung' appears on an 1831 map by surveyor Felton Mathew [285] (Appendix 4.7). It would have been an Aboriginal word used by the Aboriginal people of the area at that time.

F C Bennett believed Kourung Gourung meant 'fast running sea'.[286] Unfortunately, he did not give his source. This is an apt name however as the deep water sweeps past the point from the Rip.

*Aboriginal children spearing fish, 1905.* Modified from: Dick Thomas (Port Macquarie).

William Dawes in 1792 wrote that guru meant 'deepwater', Philip Gidley King lists in 1790-91 that carrigerang or caragarang meant 'sea' and David Collins also recorded garrigarrang as meaning 'sea'. Daniel Southwell however in 1788 said that the word garungarung meant 'pretty'.[287] Jeremy Steele offers quite a few interpretations of the words gurang gurang and similar but believes that karr-ong-gorong from the Karree language from around the Hawkesbury River is the closest to our Kourung Gourung and it means 'pelican'.[288]

The tip of the point at Wagstaffe has retained the name Kourung Gourung. It has many spelling variations, e.g. Gurrumguma, Gurrum Gina, Kourang Gourang but the official spelling is that of 1831, Kourung

## "KOURUNG GOURUNG MEANT 'FAST RUNNING SEA'." - F C BENNETT

Gourung Point being officially named in 1974.[289]

### HISTORY

Patrick and Rachel Mulhall were the first European settlers to have lived at Kourung Gourung, the area we now know as Wagstaffe. Patrick was promised land at Brisbane Water in 1821 and by 1828 was farming it.[290] A letter sent to the Colonial Secretary in 1841 requesting the deed for the land to be prepared, is headed 'Gorangorang or Mount Pleasant'. Patrick Mulhall states: 'The above is the original name and the other I wish to give it'.[291] In the Mulhalls' wills the spelling is 'Gurrumguma'.[292]

For further information about the Mulhall family see the entry for MULHALL STREET.

William Spears was granted 50 acres in 1835 at Kourung Gourung, Brisbane Water and opened a hotel called 'The Crooked Billet'. That land is now called Pretty Beach. For further information about William Spears see the entry for PRETTY BEACH.

*Kourung Gourung painted bus shelter at Wagstaffe, 2020.* Artist: Virginia Henderson, 2025. Photo: Myfanwy J. Webb.

SIGNPOSTS TO THE PAST

[ *Listing of Place & Street Names: C to P*

*Anthony Crescent and Linda Street, Killcare, 1973.* Photo: Bouddi Photos Past and Present, Flickr, CC BY 2.0.

## LINDA STREET,
### KILLCARE

### BEGINNINGS

It is probable that Linda Street was named after Linda Newhouse. Linda's father and Arnold Newhouse, the developer were first cousins and Linda, during the 1960s, was very close to George Newhouse, Arnold's oldest child.[293]

### HISTORY

Linda Street is a cul-de-sac within Anthony Crescent and is depicted in the 'Kilcare [sic] Beach' Estate (Appendix 1.1). It was kerbed, guttered and bituminised at the time it came onto the market in 1967. Electricity was available but there was no water or sewerage connected.

For further information about the Newhouse family see the entry for ANTHONY CRESCENT.

## LITTLE BEACH,
### BOUDDI NATIONAL PARK

### BEGINNINGS

Little Beach is a small, delightful beach south of MacMasters Beach and in Bouddi National Park. It is accessible by a short walk from the end of Grahame Drive, MacMasters Beach.

### HISTORY

When surveyor Felton Mathew passed this way in 1831, he wrote on his map alongside the creek which flowed into what we now call Little Beach, the words 'Running Creek Semi fresh Water'; an important fact to note when exploring new territory.[294]

Roy Dunlop subdivided some of his land at Little Beach in 1927, each of about 2 hectares and then in the 1950s he subdivided more into smaller residential sized lots. In 1941 Dunlop built 2 tourist cabins on the edge of the Bouddi Natural Park for walkers who didn't like camping, but they were not successful.

One portion on the east side of The Scenic Road was mined for sand in the 1970s and was finally sold to the National Parks and Wildlife Service. Roy Dunlop also contributed a small piece of steep land on The Scenic Road for inclusion in the Bouddi Natural Park.[295]

There is a natural feature which locals call the 'Indian Head'. The southern cliff face if viewed from a certain angle looks like the silhouette of an American Indian head.

When Bouddi Park was first reserved in 1935 there were plans to have an aeroplane landing ground built near Little Beach. *The Sydney Bush Walker Annual* reports: 'This is the spot where the District Surveyor stood admiringly and said, 'Golly! What a glorious place for a park! Think how many cars could be parked here!".[296] Fortunately, neither the aeroplane landing ground nor the car park for 'many cars' has eventuated.

There are six sites available at Little Beach for campers who need to carry in all supplies and water, although there is a gas barbecue and toilets. Fishing is allowed as the beach is not included in the Bouddi National Park Marine Extension Sanctuary.

It was officially named in 1977.[297]

*Listing of Place & Street Names: C to P*

'Indian Head' at Little Beach, 2020. Photo: Myfanwy J. Webb.

Little Beach at low tide, 2025. Photo: Myfanwy J. Webb.

*Listing of Place & Street Names: C to P*

*View of Little Box Head, 2024.* Photo: Myfanwy J. Webb.

*Little Tallow Beach with sand removed by large waves 2024.* Photo: Myfanwy J. Webb.

# LITTLE BOX HEAD,
## BOUDDI NATIONAL PARK

## BEGINNINGS

Little Box Head is a headland in Bouddi National Park and is the most westerly point of the Bouddi Peninsula. It is 1.3 km North West of Box Head and can be recognized by the survey mark mounted on a concrete pillar perched on the point. Vessels are warned that the depth of the water in the channel beginning at Little Box Head and extending to Lobster Beach can be reduced due to changing movement of sand and caution is required.

For information about the origin of the name see the entry for BOX HEAD.

## HISTORY

The name 'Little Box Head' was in use in the nineteenth century, mention of it appearing in the *Sydney Mail* on 7 September 1861 in a serial column entitled 'My Holiday'. The author looking from the top of Barrenjoey Headland mentions a constantly shifting channel from Little Box Head to near Mount Elliott, now called Lion Island. Little Box Head forms the most southern point of the narrow channel which leads into Brisbane Water.

The name was formally assigned in 1974.[298]

For further information about this channel see the entry for WAGSTAFFE BAR.

# LITTLE TALLOW BEACH,
## BOUDDI NATIONAL PARK

## BEGINNINGS

Little Tallow Beach is a small ocean beach between Tallow Beach and Box Head and is within Bouddi National Park.

For information about the origin of the name Tallow see the entry for TALLOW BEACH.

## HISTORY

In February 1940 three men and a boy of nine spent nearly 24 hours cold and hungry on Little Tallow Beach. They had set out to go fishing three miles off Barrenjoey Head in a 20-foot launch, when the engine cut out and they began drifting out to sea. They rigged up a sail and came within half a mile of the shore when a southerly gale sprang up. Within ten minutes the raging seas buffeted the launch. They saw Little Tallow Beach in the distance and tried to make for it. They donned lifebelts then two of the men were washed overboard and then the boy and the owner of the boat dived overboard as the launch capsized. All of them reached the beach, and spent the night huddled around a fire. They were rescued later the next day by the storekeeper on Barrenjoey.[299]

Little Tallow Beach was officially assigned its name in 1977.[300]

*Listing of Place & Street Names: C to P*

*Little Tallow Sunrise, 2022.*
Photo: Myfanwy J. Webb.

# LOBSTER BEACH, BOUDDI NATIONAL PARK

## BEGINNINGS

The name Lobster Beach has been in use since at least 1826 when it is mentioned in a newspaper account of an excursion from Sydney Harbour to Brisbane Water.[301]

Lobster Beach was named because of an abundance of rock lobsters there or near there. Charles Swancott relates that Joe Wilson pioneered lobster fishing in Brisbane Water. 'He made pots of fish net placed on iron circles about four feet in diameter and attached buoys along the foreshore between Half Tide Rocks and North [Box] Head'. Often, he would trap 70 or 80 dozen a night and would place them in traps in the water fronting his Blackwall cottage until he was ready to take them to market in Sydney in his ketch. He would take about 200 dozen each trip, covered with wet bags to keep them fresh and sell them for ten shillings a dozen.[302]

This naming of the beach is also supported by the story of Alwyn Koletzke, a young fisherman known as 'the lobster man' who lived in a shack on Lobster Beach. He set traps to catch lobsters which he sold to support himself. In December 1921 Alwyn and a friend drowned when they went to inspect the lobster traps near Box Head and his skiff capsized in strong winds and rough seas. He managed to cling to his craft for three hours before succumbing. A launch sent to help him was forced to turn back because of the rough weather.[30] Ironically Alwyn had saved another man from drowning only a few weeks before.

There is a plaque at Lobster Beach dedicated to his heroic action erected by his friends.[304] The plaque reads:

*This Tablet*
*commemorates the heroic action of*
*ALWIN KOLETZKE,*
*in rescuing one man from drowning,*
*and returning to attempt*
*the rescue of another.*
*Within a few days, he himself*
*drowned, together with his friend*
*CHARLES HESKETH on 28th Dec. 1921.*
*Erected by his friends.*

*The "Lobster Man" Alwyn Koletzke on Lobster Beach, date unknown.* Photo: Courtesy of Central Coast Council.

*Alwyn Koletzke plaque, 2024.* Photo: Myfanwy J. Webb.

## HISTORY

There is a very narrow deep-water channel running alongside Lobster Beach from Half Tide Rocks as far as Little Box Head. This channel often becomes silted up with sand, making the navigation of boats difficult and dangerous. For further information about the channel see the entry for WAGSTAFFE BAR.

Traditionally Pearl Beach has always been thought to be the site of Governor Phillip's first landing in the area in 1788. Stephen Jones and others present a case for Lobster Beach being the more likely place.[305]

Once the railway opened as far south as Gosford, the beauty of Brisbane Water began to attract tourists. An article in the *Maitland Mercury* in 1887 says 'There is a very pretty beach just inside the bar, called Lobster Beach; this makes a good picnic ground and the bush in the vicinity abounds in wildflowers, ferns etc, quite a paradise for anyone fond of botany'.[306]

As far back as at least 1915 until the 1970s, holiday makers would camp on Lobster Beach.[307] It was also used during the 1930s Depression as a home for some and rough huts were erected. Over the years fishermen and rock climbers have named some of the features around Lobster Beach with names like Dog Face Rock also called Top Rock, and Lobster Cave.

Helen Monks has recorded many of the fishing spots along the water's edge from Half Tide Rocks to Little Box Head, with names such as Flathead Rock Oyster Rock, Cungi Rock, The Shoe and The Pinnacles. The channel off the beach was known as Shark Alley. Lobster Beach is now in the Bouddi National Park and all the early dwellings have been removed and camping prohibited. Helen Monks has written extensively about Lobster Beach in The Bouddi Peninsula [CD-ROM]. [308]

It is a popular picnic beach which is still only reached by water or walking and was officially named in 1974.[309]

*Rock climbing in Lobster Cave, 2024*. Photo: Myfanwy J. Webb.

*View from Lobster Cave, 2024*. Photo: Myfanwy J. Webb.

[BACKGROUND SPREAD]

*Lobster Beach, 2024*. Photo: Myfanwy J. Webb.

[ *Listing of Place & Street Names: C to P*

## LOBSTER BEACH - 1940s

*Lobster Beach, 1940s.* Photo: Bouddi Photos Past and Present, Flickr, CC BY 2.0.

*Listing of Place & Street Names: C to P*

## LOBSTER BEACH - 2024

*Lobster Beach, 2024.* Photo: Myfanwy J. Webb.

[ *Listing of Place & Street Names: C to P*

# LOBSTER BEACH TRACK,
## BOUDDI NATIONAL PARK

### BEGINNINGS

From the early days of settlement, the informal track beginning at Pretty Beach and Wagstaffe to Lobster Beach went through private land. This was not a concern until landholders began to build on the traditional pathways.

For information about the name Lobster see the entry for LOBSTER BEACH.

### HISTORY

As far back as 1915 the need for a public thoroughfare to Lobster Beach was voiced in the local newspaper. 'It is proposed to open a public thoroughfare through Mr. E. S. Cox's property, Pretty Beach to Lobster Beach'.[310] However no action appears to have been taken following this statement.

In the 1990s the National Parks and Wildlife Service built steps up from High View Road to Lobster Beach on a strip of land it had acquired from the block next to it. There is a signpost in High View Road a few houses up from Venice Road.

In the early 1960s a fire trail was formed from the end of Albert Street into Bouddi National Park, linking Wagstaffe to Hawke Head Road for bush fire control. It also gave a track for walkers to reach the southern end of the park. However, the fire trail went across private land. As the number of walkers increased, especially after ferry services from Palm Beach to Wagstaffe began, access over private land caused problems with landowners who feared liability litigation.

In 1985 the track was closed when one landholder no longer allowed walkers to cross his land and the short cut from Albert Street to Lobster Beach was closed. Both the State government and the NPWS agreed to provide an alternative route, but no timetable was set for the new track to be built.[311]

While it would have been ideal to retain a fire trail for the use of emergency vehicles, this proved too difficult and expensive. To retain access for the community, one landholder Graeme Anderson, consulting with the NPWS, local community associations and affected landowners worked to form a legal Right of Way from part way up the Lobster Track across private land to join up to the national park in the south. A proposal was made to NPWS in 2003 and Graeme worked hard to get an agreement accepted. It was finally granted in January 2009. While the National Parks paid for most of the legal fees, the community also contributed, and Graeme Anderson gifted the remainder.

Now through the generosity of five landholders this pedestrian Right of Way links the Lobster Beach track with the Flannel Flower Track and gives walkers from Wagstaffe and Pretty Beach access to other areas of the Bouddi National Park.[312]

*Residents at handover of land for Lobster Beach walking track, 2009.* Photo: Bouddi Photos Past and Present, Flickr, CC BY 2.0.

*Listing of Place & Street Names: C to P*

*Lobster Beach facing Broken Bay, 2024.*
Photo: Myfanwy J. Webb.

*Near Lobster Beach Track, 2024.* Photo: Myfanwy J. Webb.

*Lobster Beach, National Park Sign, 2024.*
Photo: Myfanwy J. Webb.

[ *Listing of Place & Street Names: C to P*

# MACDONALD STREET,
## KILLCARE HEIGHTS

### BEGINNINGS

Macdonald Street commands stunning views over Killcare/Putty Beach and across to Barrenjoey Headland and down the coast to Manly, a suburb of Sydney.

The origin of the name Macdonald Street is unknown.

### HISTORY

Macdonald Street first appears on subdivision of land 'Killcare Heights Estate' 1928 which was owned by Sir Ernest Keith White (Appendix 1.4). Most streets in this subdivision were named after White's relatives but so far, no family or business connection has been found.

For further information about Ernest White and the Killcare Heights Estate see the entry for PAULINE AVENUE.

# MACMASTERS BEACH,

### BEGINNINGS

MacMasters Beach lies at the northern fringe of the Bouddi Peninsula and is named after Allan MacMaster an early settler. The Aboriginal people called the area 'Cockrone' and the beach 'Tudibaring'. Tudibaring is the name of the headland 450 metres north of the MacMasters ocean pool. Tudibaring means 'where waves pound like a heart beating'. The bay itself is called 'Allagai Bay' and is believed to mean a 'place of snakes'.[313]

The southern headland of MacMasters Beach is called Mourawaring Point. For more information see the entries for SECOND POINT and MOURAWARING POINT.

### HISTORY

The first resident landowner in the area was Peter Campbell who was farming there by 1826. Two years later he

*Listing of Place & Street Names: C to P*

*MacMasters Beach ocean pool with Bulbararing (First Point) on northern side of Allagai Bay, 2024.* Photo: Myfanwy J. Webb.

[ *Listing of Place & Street Names: C to P*

sold his farm to Robert Henderson, and Thomas Humphreys purchased an adjoining 160 acres in 1837. This land was at the head of Cockrone Creek.

Allan MacMaster, after which the area is named entered the scene in 1855. He bought 600 acres of land close to the beach which included Lake Cockrone and proceeded to cultivate a small area of land and raise cattle.

The first road was surveyed from Kincumber in 1866, legalising the track through Henderson and Humphrey's land and MacMaster's land to the beach. Another track went towards Little Beach via Dajani Drive. By 1899 George Frost who had purchased part of the MacMaster property was given legal right of way from the south-west boundary and this was later to become part of 'The Scenic Drive'.

The name MacMasters Beach was being used in the early 1890s and it was formally assigned for the beach itself in 1975 and for the suburb in 1991.[314]

*Totem by Kevin Duncan, commemorates the nearby midden, 2025.* Photo: Myfanwy J. Webb.

*Macmasters Beach facing Mourawaring Point, (Second Point) 2024.* Photo: Kalena V. Webb.

*Wreck of S.S. Maitland, Cape Three points, Maitland Bay, Bouddi Peninsula, 1898.* Photo: Courtesy of Central Coast Council.

# MAITLAND BAY,
## BOUDDI NATIONAL PARK

### BEGINNINGS

Maitland Bay facing the Tasman Sea is situated within the Bouddi National Park and the Bouddi National Park Marine Extension.

Maitland Bay was originally called Boat Harbour as it was a sheltered spot, except during storms. Marie Byles tells us how the change of name happened: 'Among the early bushwalkers was Dorothy Lawry who visited the place in 1930. She pointed out that Boat Harbour as it was then called, was not a suitable name for there were many boat harbours up and down the coast. This one was the only one which had the wreck of the *Maitland* upon it; therefore, it should be called Maitland Bay. The name stuck and later on we had it officially put on the map'. [315] For further information about Marie Byles see the entry for MARIE BYLES LOOKOUT.

### HISTORY

The paddle steamer, *SS Maitland*, was wrecked here in May 1898 during a severe storm on route from Sydney to Newcastle. The furnaces were extinguished by the force of sea water rushing into the engine room and the then uncontrollable vessel was swept towards the cliffs. It was lifted on mountainous waves and the stern slammed down on the rock platform. It immediately broke into half, the stern remained on the rock shelf and the bow half was lifted on a huge wave and thrown away about 70 feet. All those on the bow were thrown into the sea and most drowned. A remarkable effort was made as crew and passengers worked together to get everyone safely off the wreck by organizing a line to the shore. However, at least 27 people drowned. A few remnants of the wreck can still be seen today on the rock shelf. Geoff Potter believes that if the *SS Maitland* had hit the bombora rather than the rock shelf it would have been smashed to pieces with loss of all lives. For a comprehensive account see the book by Geoffrey Potter

[ *Listing of Place & Street Names: C to P*

the 'Wreck of the Maitland'.³¹⁶

It was through the efforts of Marie Byles who wanted Maitland Bay and the surrounding area reserved for public recreation that the Bouddi Natural (later National) Park was established in 1935. Marie and three girlfriends first explored Maitland Bay in 1922. The bushwalking movement began in the late 1920s and the newly formed Federation of Bushwalking Clubs took up the challenge.

The first working bee was held at Maitland Bay in 1940 and sixty bushwalkers turned up with tools. A water tank was installed; a shelter shed erected, and work began on building a properly graded and drained track down to the beach.

*'Good water in ferns' etching, 1930s*. Photo: Bouddi Photos Past and Present, Flickr, CC BY 2.0.

Maitland Bay, which said 'Good Water in Ferns' with an arrow pointing into the Bouddi Grand Deep.³¹⁷ Sadly this historic sign has been chipped away (although still decipherable), as it was thought that buildings above on The Scenic Drive would have polluted the water. The name Maitland Bay was officially assigned in 1977.³¹⁸

Maitland Bay is said by some to be the 'jewel in the crown' of Bouddi National Park and it is popular with bushwalkers and picnickers. Fishing, however, is not permitted as the bay is within the Bouddi National Park Marine Extension sanctuary zone. Access to Maitland Bay is still only by foot or by boat. For further information see 'Bouddi Peninsula [CD-ROM]'.³¹⁹

*Marie Byles (standing foreground) with Sydney Bushwalker Club friends, 1930s*. Photo: Bouddi Photos Past and Present, Flickr, CC BY 2.0.

*Marie Byles Working Bee Tent City Maitland Bay, 1941*. Photo: Bouddi Photos Past and Present, Flickr, CC BY 2.0.

The tank and shed were floated in by boat. John Wall who owned the Maitland Bay Store in the 1940s and 50s, now the Maitland Bay Information Centre, chipped a sign into a rock next to the steps leading down to

*Listing of Place & Street Names: C to P*

*Boiler from 'SS Maitland', date unknown.* Photo: Photo: Bouddi Photos Past and Present, Flickr, CC BY 2.0.

*Maitland Bay Wreck remains, 2000.* Photo: Donald G. Runcie.

*Maitland Bay, 2010s.* Photo: Bouddi Photos Past and Present, Flickr, CC BY 2.0.

[ *Listing of Place & Street Names: C to P*

## MAITLAND BAY DRIVE, KILLCARE HEIGHTS

### BEGINNINGS

Maitland Bay Drive meets Wards Hill Road at the top of the hill from Empire Bay Drive and then stops at The Scenic Road opposite the Maitland Bay Information Centre and the beginning of the track which leads down to Maitland Bay.

For the origin of the name see the entry for MAITLAND BAY.

### HISTORY

Maitland Bay Drive forms one side of The Triangle. For more information see the entry for THE TRIANGLE.

Part of the northern side of the road is Bouddi National Park. It was partially sealed by 2006 and fully sealed about 2014.

Along this road at No.27, 'Bouddi Nursery' opened in 1978 and propagated and sold native plants for twenty-five years.

## MAITLAND BAY INFORMATION CENTRE, BOUDDI NATIONAL PARK

### BEGINNINGS

The Maitland Bay Information Centre is situated on The Scenic Road opposite Maitland Bay Drive and at the head of the track down to Maitland Bay. For information about the name Maitland Bay see the entry for MAITLAND BAY.

### HISTORY

The building was originally a privately owned house built by John & Dulcie Wall. The original section downstairs was built in the mid-1940s, and the upstairs section was added in 1950 and became a small shop and cafe called 'The Maitland Store'. In 1957 divers discovered the bell from the *SS Maitland* and the Walls carried it up to the store for safe keeping. The stone cairn nearby commemorating the disaster contains a replica of the bell while the bell itself is on display at West Gosford in the Brisbane Water Historical Society's collection.[321]

Ron and Thelma Hall bought the property in 1959 and became known for their Devonshire Teas, and in the 1960s Ron became the first full-time ranger employed in Bouddi Natural Park.

The property was bought by the National Park and Wildlife Service in 1970 and the superintendent of the Bouddi National Park lived there until 1974. It then fell into disrepair and was restored as a visitors' centre with the help from local volunteers and officially opened as the Maitland Bay Information Centre in 1990.

Another major revamp of the inside took place in 2010 - 2011 and the Centre provides information, maps, brochures, and interactive displays for children. It is staffed by volunteers at weekends and public holidays. The building has been listed by Gosford City Council as a heritage site.[322]

*SS Maitland replica bell, 2025.* Photo: Myfanwy J. Webb.

*Listing of Place & Street Names: C to P*

*Maitland Bay Information Centre with local volunteer Don Runcie.* Photo: Beverley J. Runcie.

## MAITLAND BAY BOMBORA,

See the entry for BOMBORA.

## MANLY VIEW ROAD, KILLCARE HEIGHTS

### BEGINNINGS

Manly View Road commands stunning views over Putty and Killcare Beach across Broken Bay to Pittwater and Palm Beach and down the coast. It is a descriptive name as Manly; a suburb of Sydney, can be seen to the far south.

*Manly View Road, date unknown.* Photo: Bouddi Photos Past and Present, Flickr, CC BY 2.0.

SIGNPOSTS TO THE PAST

[ *Listing of Place & Street Names: C to P*

## HISTORY

Manly View Road first appears on the subdivision of land 'Killcare Heights Estate' 1928 which was owned by Ernest Keith White (Appendix 1.4). For further information about Ernest White see the entry for PAULINE AVENUE. Only the eastern part of Manly View Road was included in this land release and included those houses up to and including No.47 and Nos.50 and 50A. The western end of Manly View Road was not developed until the 1960s. It had been owned by Martha Jane Fraser and she decided it was too costly to keep and so offered it to her daughter, Eileen. Eileen sold it to N & K Developments who subdivided it and advertised it in 1964. With blocks slow to sell N & K advertised the 'Kilcare Beach' estate which included not only Manly View Road but the subdivision under the cliff face. A map appeared in the 'Sun-Herald' in 1967 with no street names and in diagrammatic form (see Appendix 1.1). The artist obviously had no knowledge of the landscape and thought it was all flat ground making the map quite misleading .

*Looking up at Manly View Road from Putty Beach, 2024.* Photo: Myfanwy J. Webb.

Manly View Road is in two sections, the first beginning at The Scenic Road and ending at the end of Pauline Avenue. It includes Nos.88-100 and Nos.91-93 and is a 'no through road'. This is where there is a very steep area making it difficult for road building. The second section begins 30m beyond, and runs towards and then along the top of the cliff to join The Scenic Road further west. There are steps to link the two sections of Manly View Road.

# MARIE BYLES LOOKOUT,
## KILLCARE HEIGHTS

### BEGINNINGS

There are stunning panoramic views from the Marie Byles Lookout at Killcare Heights on The Scenic Drive. The views take in Pittwater, West Head, Palm Beach and further south, Whale Beach headland, Long Reef and Manly and the high-rise buildings at Bondi Junction on the skyline. To the west Broken Bay, Lion Island, Box Head, Tallow Beach and Killcare Beach can be seen. To the east is a vast expanse of the Pacific Ocean.

The Marie Byles lookout is named to honour Marie Byles whose passion was to create access to the Bouddi area for everyone to enjoy. Read further in this entry about her influence.

*Marie Byles graduation, 1924.* Photo: Bouddi Photos Past and Present, Flickr. CC BY 2.0.

*Listing of Place & Street Names: C to P*

# "THE LONG UNINHABITED COASTLINE BEYOND THE RUBY LIGHT OF BARRENJOEY HAD AN INCREASING FASCINATION FOR ME..."

*Bouddi Peninsula from Barrenjoey Lighthouse Lookout, 2023.* Photo: Myfanwy J. Webb.

## HISTORY

A lookout was first proposed by Councillor Tom Humphrey in 1928 who suggested providing 'a strip of reserve from which the public may always enjoy the panorama, particularly fine from that locality'.[323]

It was originally named 'Killcare Heights Lookout' and that name appears on some earlier maps and post cards. The Geographical Names Board of New South Wales has not yet recognised Marie Byles Lookout as the new name. The Lookout was refurbished in 2009.

Marie Byles (1900-1979) was NSW's first female solicitor, a keen bushwalker, mountaineer, author, feminist and conservationist. She was instrumental in the establishment of 'Bouddi Natural Park' in 1935 which was expanded to become 'Bouddi National Park' in 1974. As a child she would look from her parents' holiday house at Palm Beach with her telescope and wonder about the coast and bushland on the other side of Broken Bay. Marie wrote 'The long uninhabited coastline beyond the ruby light of Barrenjoey had an increasing fascination for me... Those unknown lands seemed like the 'Faery Lands Forlorn' of Keat's 'Ode to a Nightingale' and I wished I were a nightingale and could fly over and explore them'.[324]

In 1922 with three girlfriends, she visited Maitland Bay which was very remote in those days there being no direct road and certainly no walking tracks. This was the beginning of her drive to have the area declared a national park so everyone could enjoy it.

Marie wrote an article for the National Parks Association Bulletin not long before she died which outlines the battle which eventually ended with a sizeable area of the coast declared as National Park.[325] See 'The Bouddi Peninsula [CD-ROM]' and 'The Summit of her Ambition' by Anne McLeod for further information about Marie Byles.[326]

*Marie & Marjorie on mountain NZ, date unknown.* Photo: Bouddi Photos Past and Present, Flickr, CC BY 2.0.

[ Listing of Place & Street Names: C to P

# MARTHA JANE AVENUE, KILLCARE

*Martha Jane signpost, 2024.* Photo: Myfanwy J. Webb.

## BEGINNINGS

Martha Jane Avenue was named by Charles Fraser after his mother Martha Jane Fraser.

## HISTORY

Martha Jane Fraser (née Munro) married Thomas Fraser in 1894. They retired to Killcare and purchased 32 acres in 1916 which was part of the 'Killcare Beach Estate' (Appendix 1.2). The family home was built at No.27 Killcare Road. Martha expected her children to work hard in the home believing in the ethic 'Idle hands make mischief'. Martha (Doll) Fraser was well known for her hospitality and along with her daughter Eileen for her excellent cooking skills.[327]

On the death of Martha Jane and Thomas the land passed to their daughter Eileen, and son, Andy. However, as son Charles was not included in the will, Eileen gave him part of her property. The subsequent purchase of No.46 Araluen Drive gave Charles access to his land, and he proceeded to subdivide in two stages in 1972 and 1974.

The land on Martha Jane Avenue was advertised for sale in 1973 with the blocks large and bushy. The family helped with the clearing of blocks ready for sale. Initially the blocks were slow to sell because Charles had put a caveat on them which decreed that only brick houses were to be built.[328] There are excellent views over Hardys Bay from houses in the avenue.

*Forming Martha Jane Avenue, date unknown.* Photo: Bouddi Photos Past and Present, Flickr, CC BY 2.0.

*Listing of Place & Street Names: C to P*

*Building Martha Jane Avenue, date unknown.* Photo: Bouddi Photos Past and Present, Flickr, CC BY 2.0.

## MASSON LANE, KILLCARE

### BEGINNINGS

Masson Lane connects Beach Drive and Putty Beach Drive and originally provided access for carts removing sewerage from outdoor 'dunnies'. It is named after the early owner of the land, William Masson.

### HISTORY

In 2000 Gosford City Council threatened to close this lane to through traffic. The Pretty Beach/Wagstaffe Progress Association and the Killcare Rural Fire Service opposed the closure and after some lobbying the Council allowed it to remain open.[329]

Naming this previously unnamed lane became necessary in 2009 when Gosford Council requested residents of 2, 2A, 4 & 4A The Scenic Road to locate their mailboxes in the lane. This was to ensure safer delivery of mail as The Scenic Road is very narrow outside these houses and it was considered dangerous to stop safely at each mailbox.

After public consultation the laneway was named Masson Lane after William John Masson (1889-1954) who owned land adjoining the laneway. His parents Charles Masson and Catherine MacDonald migrated from Scotland in the 1880s and William was the second child of six children. William was a journalist with the *'Sydney Sun'* newspaper and was sent to Melbourne in 1923 to cover the 'Buckley Murder' case. Unfortunately, he was involved in a car accident and became a quadriplegic. This meant he was unable to visit Killcare regularly but, he kept the house which he had named *'Catherine'* after his mother. After his death the property passed to his daughter Mercia, also a reporter, and interestingly an Australian Security Intelligence Organisation (ASIO) agent during the 1950s. She maintained a relationship with ASIO until her death in 1975.[330] The property then passed to her daughter Cynthia Dobbin, who grew up there in the 1940s and who still owns some of the land [2022].[331]

*2 Masson Lane, William Masson's original house, 1920.* Photo: Bouddi Photos Past and Present, Flickr, CC BY 2.0.

[BACKGROUND IMAGE] (LEFT & RIGHT)

*Ferns. 2024.* Photo: Photo: Myfanwy J. Webb

SIGNPOSTS TO THE PAST

[ *Listing of Place & Street Names: C to P*

# MOUNT BOUDDI
## BOUDDI NATIONAL PARK

### BEGINNINGS

For information about the name 'Bouddi' see the entry for BOUDDI.

### HISTORY

Mount Bouddi which is accessed from Mt Bouddi Road is the highest point of the Bouddi Peninsula at 160 metres above sea level. It is within Bouddi National Park.

# MOUNT BOUDDI LOOKOUT
## BOUDDI NATIONAL PARK

### BEGINNINGS

See the entry for BOUDDI LOOKOUT.

*Dingeldei Picnic Shelter at Mount Bouddi, 2024.* Photo: Myfanwy J. Webb.

*Listing of Place & Street Names: C to P*

# MOUNT BOUDDI PICNIC AREA

## BOUDDI NATIONAL PARK

### BEGINNINGS

This small picnic area is in Bouddi National Park at the end of Mt Bouddi Road. From there a track leads to Mt Bouddi Lookout and down to the Bouddi Coastal Walk linking Maitland Bay, Putty Beach, Little Beach and MacMasters Beach.

### HISTORY

The picnic area includes the Dingeldei Picnic Shelter and is sometimes called Dingeldei Picnic Area. For more information about this picnic area see the entry for DINGELDEI PICNIC SHELTER. For information about the name Bouddi see the entry for BOUDDI.

*Ferns, 2024.* Photo: Myfanwy J. Webb.

# MOUNT BOUDDI ROAD

## BOUDDI NATIONAL PARK

### BEGINNINGS

This road begins at The Scenic Drive and ends at Mt Bouddi Picnic Area and is within the Bouddi National Park.

For information about name Bouddi see the entry for BOUDDI.

### HISTORY

From the picnic area, a walking track leads to Mt Bouddi Lookout and then down to meet the Bouddi Coastal Walk which extends from Putty Beach to MacMasters Beach.

*Bouddi National Park Sign, 2024.* Photo: Myfanwy J. Webb.

*Water Dragon (Intellagama lesueurii), 2024.* Photo: Myfanwy J. Webb.

SIGNPOSTS TO THE PAST

[ *Listing of Place & Street Names: C to P*

## "A VIEW FROM HIGH UP"

*Mourawaring Point (Second Point) from Little Beach, 2024.* Photo: Myfanwy J. Webb.

# MOURAWARING MOOR,
## BOUDDI NATIONAL PARK

### BEGINNINGS

For information about the meaning of Mourawaring see the entry for MOURAWARING POINT.

### HISTORY

Mourawaring Moor is in the Bouddi National Park. It lies behind Mourawaring Point, and like Bombi Moor is part of ancient, perched sand dunes which support a low coastal heath. In Spring the Moor has a spectacular display of wildflowers and attracts beautiful nectar eating birds especially honeyeaters.[332]

# MOURAWARING POINT,

### BEGINNINGS

'Mourawaring' first appears on an 1831 map by surveyor Felton Mathew [333] (Appendix 4.7). Mourawaring is a local Aboriginal word F C Bennett said meant 'a view from high up'. Unfortunately, he did not give his source and so far, the meaning has not been authenticated.[334]

### HISTORY

Mourawaring Point is the headland at the southern end of MacMasters Beach. This is the second point of the three points of 'Cape Three Points' and is between MacMasters Beach and Little Beach in Bouddi National Park. Captain James Cook named 'Cape Three Points' as he sailed northwards in May 1770; however, he did not name the individual points.[335]

Mourawaring still appears on many current maps, but it is now officially named 'Second Point'.

# MUD FLAT CREEK,
## KILLCARE

### BEGINNINGS

Mudflat Creek is a descriptive name, as the silt brought down the creek covers the sandy flat as it spreads out

*Listing of Place & Street Names: C to P*

into Hardys Bay.

## HISTORY

Mud Flat Creek originates from a spring in Killcare Heights. Runoff water from The Scenic Road, Wards Hill Road and the Stewart Street area flows down through Fletchers Glen and drains into Mudflat Creek bringing with it silt. The water then flows through gardens of properties and into Hardys Bay.

The creek opens out to mudflats seen at low tide. It has a piped crossing over Fraser Road and a road bridge at Noble Road. Over the years it has been notorious for the flooding of residents' properties along its banks after heavy rain.[337]

Gosford City Council commissioned the 'Mudflat Creek Flood Plain Risk Management Study' in 2004 and the resulting Plan was published in 2008.[338] Council began remediation works in 2014 and by 2016 the problem had largely been alleviated.[339]

*Sandpipers (Scolopacidae), 2024.* Photo: Myfanwy J. Webb.

# MULLHALLS POINT,

See the entry for WAGSTAFFE POINT.

# MULLHALL STREET,
## WAGSTAFFE

### BEGINNINGS

Mulhall Street, named after the Mulhall family, first appeared on the developer's plan for 'Wagstaffe's Point Estate Woy Woy' in December 1906 (Appendix 1.8). An early postcard shows it as The Hill Road.

Patrick Mulhall was the first landholder of the Wagstaffe area, and his family lived there for nearly 60 years. Patrick was an Irishman who arrived in Port Jackson as a convict in 1806 and Rachel his wife, also a convict arrived in 1804.

### HISTORY

In 1820 Patrick Mulhall requested some land and was granted 50 acres at Brisbane Water in 1821. For some years Patrick and his family lived in Sydney but also worked the land. The 1828 census shows that of the 50 acres he held he had cleared 14, had 7 in cultivation and 35 head of cattle. In 1841 he requested the deed for the land to be made up and headed his letter 'Gorangorang or Mount Pleasant' stating 'The above is the original name and the other which I wish to give it'. Gorangorang is a variant spelling of Kourung Gourung.

*Mud flat near Mud Flat Creek, 2024.* Photo: Myfanwy J. Webb.

[ *Listing of Place & Street Names: C to P*

After the death of Patrick and Rachel, the land stayed in their sons' hands until the land came up for sale in 1861. Advertisements in *The Sydney Morning Herald* give an interesting description of the land and buildings on it, extolling its excellent farming qualities. However, it did not sell immediately and in 1886 it was sold to Francis Gerard. By 1890 Mulhall's land came into possession of George Wagstaffe.[340]

Mulhall Street leads from Albert Street down to Wagstaffe Square and Wagstaffe Wharf, which was a focal meeting point for early residents and holiday makers. This led to some of the owners in Mulhall Street producing goods for sale.

Walter Sydney (known as Syd) Osborne opened 'The Wonderland Greengrocer' in 1936. This was in Mulhall Street opening onto Wagstaffe Square but now the building faces Wagstaffe Avenue (No.57). It is the building opposite the Wagstaffe Community Hall close to the wharf. To supplement his income Syd ran a General Carrier business taking both goods and people. After selling the shop he bought six blocks of land in Mulhall Street and planted grape vines, selling table grapes, and making wine mostly for home consumption. He built a house at No.25 and had a thriving orchard. He later went into poultry farming and finally he sold off the land and kept Nos.23 & 25. Here he grew orchids in a huge greenhouse which were sent to Sydney and exported.[341]

It remained a grassy and muddy road for many years but by 1959 the Council had referred the Progress Association's concern to its works program for action. However, it remained a problem and by 1977 the condition of Mulhall Street was so poor it was mentioned almost every month at the Pretty Beach & Wagstaffe Progress meetings. When Council did nothing the Gosford Express newspaper was approached 'to run an article showing the … dangerous aspects of Mulhall Street'.[342] The road was finally sealed and in 2025 remains without kerbing or guttering.

Mulhall Street is now the only local reminder of the pioneer Mulhall Family.

*Looking down Mulhall Street, 1943.* Photo: Bouddi Photos Past and Present, Flickr. CC BY 2.0.

*Mulhall Street, 2010.* Photo: Bouddi Photos Past and Present, Flickr. CC BY 2.0.

*Listing of Place & Street Names: C to P*

## NUKARA AVENUE,
### HARDYS BAY

### BEGINNINGS

'Nukara' is an Aboriginal word meaning 'mine' or 'my own'. The name is not necessarily from this area and was chosen by Gosford Shire Council officers from S J Endacott's book 'Australian Aboriginal Words and Place Names'.[345]

### HISTORY

Barney Reeves recalled: 'In [the early] days... People walked over the hill, along a track established by the milkman, which is now Nukara Avenue'. In fact Nukara was originally named Government Road. This appears on the subdivision map of the Killcare Estate in 1916 (Appendix 1.2). Government Road began near the junction of Killcare Road and The Scenic Drive and continued westwards down to meet Hardys Bay just before the creek near the Hardys Bay Club. It then turned east and followed the shoreline turning right into what is now Fraser Road.

In 1970 Nukara Avenue was officially named, commencing at the corner of Beach Drive and running west to the intersection of Flora Avenue. The last section is now a closed road and steps lead down to Araluen Drive.[347]

*Emma Augusta Noble, 1890-1943.* Photo: Bouddi Photos Past and Present, Flickr, CC BY 2.0.

## NOBLE ROAD,
### KILLCARE

### BEGINNINGS

This road first appears on the 'Killcare Extension Estate' subdivision in 1920 (Appendix 1.3).

Rev. Richard Heath Rickard (1858-1938) was the brother of Sir Arthur Rickard who was the developer offering the land for sale. Richard had married Emma Augusta Noble (1860-1943) and their eldest son was named Stanley Noble Rickard. So, it appears the family wished to acknowledge the family name. Both Stanley Street and Noble Road appear on this subdivision.

### HISTORY

In 1978 Noble Road was extended when a section of Araluen Drive, between Stanley Street and Noble Road was renamed Noble Road.[343]

Mud Flat Creek enters Hardys Bay underneath the road bridge in Noble Road. A new road bridge was constructed in 2015 as part of Council's plan to overcome the flooding of properties which occurred when Mud Flat Creek became silted up.[344]

*Aboriginal man collecting oysters, 1905.* Photo: Dick Thomas (Port Macquarie)

[ *Listing of Place & Street Names: C to P*

# OROO STREET,
## PRETTY BEACH

### HISTORY

Oroo Street is named from an Aboriginal word for 'nankeen coloured crane' or more accurately 'nankeen night heron'. The name is not necessarily from this area and was chosen by Gosford Shire Council officers from S J Endacott's book 'Australian Aboriginal Words and Place Names'.[348]

Gwen Perrie, a long-time resident, related a colourful story. When she was young, as the children ran down this street (which was then unnamed) to go to school they would call out to their mothers 'hooroo' or 'ooroo'; Australian slang for 'goodbye' and this was the basis of the name.

### HISTORY

This is a very short street which links Pretty Beach Road and Venice Road and runs alongside the tennis court in Turo Reserve. As Oroo Street begins opposite the Pretty Beach wharf it is likely that a track was made in the very early days to reach 'The Crooked Billet Inn' which was built in Venice Street at the top of the hill. Oroo Street remained officially unnamed until it was gazetted in 1970.[349]

*Oroo Street signpost, 2025.* Photo: Myfanwy J. Webb.

# OTELLA AVENUE,
## HARDYS BAY

### BEGINNINGS

The name Otella is from an Aboriginal word meaning 'eagle'. The name is not necessarily from this area and was chosen by Gosford Shire Council officers from S J Endacott's book 'Australian Aboriginal Words and Place Names'.

### HISTORY

Otella is a short avenue running between Heath Road and Araluen Drive. It is not a through road for vehicles to Heath Road but there are stairs near the top to link up with Heath Road. It was declared a road in 1970.[351]

*Oroo Street at the end of Pretty Beach wharf is just a foot track, date unknown.* Photo: Bouddi Photos Past and Present, Flickr, CC BY 2.0.

*156, 158, 160 Araluen Drive Butchers shop and neighbours on Otella corner, date unknown.* Photo: Bouddi Photos Past and Present, Flickr, CC BY 2.0.

## PATRICIA PLACE, KILLCARE

### BEGINNINGS

Patricia Place is a small cul-de-sac on the hill overlooking the Killcare Surf Lifesaving Club House and the Bogey Hole and with magnificent views encompassing Putty Beach to the east.

Bert Myer reported that Ron Walters named Patricia Place after his wife 'Patty' (née Thomas) when he subdivided the land.

### HISTORY

Bert said, 'Before her marriage in 1954 Patricia lived with her aunt and uncle, Lorna and Jim Annand, who lived in an old, closed shop next to the Old Killcare Store, where units have now been built. Ron's parents owned a farming property on Wards Hill Road, Killcare Heights where they had an orchard and tennis courts. The house is still there and was owned for many years by Mr Miles who runs goats on the property [2010].'[354] The closeness to the beach, the views over the beach and ocean, and the quietness of a cul-de-sac has meant a sharp increase in property prices in Patricia Place.

*Otella Avenue, 2025.* Photo: Myfanwy J. Webb.

## OWANDA CRESCENT, KILLCARE

### BEGINNINGS

Owanda is an Aboriginal word meaning 'heat'. The name is not necessarily from this area and was chosen by Gosford Shire Council officers from S J Endacott's book 'Australian Aboriginal Words and Place Names'.[352]

### HISTORY

This road was officially named in 1970 and runs from Stanley Street around a small park to Noble Road.[353] In the park there are swings and a climbing frame for children. There is also a small electricity substation in one corner.

*Houses in Patricia Place can be seen up high.* Photo: Bouddi Photos Past and Present, Flickr, CC BY 2.0.

[ *Listing of Place & Street Names: C to P*

*Lady Pauline White (née Mason) daughter of Jeremiah J. Mason of Gosford, date unknown.* Photo: via Gwen Dundon. Courtesy of Central Coast Council.

# PAULINE AVENUE, KILLCARE HEIGHTS

## BEGINNINGS

Pauline Avenue is named after Lady Pauline Marjory White (1893-1984), wife of Sir Ernest Keith White (1892-1983) who purchased and subdivided the land called the 'Killcare Heights Estate' in 1928 (Appendix 1.4).

## HISTORY

Three streets in Killcare Heights are also named after their children: Babs (Babette), Jacqueline and Baden.

Pauline's parents were Jeremiah Mason and Jessie Fanning. Masons Parade in Gosford is named after her father who was Mayor of Gosford. Pauline was a primary schoolteacher and coming from a very musical family, was a fine singer appearing in concerts from a very early age. Newspaper reports show Pauline and her siblings all appearing in local Gosford events. Pauline was a pupil of Percy French and was well received by audiences and reviews in the Sydney newspapers. She performed at a Concert and Variety Entertainment held by the Gosford District War League in October 1915, a month before she was married, singing 'Your King and Country Need You'.[355]

Pauline's husband Ernest White left for overseas duty in World War I shortly after their wedding. During his absence she designed and made hats which she sold to David Jones Pty Ltd. the up-market department store in Sydney. Hats Street was named to acknowledge this. The money she saved went to help her husband set up a business when he returned from the war. Pauline died aged 90 in 1984 less than a year after her husband.

Pauline loved her grandchildren dearly; they in turn loved her and she had a great influence on them.[356]

Her husband Ernest White, whom she married in 1915, was born in East Gosford and grew up in Gosford. Sir Ernest's parents were Robert John White and Bertha née Davis. He was a remarkable man. Leaving school at the age of twelve he educated himself and became a very successful businessman and was awarded a knighthood.

After serving with distinction in World War I and being awarded the Military Cross for twice reconnoitering the front line while under heavy fire, he entered his father's timber business. The business expanded to supply logs from the north and south coasts of New South Wales, for use as telegraph poles, wharf piles and railway girders and sleepers. These were shipped within Australia and also exported to New Zealand, Egypt, China, South Africa, Hong Kong, Pakistan and India.

*Listing of Place & Street Names: C to P*

He was also active in R J White & Co Real Estate, purchasing and subdividing land around the Central Coast, although it appears the Killcare Heights land was bought in his private name.

He assisted in the formation of the Australian-American Association and the formation of the Democratic Liberal Party which later combined with others to form the Liberal Party. In 1954 he was appointed Officer of the Order of the British Empire (OBE) elevated to Commander of the Order of the British Empire (CBE) in 1967 and was knighted in 1969.

See also the entries for BABS ROAD, BADEN STREET, JACQUELINE AVENUE & HATS STREET.

*Sir Ernest K. White, son of R.J. White who had grazing, timber and shipping interests around the Gosford district, 1914-1918.* Photo: via Gwen Dundon, Courtesy of Central Coast Council.

# PRETTY BEACH,

## BEGINNINGS

The name Pretty Beach first appears on the subdivision 'Pretty Beach Estate' offered for sale at auction in March 1910 (Appendix 1.6). It is now the name of both the suburb and the beach.

Pretty Beach is probably a descriptive name as the beach was sandy and wider than it is today. An advertisement for an auction sale of land on Easter Saturday 1910 states blocks. 'It fronts a beautiful half-moon beach of hard sand'.[358] Frederick Smith remembered Pretty Beach when it was 'pretty' and he said until 1925 it had good yellow sand. Unfortunately, silt has gradually covered the sand.[359]

Daniel Southwell in 1788 noted the Aboriginal word 'garungarung' meant 'pretty'.[360] As Kourung Gourung was the name first given to Pretty Beach, could that meaning have remained in public consciousness in 1910 when the estate was first opened?

Shirley Hood believed it to be named after a Mr Pretty who owned the land and so it was called 'Pretty's Beach' but no evidence of this has been found.[361]

## HISTORY

When the Pretty Beach Estate first came on the market in 1910, prices ranged from £15 to £90 for the weekend sites and £5 to £15 per acre for the larger blocks.[362] It appears that all blocks were sold by 1911 and so in 1912 adjoining land was advertised for sale as the 'Pretty Beach Extension Estate' (Appendix 1.6).[363] This land ran from the boundary of the original estate to Hardys Bay. Both Estates were offered for sale by Arthur Rickard and Co. Ltd. For further information about Arthur Rickard see the entry for ARTHUR STREET.

The area originally was known as 'Kourung Gourung' and William Spears was the first to settle here when he was granted 60 acres of land facing the bay and called his land 'Somerset Place'. He had been promised the land in 1824. In 1834 he also purchased the adjoining portion which later became part of the Pretty

[ *Listing of Place & Street Names: C to P*

"IT FRONTS A BEAUTIFUL HALF-MOON BEACH OF HARD SAND"

*Pretty Beach, 1954.* Photo: Bouddi Photos Past and Present, Flickr, CC BY 2.0.

Beach Extension Estate. Spears is perhaps best known as the first innkeeper in the area, setting up a public house selling liquor which he called 'The Crooked Billet Inn'.[364] The Inn was situated high on the hill in what is now Venice Road, just west of Oroo Street.[365] It was a successful business as it was often visited by sailing ship crews entering or leaving Brisbane Water who needed to shelter when the wind or the tide was against them. The inn is believed to have closed in the 1880s after the decline in sailing ships and the coming of the railway.[366]

Pretty Beach the suburb was officially named in 1974 and 1991 and the beach was officially named in 1977.[367]

# PRETTY BEACH ROAD, PRETTY BEACH

## BEGINNINGS

For information about the name PRETTY see the entry for PRETTY BEACH.

## HISTORY

Originally there was no road along the waterfront at Pretty Beach. The 'main' road from Pretty Beach to Wagstaffe went via Como Parade, then along Venice Road to Wagstaffe Avenue.[368] Como Parade and Venice Road at that time were linked.

Pretty Beach Road was shown, but not yet named in the subdivision map of 1910 (Appendix 1.6).

Gradually it came into common use as it met the road from Hardys Bay forming a valuable link between Hardys Bay and Wagstaffe. It was not until 1957 that the road was officially named 'Pretty Beach Road' after objections were made to the Gosford Shire Council's plan to name it Wagstaff Avenue.[369]

'The waterfront at Pretty Beach underwent two periods of reclamation to widen and establish the road which became Pretty Beach Road'.[370] It was well constructed in late 1934. The road level was raised first as it was often submerged at high tides in some places. It had a good sandstone base to a depth of nine inches (23cms) and was rolled and topped off with gravelly loam. At the Wagstaffe end, extensive drainage was also carried out.[371] After the road was completed there was a fear that 'visiting motorists use this as a speedway and frequently pass through the village at 40 to 45 miles an

*Pretty Beach Wharf.* Photo: Bouddi Photos Past and Present, Flickr, CC BY 2.0.

*George McDonald at Boat Ramp on Pretty Beach Road, 2011.* Photo: Bouddi Photos Past and Present, Flickr, CC BY 2.0.

*Group on lookout above Pretty Beach, date unknown.* Photo: Courtesy of Central Coast Council.

*Pretty Beach Road, date unknown.* Photo: Bouddi Photos Past and Present, Flickr, CC BY 2.0.

hour.'[372] This equates to 64 to 70kms an hour and today more than 80 years later the speed limit is set at 50kms an hour.

In 1973 Pretty Beach Road along the waterfront had been filled and widened and in 1995 it had been widened a second time and sealed.[373]

Because of the easy access to the wharf at Pretty Beach, some shops began to appear in Pretty Beach even before Pretty Beach Road was formed. Lucas General Provider was the first store to open right on the waterfront and adjoining it was a hall where dances were held. Later that land was reclaimed to form the road. Originally part of the Lucas stores a shop was built on the site where the tennis courts are now, on the corner of Oroo Street. While the shop remained a mixed business it became known as 'The Milk Bar' selling ice

[ *Listing of Place & Street Names: C to P*

*John, Rene, Elsie and Les Thompson Pretty Beach Wharf, 1925.* Photo: Bouddi Photos Past and Present, Flickr, CC BY 2.0.

*Pretty Beach Store Steedman & Turner's Store, 1948.* Photo: Bouddi Photos Past and Present, Flickr, CC BY 2.0.

*Pretty Beach Boats, date unknown.* Photo: Bouddi Photos Past and Present, Flickr, CC BY 2.0.

cream and soft drinks and later included a fish shop and refreshment rooms.

A bakery was established on the other corner of Oroo Street and Pretty Beach Road. Timber for the wood-fired ovens was cut from the hills behind the beach. Next to the bakery was another mixed business at No.38. Terry Baker has his wood-turning studio there now, called 'The Crooked Billet'. Further along towards Wagstaffe Avenue was Whitings' shop, later Stewarts'. This was also a mixed business and the shop was tucked into the corner where Pretty Beach Road meets Wagstaffe Avenue which is now informally called Whitings Corner'.[374] Turo Park was established in the early 1980s and has been extended to both sides of the creek. New amenities continue to be added to the park. See TURO.

On the corner of Como Parade and Pretty Beach Road at No.16 was Baldwin's Ice Works. The ice would be brought by carrier from Woy Woy via Gosford and supplied residents and holiday makers with much welcomed ice to keep meat, milk and butter etc. fresh.[375]

The establishment of Pretty Beach School at the junction of Pretty Beach Road and Heath Road was important for the people of the area. A 'Gala Day' was held in December 1926 when the NSW Minister for Education opened the school which was then ready to welcome the first teacher and students in January 1927. The community had been pushing for a school since 1920, the children having to go by ferry from Wagstaffe Point to Woy Woy and back each day. The swimming baths opposite were included in school activities and had been completed by 1928. Another feature at the junction of Pretty Beach Road and the Dog Track for which the community lobbied the Council, were boat ramp improvements which were completed in 2006.[376]

# PUTTY BEACH, KILLCARE

## BEGINNINGS

Putty Beach is the official name for the main surf beach. However, it is often called Killcare Beach, so the Geographical Names Board of NSW has named Killcare Beach as a variant.[377]

The origin of the name Putty is unknown. There are various possibilities:

A booklet published around 1938 says 'Killcare Beach (The Manly of Brisbane Water) was called Putta by the Aborigines and the name was corrupted into Putty Beach'.[378] Judy Adderley, a long-time resident, said it was called Putty from the Aboriginal words 'putta putta'.[379] The meaning of putta has not been determined.

There is a place named 'Putty' near Windsor, NSW which is derived from an Aboriginal word 'puttee'. Benjamin Singleton, attempting to reach the Hunter Valley from Windsor in 1818, records that they had 'got into a place called Putty' Andy Macqueen says in his book *Somewhat Perilous:* 'The name Putty or Puttee was certainly recognised by Singleton and [John] Howe [1819]—Howe wrote on his sketch map that it was "called by the Natives Puttee". He also mentions that the early settlers of Putty referred to the locality as 'Bootty".[380] Peter Prineas also states: 'This Aboriginal name for the area was also rendered by early settlers and travellers variously as 'Bootty' or 'Pootie'.[381] In 1823 Commissioner Bigge reported: 'a place that is called by the natives Boottee'. There are three other instances reported in 1819 and 1825 where one of the places was spelled 'Bootie', a mention of Mrs. Laycock's Station at 'Booty' and from Allan Cunningham's diary "he reached an alluvial flat named Booty or Pooty by the Aborigines.[382] So there is evidence that 'Putty' was initially pronounced 'Pootee' in the early discovery and settlement of the area.

Local residents of Putty Valley think the name Putty was 'derived from an Aboriginal word which sounded like 'Booty or Parbooty' and was understood to mean 'place of plenty'.[383]

If the word (from near Windsor) 'Putty' was pronounced 'Pootee' then it is possible that 'our' word Putty may originally have been pronounced the same. If this is so, then it sounds very like the word 'Bouddi' which had already been noted on the Felton Mathew map of 1831 (Appendix 4.7). We pronounce 'Bouddi' as Boodee (see the entry for Bouddi for a little more on the original pronunciation of Bouddi) so perhaps our Putty Beach was originally Bouddi Beach. Kevin Duncan from the Darkinjung Aboriginal Land Council believes the name Putty relates to the name Bouddi.[384]

The Darkinjung people lived as far west as the Putty region, and it is generally believed that they inhabited the land as far east as the Central Coast. If this is so then the word 'Putty' could have been used for Putty Beach as it too was a 'place of plenty'.

Another possibility could be that it is from the Aboriginal word 'putu' meaning bloodwood tree (*corymbia* [previously eucalyptus] *eximia*) which extends from the Howes Valley (which is near Putty) to the west, and to Nowra to the south.[386]

Jeremy Steele has found the word 'puti' meaning oil as in 'anointing with oil' from the Awabakal people in Reverend Threlkeld's translation of the Gospel according to Luke.[387]

Marjorie Whiting believed Putty Beach was named by an Irishman who meant Pretty Beach[388]. This is also mentioned in the local newspaper in 1924. Here is the story: 'Years ago there resided at Hardy's [sic] Bay an Irishman who always referred to the ocean beach as 'Purty' beach. Paddy's corruption was carried a stage further, and today we have 'Putty' Beach – certainly not much of an improvement on Paddy's nomenclature'.[389]

So, there are many ideas about the derivation of the name 'Putty'. We may never know for certain why the beach is called 'Putty Beach'.

## HISTORY

Putty Beach is mentioned in *The Sydney Morning Herald* as early as June 1850 when a boat belonging to the ketch 'Scud' which was reported missing with a cargo of coal from Newcastle, 'washed ashore on Putty Beach (Broken Bay)'.[390]

Many residents call the western end 'Killcare Beach', and the eastern end 'Putty Beach'. The Killcare Surf Club and the Bogey Hole are at the Killcare Beach end and the Putty Beach end is also known as 'Fishermens End' and is popular for fishing from the rock shelf and the beach. This end is also called 'Grannys End' and 'Grannys Beach' as it provides sheltered water in the groin of the headland for swimming. Central Coast Council manages the western end covering about two thirds of the length of the beach and about one third at the eastern end falls within the Bouddi National Park. Just behind the beach in the National Park there is a camping area and picnic area.

In the first half of the 20th century local fishermen set up a tripod with a ladder at the Fishermen's end of the beach. From here they watched for schools of fish and on sighting one, the watchman would direct the men in their boats with their nets ready Professional fishing continued at Fishermens End into the 21st century with a break while the beach was being mined for rutile.[391]

During the 1950s and 1960s the beach was mined for rutile and the very high sand dunes which could be seen so prominently from Palm Beach were removed along with thick vegetation behind them. Unfortunately, after mining ceased, the South African plant Bitou Bush was planted to stabilise the remaining sand and has now become a highly invasive weed which is difficult to eradicate.[392]

In 1942 during World War II the 33rd Battalion Horse Guard soldiers came to Putty Beach to lay barbed wire along the beach for defence purposes. They brought with them dozens of horses and set up camp at Fisherman's End. This may not have been as pleasant as

*Mullet Fishing eastern end of Putty Beach, 1930.* Photo: Bouddi Photos Past and Present, Flickr, CC BY 2.0.

*Putty Beach after heavy rain, 2022.*
Photo: Myfanwy J. Webb

[ *Listing of Place & Street Names: C to P*

*Putty Beach Beach Fishing.* Photo: Bouddi Photos Past and Present, Flickr, CC BY 2.0.

*Boy (Jeremy J. Webb) and his dog Wasp on Putty Beach.* Photo: Myfanwy J. Webb.

it sounds as at that time sewerage was collected in pans and emptied up this end of the beach.[393]

In 2004 the middle section of Putty Beach, outside the National Park, was declared an area for dogs to exercise off leash.[394]

# PUTTY BEACH DRIVE, KILLCARE

## BEGINNINGS

Initially the beginning of Putty Beach Drive was named Killcare Road as it was an extension of Killcare Road crossing over The Scenic Drive. At that time, the road only went as far as the bend where it now turns left and runs parallel to the beach. The name change to Putty Beach Drive was officially made in 1970 and included the rutile company's road to the eastern end of Putty Beach.[395]

For information about the name Putty see the entry for PUTTY BEACH.

## HISTORY

A track was made behind the beach originally for the disposal of sewage behind the dunes at the eastern end of Putty Beach during the 1940s.[396]

Putty Beach Drive was first formed for vehicles in 1956. The Crescent Rutile Ltd. put in the road which ran from The Scenic Drive parallel to Putty Beach behind the sand dunes to the company's rutile recovery plant site at the eastern end.[397] When the rutile company left in the early 1960s the road was in a very 'bad' condition and the Council was asked to repair it.[398] For further information about the sand mining see 'The Bouddi Peninsula' [CD-ROM].[399]

Past the bend running parallel to the beach, Putty Beach Drive has the Putty Beach Reserve on either side until the gate of the Bouddi National Park is reached. This land is COSS (Coastal Open Space System) land owned by the Central Coast Council and is proposed by the Council to be zoned E2 Environmental Conservation. COSS is a network of bushland reserves set aside and managed for their natural beauty and nature conservation values. The COSS was created in 1984 by Gosford Council and land continues to be actively purchased as it becomes available. One of its important aims is to allow wildlife corridors to exist. In December 2020 the Australian Conservation Foundation raised concerns that the proposed E2 zoning of COSS lands posed a threat as it allowed secondary developments and housing and COSS really required a 'special environmental zone'. The land is currently a Deferred Matter (DM).[400] The Putty Beach Reserve, although weed infested in many places, has a long-term management plan and a regular bush regeneration group is working from the western end.[401]

When the Kilcare [sic] Beach Estate was opened in the 1960s Putty Beach Drive was upgraded, as it leads to Taworri Road, Anthony Crescent and Linda Street. It remained gravel until the early 2000s when the surface was sealed.

Putty Beach Drive also leads to the camping and picnic area in Bouddi National Park and gives access to the Bouddi Coastal Walking Track which leads to Bullimah Beach and on to Maitland Bay, and Little Beach finishing at MacMasters Beach.

CHAPTER SIX

# 6

# LISTING OF PLACE & STREET NAMES

## R-Z

[ *Listing of Place and Street Names: R to Z*

[PREVIOUS SPREAD]

*San Toy rockpool, 2024.* Photo: Myfanwy J. Webb.

# THE RESERVE,
## HARDYS BAY

### BEGINNINGS

The western end of Araluen Drive, from where it meets Heath Road to the beginning of the Dog Track at the point, was called The Reserve by locals in the early days of the settlement.

### HISTORY

There was a designated reservation 100 feet wide extending around the foreshore to Pretty Beach when the Pretty Beach Extension Estate was first opened up in 1912 (Appendix 1.7). As The Reserve was a wide grassy area it was a common sight to see local dairy cows grazing there.

For more information see the entry for ARALUEN DRIVE.

*Nocks Wharf and the Reserve, date unknown.* Photo: Bouddi Photos Past and Present, Flickr, CC BY 2.0.

# RILEYS BAY,

### BEGINNINGS

Rileys Bay is located between Daleys Point and Hardys Bay and was named after the Riley family who remain well known in the Brisbane Water district today. Part of the bay to the east of the Rileys' house is included in

*Wedding portrait of William & Isabella Riley, 1894.* Photo: via Gwen Dundon, Courtesy of Central Coast Council.

Bouddi National Park.

### HISTORY

The first settlers in the bay were Elizabeth and John Murray who took up the land in 1835. Remains of their house foundations can still be seen today. The bay was also referred to as Murrays Bay in the early days.[402] The Murrays and the Rileys lived near each other for many years.

John Riley of London aged 18 was tried and convicted of stealing a hat valued at 2 shillings and a handkerchief valued at 6 pence in 1827. He arrived at Sydney Cove in the following year and by 1838 he was living at Brisbane Water. He settled on Rileys Island, previously named Shell Island (for the large amount of shell middens there) in the 1850s.

It was his son William Riley (1841-1910) by John's second wife Elizabeth who took up the land at Rileys Bay in the 1870s. Initially William captained his father's vessel, *Maggie Riley*, and later came to own his own vessels. He transported cargo to Sydney from Brisbane Water and returned with supplies for the locals. Some of the goods he took to Sydney for sale were baskets of shells, hides, skins, horns, tallow, timber, fowls, eggs and oysters. Later in life William became an oyster farmer, with a lease off Rileys Bay made from sandstone blocks taken from the Murrays' old house. In 1920 the present Riley house was built and named Mount Earl. William's widow, his second wife Isabella, lived there, without electricity or running water until her death in 1953. Members of the Riley family lived there for most of the twentieth century and owned the land until 2005.[403]

*'Mount Earl' Rileys Bay, date unknown.* Photo: Bouddi Photos Past and Present, Flickr, CC BY 2.0.

In the twentieth century, Rileys Bay had a shell crushing factory. There was a steam engine and wheel for grinding the shells which were collected from a nearby sand bar. The shell grit then went to farmers for fertiliser and to Sydney by boat for use in the building industry. The Rileys also ran dairy cattle and when that ceased, they kept a few to keep the grass down. Timber getting was important in the area and in the 1930s there remained a sawmill at the end of Hardys Bay Parade.[404]

Rileys Bay was formally assigned the name in 1977.[405]

*Aboriginal Midden, Rileys Bay, date unknown.* Photo: Bouddi Photos Past and Present, Flickr, CC BY 2.0.

# THE RIP,
## BRISBANE WATER

### BEGINNINGS

The Rip was originally called Webb's Reef, after Brisbane Water's first permanent settler James Webb who settled on the western shore at what is now called Blackwall in 1823.[406]

The Rip is a descriptive name and can be a warning to watercraft. It is a narrow stretch of water extending from Daleys Point to Booker Bay. The narrowness (about 200 metres) and the high tidal flows produce a fast-running current which is clearly visible from the bridge above.

### HISTORY

Vessels entering Brisbane Water were often prevented from continuing into Brisbane Water due to the strength of The Rip and were forced to wait until the tide changed.

The first Europeans to tackle The Rip were those in an exploring party led by Governor Arthur Phillip who entered Brisbane Water on 2nd March 1788 only five weeks after their arrival in Port Jackson. William Bradley describes part of the journey;

*As we proceeded up this branch after passing a very flat shoal and two or three Coves, we found [the ebb tide] set out so strong that we could not pull ahead through between two projecting points.*[407]

The coves mentioned were probably Pretty Beach, Hardys Bay and Rileys Bay, and The Rip Bridge now spans the 'projecting points'. After the tide had slackened the party was able to negotiate The Rip and explore further.

It is registered by the Geographical Names Board of NSW as a strait and the name was assigned in 1974.[408]

# RIP BRIDGE,

### BEGINNINGS

The building of the Rip Bridge was important for

[ *Listing of Place and Street Names: R to Z*

[IMAGE LEFT]

*Rip Bridge during late construction stages, 1973.* Photo: via Gwen Dundon, Courtesy of Central Coast Council.

providing better access to the Bouddi Peninsula and meant the end of relying on ferries. Access to the peninsula was originally by water and later by a road via East Gosford and Kincumber and along The Scenic Road.

For information about the name RIP see the entry for THE RIP.

## HISTORY

Residents after World War II expected an increase in the population and believed while a bridge would eventually be necessary from Ettalong across to the Bouddi Peninsula it was thought a short-term solution could be using a punt. This did not eventuate and so in the 1950s and 1960s there was a plan to build a bridge from Ettalong to Wagstaffe which was to be built along the Wagstaffe ridgeline. The Pretty Beach Wagstaff [sic] Citizens Association formed a committee which worked towards this.

However, it was not to be and finally a bridge was decided on to link Booker Bay and Daleys Point across The Rip.[409] At the time the construction of the bridge was controversial as some felt that so few people lived on the eastern side it was a waste of money. A local newspaper reported 'The Rip Bridge was branded the Bridge to No-where' by a former shire president.[410]

The cantilevered Rip Bridge was opened in June 1974 and for the first time linked the Woy Woy Peninsula to the other shore. This prompted a realignment of Empire Bay Drive and an upgrade of Wards Hill Road. Combined with a faster motorway from Sydney it meant the Bouddi Peninsula was much more accessible for workers, holiday makers, weekenders and retirees.

At mean high water the maximum clearance at the centre of the bridge arch is 17.2 metres and so restricts larger vessels from entering Brisbane Water.[411]

For those who would like to know more, The NSW Department of Main Roads released a short film about the construction of the bridge entitled 'The Rip Bridge' produced by Max Lemon. It is available on YouTube by searching 'The Rip Bridge Construction Work'.

*View of Rip Bridge from Booker Bay wharf, 2025.* Photo: Myfanwy J. Webb.

*Listing of Place and Street Names: R to Z*

# THE RIP ESTATE,

## BEGINNINGS

The Rip Estate is really a case of 'The Estate that wasn't'. It was named this because it is close to the The Rip in Brisbane Water (Appendix 1.10). This estate included part of Riley's Bay and land which abutted The Killlcare Extension Estate (Appendix 1.3).

## HISTORY

The land was first owned by William Nash who is believed to have been promised the first land grant in Brisbane Water in 1811. The deeds were not prepared until 1838. William had arrived as a convict in 1798 and after his term was served, he became a farmer in the Wisemans Ferry area. He probably never lived on the Brisbane Water land as he sold it three years after he received the deeds.

The land changed hands a few times until the McDonnell family advertised it for sale as 'The Rip Estate' in 1908. The auctioneers offered prospective purchasers 'Cheap railway fares, free launches, free luncheon [and] free tents for campers'.[412] However the sale failed to go ahead apparently due to problems providing the Torrens Title. Torrens Title was applied for and granted in March 1939 but the land has never been densely settled as had been planned in The Rip Estate of 1908.[413] For more details see the Bouddi CD-ROM, Chapter 9, Early European settlers and their land.

# ROCKY POINT,
## KILLCARE

### BEGINNINGS

Rocky Point is a descriptive name as there is a rocky reef in the water off the Point. This has provided an excellent area for oyster growing in the past but does remain a hazard for vessels.

### HISTORY

The point on the southern end of Rileys Bay is named Rocky Point and on the ridge above it is Allen Strom Lookout. The Rocky Point walking track begins in Wards Hill Road nearly opposite the intersection with Maitland Bay Road and leads to the Lookout through the Bouddi National Park. Rocky Point was officially named in 1977.[414]

For more information see the entry for ALLEN STROM LOOKOUT.

*Rocky Point at sunset, 2024.* Photo: Kalena V. Webb.

SIGNPOSTS TO THE PAST

[ *Listing of Place and Street Names: R to Z*

*San Toy Resort, 1956.* Photo: Bouddi Photos Past and Present, Flickr, CC BY 2.0.

*San Toy swimming pool, late 1950s.* Photo: Bouddi Photos Past and Present, Flickr, CC BY 2.0.

*Collapse of San Toy after 7ft 6in high tide, 1956.* Photo: Bouddi Photos Past and Present, Flickr, CC BY 2.0.

# SAN TOY ESTATE, WAGSTAFFE

## BEGINNINGS

The San Toy Estate was an informal estate at the end of Wagstaffe Avenue in Bulkara Street named by the Radford Family. Read the following history to hear why it was named San Toy.

## HISTORY

In 1939 Ernest Radford (1893-1956) and his wife Isobel (1897-1987) (née McDonald) bought a holiday cottage at Wagstaffe Point in Bulkara Street. They bought two more blocks and built holiday houses on them also.

Next to the Radfords' blocks were two blocks owned by the Horne Family of Tamworth. They loved music and called a building with an oriental shaped fascia board on the waterfront *San Toy*. This was after an 1899 musical comedy 'San Toy, or, The Emperor's Own'. The Hornes rented out three cottages.

When the Radford's acquired the Hornes' adjacent land with two cottages they decided to call all the area they owned with its holiday cottages the 'San Toy Holiday Estate' and later the 'San Toy Estate', after the San Toy cottage.

Unfortunately, during a winter storm in 1956 tidal water rose well above the normal height and inundated low lying land. San Toy cottage which was built over the water on piles was lifted up and destroyed. The Radfords set to work reclaiming some of the land washed away. They had already started building a sea wall as early as 1938 to protect the beach and cottages.

Gradually as the holiday rentals began to decline, some of the houses became permanent rentals for not-so-well-off locals. However, sadly, the San Toy Estate was dismantled when the Radfords found they were paying more land tax, rates and upkeep than they received from their rentals. So the individual blocks had to be sold, the Radfords retaining their own block and house.

Ernest and Isobel Radford had one son (Ernest) Rod (1920-2017) who studied at the University of Sydney and became a pharmacist at Umina and Ettalong. He married Patricia Coxon (1921-2010). Rod lived on the San Toy Estate at No.7 Bulkara Street and travelled by boat from Wagstaffe across to Ettalong. In the 1960s he bought a German made amphicar which meant he could travel not only on land but across the water. He would pick up orders from the Old Killcare Store and

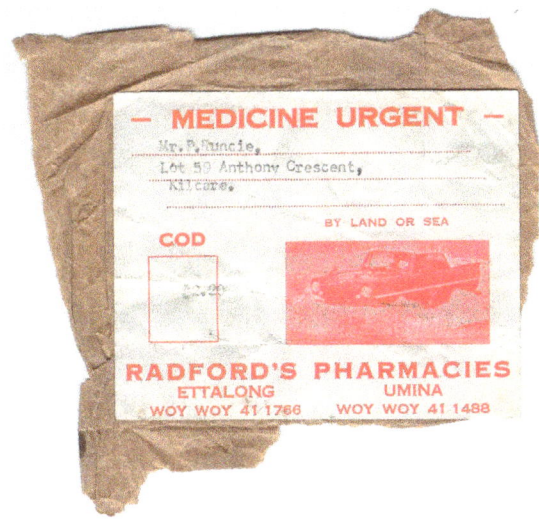

*Radford's Pharmacy label with amphicar, 1970s.* Photo via: Beverley J. Runcie.

*Rod Radford in his Amphicar amphibious car, 1960s.* Photo: The Daily Telegraph.

[ *Listing of Place and Street Names: R to Z*

*Mooring at Radfords, date unknown.* Photo: Bouddi Photos Past and Present, Flickr, CC BY 2.0.

*Don Radfords Fishing Boat, date unknown.* Photo: Bouddi Photos Past and Present, Flickr, CC BY 2.0.

bring the medicines across in his amphicar. Rod delivered to other places on the bay as well. Rod Radford died aged 97.

Now those houses have disappeared and have been replaced by very different ones. The Radford is

*Car and Opera House, Sydney, date unknown.* Photo: Bouddi Photos Past and Present, Flickr, CC BY 2.0.

recognised by a plaque at the old gate to the San Toy Estate in Bulkara Street acknowledging the Radford family's reclamation of land and their contribution to the community. The old gateway is built with local cut sandstone from the demolition of one of the houses, *Silver Spray*.[415]

# THE SCENIC ROAD, KILLCARE, KILLCARE HEIGHTS, MACMASTERS BEACH

## BEGINNINGS

The Scenic Road commences at the roundabout at Empire Bay Drive, Kincumber and finishes at the intersection of Beach Drive and Nukara Avenue, Killcare.

The Scenic Road is a descriptive name and even after considerable human impact over the years and the growth of trees, the views, especially from Killcare Heights to Barrenjoey and down to Manly and across Brisbane Water live up to the name.

## HISTORY

By 1855 there was a track from Kincumber to Cockrone Lake at MacMasters Beach but not as far as Killcare. By the end of the 19th century there were only two formal roads in the area, one linking Kincumber to Little Beach

*Signpost cluster at Scenic Road, 2025.* Photo: Myfanwy J. Webb.

via Dajani Road and one which led to Wagstaffe via Fraser Road.[416] The main access to the Bouddi Peninsula however remained by boat and ferry for the first half of the 20th century.

During the 1920s Councillor Thomas Humphrey took up the fight to have The Scenic Road made and opened for motorists. In February 1926 he travelled in his sulky with reporter R. Norman Mawer through MacMasters Beach and up onto the ridge, passing Maitland Bay (then called Boat Harbour) extolling the view from Killcare Heights as they gazed down to Manly and then viewed Brisbane Water up towards Gosford. Negotiating the steep descent to Killcare and Hardys Bay it was estimated that a steady grade of 1 in 14 could be obtained and seeing the ridge had excellent road making material, the project appeared to have no insurmountable problems.[417]

When The Scenic Road from Kincumber to Killcare was being discussed it was seen by some councillors as an important part of a great projected coastal highway. This highway was to run from Wagstaffe to The Entrance and even on to Catherine Hill Bay. The project was conceived by the Erina Shire Development League and initially was known as 'Scenic Coastal Highway'. The panoramic views of lake and ocean were expected to attract many tourists.[418]

Local resident Alexander Martin became a great ambassador for the making of the road, writing long letters to the Erina Shire Council. One letter says the 'Scenic Crop' should be harvested to bring money into the Shire. He wrote 'One of the miracles wrought by the coming of automobiles is the creation… of a new cash crop, which brings to certain Shires, hundreds of thousands of pounds every year. This Crop is Scenery, and it is a crop that can be harvested summer and winter the year round… Making this marvellous region easily accessible to motor tourists… involves making a major contribution to the scenic wealth of Australia'.[419]

Pressure to construct a road appeared to propel the Council into action. By November 1926 construction was well under way and this is the first time we see the name 'The Scenic Road' used.[420] It was opened for motor traffic in early December even though there was still work to be done.[421] The local paper reported on 2nd December 1926: 'So rapid has been the progress of work on the scenic road from Kincumber to Killcare that by the end of the present week the road will be open for motor traffic. The road, it is understood, will not be

[ *Listing of Place and Street Names: R to Z*

completed for some time, but the work already done renders it fit for vehicular traffic for all time. The scenery along the road ranks with the best to be had in any part of the State, and any Gosford residents desiring to attend the opening of the new school at Pretty Beach on Saturday Dec.11, could not do better than make the trip by motor over this road. Last week the Shire Engineer, Mr. Fenton, covered almost the whole of the road with his car. Operations this week will be in the direction of finishing off the parts requiring most attention. Those who know the road declare that the beauty of the scenery will make it a very popular motor drive'.[422]

However, The Scenic Road was not sealed or any gravel laid and remained a very rough drive. A letter to the editor of *The Sydney Morning Herald* in 1932 protested: 'It is comparatively easy to get to the lake [Cockrone], as the road from Gosford to Kincumber is really good, but from there on to Hardy's [sic] Bay it is to motorists a nightmare …The Scenic Road is simply an uncleared track through about seven miles of bush'.[423] The following year some work was done on the road by labourers in the 'work-for-the-dole' scheme set up during the Depression years.[424]

In 1936 William Macleod from MacMaster's Beach and Councillor Thomas Humphrey formed the Coastal Scenic Road League 'to work for the construction of a proposed highway between Terrigal and Wagstaff, passing through Avoca, MacMaster's Beach, Bouddi, Killcare, Pretty Beach and Hardy's Bay'. With money secured from the Government's relief work scheme further work was undertaken. In appreciation, Spooners Lookout on Box Head was named after the then Minister for Public Works.[425] The name was not taken up and does not appear to be on any later maps. See SPOONERS LOOKOUT.

The first bus service along The Scenic Road from Gosford to Wagstaffe began in 1945 by Rowles Bus Service. The road between Kincumber and Killcare was gravel with many potholes and was graded only once or twice a year with a grader towed by a crawler tractor. 'It was a two-man operation with a caravan towed along behind for accommodation. The Scenic Road

*The Scenic Road, Killcare, date unknown.* Photo: Bouddi Photos Past an

*Listing of Place and Street Names: R to Z*

[ *Listing of Place and Street Names: R to Z*

was topped with the local Killcare Heights red soil and marble sized round gravel, treacherous to walk on, as it would roll under foot, causing many walkers to stumble'.[426]

The Scenic Road remained a rough track until the early 1960s when the road from Kincumber to Killcare was re-formed and sealed.[427] This was done with the help of subsidies from the beach sand mining companies which mined at Bouddi beaches, and which had a processing plant at Kincumber.[428]

The Scenic Road was the primary road to the Bouddi Peninsula until the Rip Bridge was opened in 1974 and the subsequent upgrading of Wards Hill Road gave an alternate access by road to the area.

There are numerous houses of interest along The Scenic Drive which Robyn Warburton has included in her book 'More than Bricks and Mortar: Bouddi Houses & People'. See also in this listing under the headings BOUDDI FARM and STROM CENTRE.

*The Scenic Road from North Ridge Fire Trail, 2024.* Photo: Myfanwy J. Webb.

*The Scenic Road, Killcare Heights, 1925.* Photo: Courtesy of Central Coast Council.

# SECOND POINT,
## BOUDDI NATIONAL PARK

### BEGINNINGS

Second Point appears as Mourawaring on an 1831 map by surveyor Felton Mathew[429] (Appendix 4.7) and would have been a local Aboriginal name. The name Mourawaring is still shown on many current maps.

For information about the name Mourawaring see the entry for MOURAWARING POINT.

### HISTORY

This is the middle point of the three points of 'Cape Three Points' and is in Bouddi National Park. Captain James Cook named 'Cape Three Points' as he sailed northwards in May 1770. However, he did not name the individual points.[430]

Officially it is named 'Second Point' and 'Mourawaring' remains as a variant.[431]

# SMITHY STREET,
## KILLCARE HEIGHTS,

### BEGINNINGS

The origin of the name is unknown. Smithy Street first appears on the subdivision of land called the 'Killcare Heights Estate' in 1928 owned by Sir Ernest Keith White (Appendix 1.4).

### HISTORY

Sir Ernest White named the streets in this subdivision after his family, but no relative with the name 'Smith' can be found. It may refer to a person or an occupation such as a metalworker.

Assuming 'Smithy' is a surname then one possibility is Sir Charles Kingsford Smith who was popularly known by his nickname 'Smithy'. He famously was the first aviator to cross the Pacific from United States of America to Australia. Smithy was very popular around this time. Sir Ernest White advertised his land to be auctioned in April 1928 and Smithy set out on his famous Pacific flight in May 1928.[432] Ernest's grandchildren think this is a distinct possibility because he was keen on the adoption of new technology and would have admired Charles Kingsford Smith.[433]

Another possibility is that Smithy Street is named after James T S Smith who is named as a Subscriber and a First Director of the Pacific Shipping & Trading Co. Ltd. along with Sir Ernest and others as reported under New Companies Registered in the *Daily Commercial News and Shipping List* in 1935.[434] Sir Ernest may have known him before this time.

Of course, these suggestions are speculation only. For further information about Sir Ernest White see the entry for PAULINE AVENUE.

*Smithy Street signpost, 2024.* Photo: Myfanwy J. Webb.

# SMUGGLERS COVE,

## BEGINNINGS

Smugglers Cove is an inlet just south of Maitland Bay within Bouddi National Park. It was named, (with tongue in cheek) quite recently 'by the NPWS field staff when they were building bridges in the area as it looks like an ideal place for smugglers to land with a sheltered cove, a cave over the rock platform and a creek feeding into the cove'.

## HISTORY

This new name is accompanied by new lookouts, built in 2021 along the Bouddi Coastal Walk upgrade and situated along the Bouddi Coastal Walk. Marang Lookout has been constructed just to the north with a great view over Maitland Bay.[435] See BOUDDI COASTAL WALK.

# SPECKS LANE,
## KILLCARE

## BEGINNINGS

This is an unofficial road off The Scenic Road several houses down the hill from the junction of Wards Hill Road overlooking Hardys Bay.

It was named after Oskar Speck (1907-1995) and it originally led to his house. It now leads to the house (now renovated) he built for his partner Nancy. Today there is an informal signpost leading to a few houses (Nos.41-43) whose postal addresses remain 'The Scenic Drive'.

## HISTORY

Oskar Speck was an adventurer. He left Germany in 1932 in a kayak, arriving in Australia over seven years later in 1939 having travelled 50,000 kilometres. Unfortunately, he arrived on Saibai Island just north of Thursday Island during World War II, unaware Germany and Australia were at war, and was interned for the duration of the war. After his release he made his fortune on the

[ *Listing of Place and Street Names: R to Z*

Lightning Ridge opal fields and later became a successful opal merchant in Sydney.

Oskar purchased a large block of land at Killcare Heights for £25 and in 1952 began building a home. He did much of the building and extensive landscaping by himself. This house at No.21 The Scenic Drive has become a landmark and was even included in postcards promoting the area.

At one stage Oskar owned more than 180ha of land on the ridgeline between Pretty Beach and Wagstaffe in anticipation of the proposed bridge from Ettalong to Wagstaffe. Much of it became part of the Bouddi National Park.

Oskar died aged 88 and the house and land passed to his life partner, Nancy Steele.[436] In September 2002 the property sold. His land has since been subdivided. However, his renovated house remains.[437]

*Speck with fellow canoers in New Guinea, 1939.* Photo: Bouddi Photos Past and Present, Flickr, CC BY 2.0.

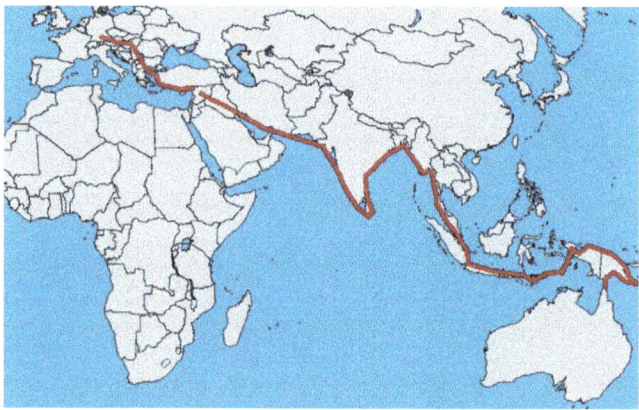
*Map of Oskar Speck journey (1932-1939) from Germany to Australia, 2016.* Photo: Ironie at the English Wikipedia, CC BY-SA 3.0.

*Oskar Speck's home and view from postcard.* Photo: Bouddi Photos Past and Present, Flickr, CC BY 2.0.

*Oskar Speck at Brisbane Water, date unknown.* Photo: Bouddi Photos Past and Present, Flickr, CC BY 2.0.

*Specks Lane, 2024.* Photo: Myfanwy J. Webb.

# SPOONERS LOOKOUT,
## BOUDDI NATIONAL PARK

### BEGINNINGS

Spooners Lookout was situated at a viewing point towards Box Head. Most likely it was situated at the end of Hawke Head Road where there is now a locked gate. It is a name no longer used and the exact location of the lookout appears to be lost to history. It was named after Eric Sydney Spooner (1891-1952).

### HISTORY

Spooners Lookout appears on a map in a booklet 'Gems of Coastal Scenery' published about 1938. The text opposite the map mentions that Eric Spooner, then Minister for Public Works, visited the area in 1937, liked what he saw and made money available 'to put the Scenic Road in good order for motor traffic, from Terrigal to Wagstaffe'.[438]

The Coastal Scenic Road League proposed to name Spooners Lookout in 1937 and there are four more mentions in the local newspaper regarding the Lookout in 1938 and 1939.[439] It could be that naming Spooners Lookout after Eric Spooner may have been to encourage him to finance the project. There appears no mention of it after those dates and it doesn't seem to have taken hold as a name.

# STANLEY STREET,
## KILLCARE

### BEGINNINGS

Stanley Street first appears on the 'Killcare Estate' subdivision map in 1916 (Appendix 1.2).

It appears that this street was named after Stanley Noble Rickard (1883-1976) who was the nephew of Arthur Rickard, the developer who offered the land for sale in 1916.

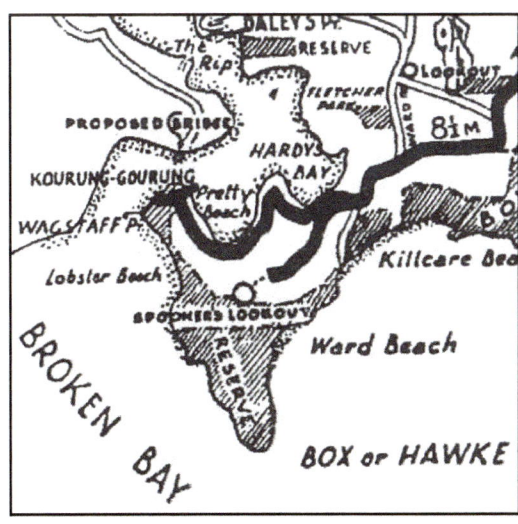

*Spooners Lookout listed in newspaper, 1925.* Photo: Erina Shire Development League Tourist Guide.

*Stanley Noble Rickard, 1883-1976.* Photo: EJ Drinkwater.

[BACKGROUND SPREAD]

*Ferns, 2024.* Photo: Myfanwy J. Webb.

[ *Listing of Place and Street Names: R to Z*

## HISTORY

Stanley's father was Rev. Richard Heath Rickard, brother of Arthur and his mother was Emma Augusta Rickard née Noble. Both Heath and Noble are named roads in the area.

Stanley Rickard was born in New Britain, part of Papua New Guinea, where his father was a Wesleyan missionary. Stanley married Ruby Chaseling in 1912 and after their divorce he married Ruth McCracken in the United States of America.

Stanley trained as an architect and became well known for his Federation Bungalow style houses. World War I interrupted his career and he served four years with the First Australian Imperial Force in France. After the war he practiced architecture in Los Angeles before returning to Australia in 1935. Some of the houses he designed have been heritage listed.[440]

The Killcare Wagstaffe Fire Brigade has its headquarters at No.4 Stanley Street. The Brigade is part of the Rural Fire Service and celebrated its 50 years of service in 2005. It was formed in 1954 as the 'South Brisbane Water Volunteer Bush Fire Brigade' to fight fires from Wagstaffe to MacMasters Beach.[441]

*Stanley St playground, 2010s.* Photo: Bouddi Photos Past and Present, Flickr, CC BY 2.0.

# STEWART STREET, KILLCARE HEIGHTS

## BEGINNINGS

The origin of the name is not known.

*Stewart family at Wagstaffe store, date unknown.* Photo: Bouddi Photos Past and Present, Flickr, CC BY 2.0.

Stewart Street first appears on the subdivision of land called the 'Killcare Heights Estate' in 1928 owned by Sir Ernest Keith White (App 1.4). It is in two sections intersected by Wards Hill Road.

## HISTORY

While the origin of this street name is not known there are a few possibilities:

It could be that Stewart Street was named after Daniel Finlayson Stewart and/or his son Neil Finlayson Stewart. They were both first subscribers along with Ernest White and his wife Pauline to R J White and Co which was registered on 17 February, 1926.[442]

Another possibility is that the street was named after (Sir) Frederick Harold Stewart (1884 -1961) who was a businessman, politician and philanthropist. In the late 1920s he founded the Australian National Airways Ltd with (Sir) Charles Kingsford Smith and Charles Ulm. Stewart also became a politician supporting the United Australia Party. Ernest White held similar political views as Frederick Stewart and if White also knew Charles Kingsford Smith, then it is possible that they were friends and Stewart Street was named after Frederick Harold Stewart. Note that both these suggestions are possibilities only.

For further information about Ernest White see the entry for PAULINE AVENUE.

*Listing of Place and Street Names: R to Z*

*Girl sitting in boat, date unknown.* Photo: Courtesy of Central Coast Council.

*Killcare Wharf, 2000.* Photo: Myfanwy J. Webb.

*Bogey Hole after Storm, Killcare Beach, 2020.* Photo: Myfanwy J. Webb.

*Beach Improvement, 1980s.* Photo: Bouddi Photos Past and Present, Flickr, CC BY 2.0.

*Pilot Whale at Maitland Bay, 2024.* Photo: Myfanwy J. Webb.

*Rock orchid (Dendrobium), 2023.* Photo: Myfanwy J. Webb.

SIGNPOSTS TO THE PAST

# STROM CENTRE, BOUDDI NATIONAL PARK

## BEGINNINGS

The Strom Centre is located at No.230 The Scenic Drive and is within the Bouddi National Park.

The Centre was formerly *'Miara'* the home of Allen and Beryl Strom and their family and was gifted to the National Parks and Wildlife Service by the late Beryl Strom when she died in 2002.

## HISTORY

It is used: 'To provide resources to facilitate research, environmental education and field work, which supports the management of Bouddi National Park. To provide educational resources including the Strom's [sic] collection of papers, photographs and other material relating to Bouddi National Park and its surrounds; and to support the administration and management of Bouddi National Park'.[443]

The very large double garage was upgraded to form the hub of the Centre and the house itself is rented out to an employee of the National Park. Currently, among other things, the Centre is used for National Park volunteer events. As it holds an excellent collection of reference books it has been used as a classroom for 'Green Army' young people and as a study centre. The Strom Centre also houses part of Allen and Beryl's personal collection.

Allen and Beryl Strom married in 1967 and in Beryl's son Gary's words, 'an amazing partnership then ensued of continued tireless dedication in the public interest in environmental education and heritage issues'. In fact the following phrase sums up the Stroms' influence: 'When developers go for their bulldozers, we go for our Stroms!'[444] An inaugural Strom talk in honour of the late Beryl and Allen Strom was held in June 2019 on World Environment Day to celebrate the natural environment of the Central Coast and the Coastal Open Space System (COSS).[445] Central Coast Council announced that the Strom talk would become an annual event.

For further details about this remarkable couple, see *The Bouddi Peninsula* [CD-ROM] and a biography of Allen Strom written by his friend and colleague Allan Fox.[447] See also the entry for ALLEN STROM LOOKOUT.

*Strom Centre and House, 2007.* Photo: Bouddi Photos Past and Present, Flickr, CC BY 2.0.

*Grass tree (Xanthorrhoea), 2024.* Photo: Myfanwy J. Webb.

*Listing of Place and Street Names: R to Z*

*Beryl Strom (1933-2002) & Allen Strom (1915-97).* Photo: Bouddi Photos Past and Present, Flickr, CC BY 2.0. Society.

*Allan Strom at work, 2020.* Photo: Bouddi Photos Past and Present, Flickr, CC BY 2.0.

[ *Listing of Place and Street Names: R to Z*

*Tallow Beach, 1974.* Photo: Gene Dundon, Courtesy of Central Coast Council.

## TALLOW BEACH, BOUDDI NATIONAL PARK

### BEGINNINGS

Tallow Beach a surf beach lies between Little Tallow Beach and Putty Beach and is in the Bouddi National Park. Why it was called Tallow is uncertain.

The name may refer to a barrel or barrels of tallow washed ashore after a shipwreck. Tallow Beach near Byron Bay was named after such an event when the *Volunteer* was wrecked in 1864 with loss of crew and 120 casks of tallow were washed ashore.[448] A similar event may have happened here.

Bert Myer, a local resident, heard that a boat was shipwrecked off the beach and drums of tallow were washed up.[449] A similar story was put forward in the local newspaper in 1924. The author of the article 'Tantalus' said: 'The name Tallow given to the beach near the north head of Broken Bay has a feasible explanation. Years ago, a resident of the place is said to have visited the beach and found a cask of tallow which was supposed to have been washed ashore from a wreck. With the aid of a horse, he brought the cask [put into kerosene tins] to the heights overlooking the beach and eventually got it and its contents away to market. During the war time a fisherman found a cask of tallow near Putty Beach. He recovered it and placed it on the market at a time when tallow was worth £55 a ton.'[450]

Early settlers found the use of tallow extremely important. Tallow is rendered animal fat usually beef or lamb. Rendering separates the fat from the bone and protein and becomes a solid. Traditionally it was used for candles and soap, treating leather and cooking. It was also important as a lubricant for engines.

There have been reports of shipwrecks with cargoes of tallow being wrecked near Broken Bay. In 1852 the schooner *'Rose of Eden'* came to grief south of Broken Bay with a cargo of tallow, hides and furniture.[451] A ketch the *Elizabeth Cohen*, was sighted off Broken Bay in October 1857 but never reached her Sydney destination. She had aboard a mixed cargo which included 45 casks of tallow.[452] So it is quite likely that the story of finding a cask of tallow on the beach is the origin of the name 'Tallow Beach'.

## HISTORY

In 1927 there was an attempt to name Tallow Beach, Ward Beach, and this name appears in a tourist guide for the area in 1928. The article says: 'It was formerly called Tallow Beach', and was named after William Ward's son, Manasseh Ward, a one-time Shire President.[453] The name does not appear to have caught on and the beach is still known as Tallow Beach.

See also the entry for WARD BEACH. For further information about the Ward family see the entry for WARDS HILL ROAD.

The first newspaper article found so far mentioning the name 'Tallow Beach' is in the *Maitland Daily Mercury* in 1922. It announced the body of local fisherman Alwyn Koletzke being found washed up on Tallow Beach.[454] For further information about Alwyn Koletzke see the entry for LOBSTER BEACH.

In October 1924 volunteers began constructing a good track from Pretty Beach to Tallow Beach. Here is a glimpse of what was planned:

'A movement is on foot to improve the track from Pretty Beach to Tallow Beach on the ocean front. It is also proposed to improve a natural 'Bogey Hole' at Tallow Beach on the ocean front. It is also proposed to improve a natural 'Bogey Hole' at Tallow Beach by blasting away a little rock and controlling a small stream of fresh water so that visitors may indulge in a refreshing shower after their dip in the salt water. In order to improve the existing fine outlook to be had from the great heights above Tallow Beach, it is proposed to erect a miniature Eiffel Tower from which a view extending almost to Gosford and up and down the coast will be commanded. At present visitors and others at Wagstaffe and Pretty Beach desiring a safe dip in the ocean, have to take a long walk to Putty Beach, where there is a good natural 'Bogey Hole', but no advantage in the form of a fresh water shower'.[455]

In just over a month the track was completed, and a number of holes had been bored in the rocks in preparation for the blasting to deepen the Bogey Hole.[456] Whether work on the bogey hole was ever completed is questionable. Certainly, the idea of an 'Eiffel Tower' was not taken up!

During the 1960s the beach was mined for rutile and zircon and the mining company formed Hawke Head Drive to enable access to the beach. However, similar

*Tallow Beach showing camping area, 1990s.* Photo: Donald G. Runcie.

to Putty Beach, after the mining company departed and 'rehabilitated' the beach dunes, the invasive bitou bush was planted as part of the rehabilitation scheme. After many years of aerial spraying and National Parks volunteers working to eradicate the weeds, weed invasion is now minimal.

# TAWORRI ROAD,
## KILLCARE,

### BEGINNINGS

Taworri is an Aboriginal word meaning 'evening breeze'. It appears to be chosen by Gosford Shire Council officers from Endacott's book 'Australian Aboriginal words and place names'.[457] It is not a local word and comes from the Kaurna people of the Ade laide region of South Australia.[458]

### HISTORY

This is a short road linking Putty Beach Drive and Anthony Crescent. There is a Council reserve on one side and Bouddi National Park on the other and there are no dwellings.

It first appears unnamed on the Kilcare [sic] Beach subdivision (Appendix 1.11) and was named when the land was offered for sale in 1967. It was officially named in 1970.[459] It was kerbed and guttered and had a bitumen surface when the development was first put on market. in 1970.[459]

# THE TRIANGLE,
## KILLCARE HEIGHTS,

### BEGINNINGS

'The Triangle' is an unofficial name for the area at Killcare Heights bounded by The Scenic Drive, Maitland Bay Drive and Wards Hill Road which forms the rough shape of a triangle.

### HISTORY

It was a small thriving farming area in the early twentieth century due to its lateritic soil which was enriched by poultry manure. There is a spring and a creek running through the centre of the Triangle which goes under the Wards Hill Road and spills over the edge via a waterfall into Fletchers Glen. This allowed the farmers

*Taworri Road looking north, 2024.* Photo: Myfanwy J. Webb.

*Aerial Maitland Bay & Triangle, 1983.* Photo: L Medley, Courtesy of Bouddi Photos Past and Present, Flickr, CC BY 2.0.

*Listing of Place and Street Names: R to Z*

[BACKGROUND SPREAD] (LEFT)

*Anthony Crescent Killcare. Photo: Myfanwy J. Webb.*

to build dams and access good water. Clyde Adrian Livingstone Walters with wife Nellie were the first family to farm and owned much of the land. They had a poultry farm and also kept pigs and grew citrus, beans and other vegetables. Produce for sale was taken down Wards Hill Road and loaded onto a boat at Palmer's Wharf and taken to Woy Woy and then transferred to the railway station to be sent to the Sydney markets.

Later the land was subdivided into rural and urban blocks. Ian McCall established a plant nursery on their property on the corner of Maitland Bay Drive and Wards Hill Road and in 1978 Sheila Wilmott and her son Chris set up a nursery at No27 Maitland Bay Drive specialising in plants native to the area.

A newer arrival in the Triangle is 'Bells at Killcare' which is accessed from The Scenic Drive. This is a boutique resort with restaurant and spa. It has cottages, suites and villas set among native trees and some overlook a small lake. There is a vegetable garden which provides the restaurant with much of its fresh produce.

Because of the elevated position of The Triangle, it has a Telecommunications Tower at No.223 The Scenic Road nearly opposite the Maitland Bay car park. On Wards Hill Road at No.37 a water reservoir was installed and in 2019 a 'super' tower to improve mobile telephone reception was proposed for the same site.[461]

# THIRD POINT,
## BOUDDI NATIONAL PARK,

### BEGINNINGS

Third Point or Bombi Point is the most southerly point of the three points of 'Cape Three Points' and is between Caves Bay and Little Beach in Bouddi National Park.

### HISTORY

Captain James Cook named 'Cape Three Points' as he sailed northwards in May 1770; however, he did not name the individual points.[462]

*Ian, Pat McCall, 'Kilcare', 1945.* Photo: Bouddi Photos Past and Present, Flickr, CC BY 2.0.

*The Triangle left The Scenic Road, top Wards Hill Road, right Maitland Bay Drive, 1964.* Photo: Bouddi Photos Past and Present, Flickr, CC BY 2.0.

*McCalls Real Estate, date unknown.* Photo: Bouddi Photos Past and Present, Flickr, CC BY 2.0.

[ *Listing of Place and Street Names: R to Z*

The name appears as 'Bombi' on an 1831 map by surveyor Felton Mathew [463] (Appendix 4.7) and would have been a local Aboriginal name. The name 'Bombi' still appears on some current maps.

However, it is now officially named 'Third Point' and 'Third Point (Bombi)' is listed as a previous name.[464] See also the entry for BOMBI POINT.

## TURO CREEK,
### PRETTY BEACH

### BEGINNINGS

Turo Creek runs through Turo Reserve/Park into Pretty Beach. For information about the name 'Turo' see the entry for TURO RESERVE.

### HISTORY

In 1996 the Killcare Wagstaffe Trust was given a grant under the NSW Government's 'Rivers Reborn' program. The grant was to make environmental improvements to the Pretty Beach foreshore and this plan included Turo Creek.

The Trust submitted a plan which included replanting mangroves along the creek bank and at the mouth of the creek to provide: erosion control, a sediment trap to reduce siltation, recycling of pollutants and

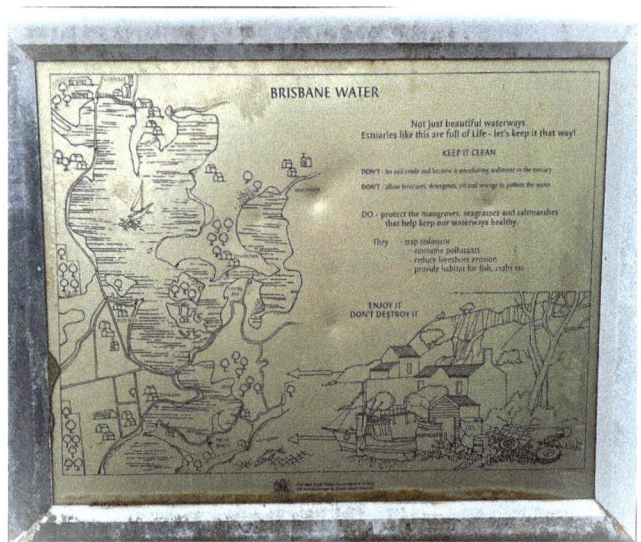

*Turo creek sign, 2025.* Photo: Myfanwy J. Webb.

*Turo creek, 2025.* Photo: Myfanwy J. Webb.

a fish breeding habitat. Native trees and shrubs were to be planted on the creek bank to provide: a safety barrier for children and an attractive complementary planting to the mangroves. A boardwalk across the creek was planned to provide a safe pedestrian access, and a viewing platform to observe estuary life was included. Also, an interpretative signage board was planned to provide information about estuarine organisms. Not everyone approved of the plan and it caused an enormous amount of dissension locally. Mangroves became the hot topic.

The Council however, approved the planting of mangroves in Turo Creek and some pupils from Pretty Beach School helped plant. A few weeks later however all the new plantings had disappeared. However, the bridge and the information board were successfully installed.[465]

Gosford City Council developed a 'Turo Creek Flood Plain Risk Management Plan' in 2007. By 2010 mangroves were blocking the water flow in the creek causing flooding and Gosford Council removed them. In addition, Council has also placed large sandstone blocks along the banks of the creek and the problem has been largely resolved. The clearing of the mangroves in the creek and at its mouth needs to be constant to prevent the silt building up.[466]

*Listing of Place and Street Names: R to Z*

# TURO RESERVE/TURO PARK,
## PRETTY BEACH

### BEGINNINGS

Originally this park was known as Pretty Beach Reserve. The name Turo Reserve which is now commonly known as Turo Park was suggested by the South Bouddi Peninsula Community Group and submitted to Gosford City Council.

Turo Park at Pretty Beach was named after Turo (Teuro) Downes (Down) (c1856-1942) a well-respected and loved Aboriginal man who lived in the Bouddi area from the late 1890s until his death. Turo signed

*Turo Downes with Pamela, Moya & Alan Kirby and Enid Bryant, date unknown.* Photo: Bouddi Photos Past and Present, Flickr, CC BY 2.0.

his name 'Tuero Down' but common usage is Turo Downes. For more about Turo see an article by Bruce Dunlop who knew Turo well and was 15 years old when Turo died. Reminiscences by others can also be found in *'Reflections from the Beach and the Bays'* edited by Jill Baxter.[467]

Before settling down at Hardys Bay, Turo helped Mrs Hyde of Paddington, a house demolition specialist, load and unload cargo from the *SS Erina* which ran from Gosford to Sydney.

During the 1930s Turo endeared himself to the local community and he was especially loved by the children. He lived in a hut made with a tree trunk timber frame, flattened kerosene tin walls and a corrugated iron roof. The hut was well placed on Heath Road for Turo to look down to the Rip and and see the ferry coming and he would go down to meet it. He greeted people by name when they arrived on the launches for their holidays even though he had not seen them for a long time. He was an excellent runner, rower, swimmer, fisherman and card player, often winning the local euchre tournament.[468]

Turo would also teach the children to fish from Hardys Bay wharf and take them on walks over to the Bogey Hole and even as far as Maitland Bay, leading the way and then 'have the 'billy' boiling for a cuppa when

*Turo Downes, 1866-1942.* Photo: Bouddi Photos Past and Present, Flickr, CC BY 2.0.

[ *Listing of Place and Street Names: R to Z*

*'Hillcrest' back view with Turo, date unknown.* Photo: Bouddi Photos Past and Present, Flickr, CC BY 2.0.

*Group including Turo Downs waiting for the Ferry, date unknown.* Photo: Bouddi Photos Past and Present, Flickr, CC BY 2.0.

everyone arrived on the beach'.[469]

Elizabeth Pope spent most summers of her childhood around Turo as his hut was just behind the Pope family's weekender at No.82 Heath Road. Elizabeth became a noted marine biologist, Deputy Director and Curator of the Australian Museum. Elizabeth became a noted marine biologist, Deputy Director and Curator of the Australian Museum. In correspondence in 1986, held by local historian Gwen Dundon, Elizabeth states:

*He was a gentleman, well mannered and much better spoken than many nowadays white Australians. According to Turo, he had been a coachman for a C. of E. clergyman at Edgecliff (Sydney) and while there received his education. Turo was a full-blood native from the Central Coast tribe. He used to go and visit his relatives at Wyong occasionally. He was not in any way Torres Strait Islander. He always claimed that the whole area round Brisbane Water belonged to his people and that he had the right to kill or use any animal or plant in the area. He certainly taught us facts about the plants you could or couldn't eat and he taught me a lot about fishing and where to and when to get bait. I used to be able to catch the giant beach worms, the squirter worms and to tread nippers (pistol prawns) whenever I need them. In fact, it was probably Turo's influence on me that led me to take up zoology at Sydney University and specialize in Marine Zoology which led to a big job in the Australian Museum.*

In 1957 a new department called Worms and Echinoderms was created with Elizabeth as the Curator. Elizabeth also states,

*'Dr Fred D. McCarthy became head of the Canberra Institute of Aboriginal Studies and is a famous anthropologist and authority in local Aborigines and actually visited us at Hardys Bay in order to meet and talk to Turo. He would confirm that he was a Central Coast (Woy Woy to Wyong) native and a full blood – probably one of the last full bloods of his tribe.'*

The NSW Death Certificate lists Flinders, Queensland as Teuro Down's birthplace however the 'informant' is listed as 'no relation' and therefore the accuracy of his birthplace is undetermined.

*The inscription on Turo's grave reads;*
*'In Loving Memory of*
*Turo Downes*
*Died 16/12/1942*
*Aged 86 Years*
*Respected by all'.*

He died in 1942 aged 86 and is buried at St Paul's Church of England, Kincumber.

## HISTORY

In 1980 when the Council acquired the land where Turo Reserve is, it had a house on the waterfront called 'Naomi' which was built about 1912. Local efforts to keep this historic house failed and it was demolished.

Plans were drawn up in 1982 for a 'passive' park and by 1985 some work had been done and it was very popular especially during school holidays.

On 20th May 1988 in the Australian Bicentennial Year, a naming ceremony took place at Turo Park as part of the Celebrations and trees were planted. Its official name Turo Reserve was assigned in March 1988. Since 2000 the park has had a facelift with new children's equipment and electric barbecues for families. In 2022 a revamp of the children's playspace began.

In 2011, Gosford City Council bought and demolished two houses adjacent to Turo Park which were on flood prone land. The land has been added to the park and is on the other side of Turo Creek. A bridge has been built and the Community Association has been active in designing the layout of the area. Since then, the Reserve has undergone improvements which continue to this day. In 2022 an upgrade of the children's playground planned. [475] It now includes a children's playground and swings, a tennis court with shelter, cricket net, basketball hoops, soccer goal and marine grade exercise equipment for adults.

[BACKGROUND SPREAD]

*Turo Downes article, date unknown.* Photo: Bouddi Photos Past and Present, Flickr, CC BY 2.0.

[ *Listing of Place and Street Names: R to Z*

*First Post Office in Venice Road at No.9.* Photo: Bouddi Photos Past and Present, Flickr, CC BY 2.0.

# VENICE ROAD,
## PRETTY BEACH

### BEGINNINGS

Venice Road first appears on the 'Pretty Beach Estate' subdivision map in 1910 (Appendix 1.6).

The names 'Venice' and 'Como', which also appears on this subdivision, are both popular tourist destinations in Italy which feature water and would have sounded very exotic holiday destinations in 1910. By 1914 advertisements for land around Woy Woy were often labelled as the 'Waterside Wonderland'.

Later in 1936 a short documentary film by Claude Flemming was released entitled '*Woy Woy: The Venice of Australia*.' This film can be viewed on YouTube.[476] So it appears that the name Venice Road may have been capitalising on the glamour of the Italian connection to encourage land sales.

### HISTORY

Originally Venice Road and Como Parade formed the original main road leading to Wagstaffe from Hardys Bay. Pretty Beach Road adjacent to the waterfront was a minor road until later and now there is no link between Venice Road and Como Road.

The first business at Pretty Beach was an inn called 'The Crooked Billet' which William Spears established as early as 1838. It is believed to have been situated up the hill from the water and wharf, where Venice Road is today. The history of the inn's name is interesting. By the year 1393, publicans in England were required by law to have signs to indicate their presence.[477] The simplest sign was an old stick from a tree and as 'billet' was such a stick; pub owners would just hang this crooked stick outside, hence 'The Crooked Billet'.

The first Post Office was at No.9 Venice Road. There was a market garden in Venice Road on both sides of Turo Creek run by Jack and Marjie Smith. During the war years (World War II) they supplied much needed fruit and vegetables to the local community. There was a dairy on the corner of Venice Road and High View Road but unfortunately it failed to flourish.[478]

By 1967 Venice Road had still not been tarred but the Council had listed it 'for future consideration'. In 1969 it had been placed in the 'future program of works' and by 1976 Venice Road had undergone repairs.[479]

168     SIGNPOSTS TO THE PAST

# WAGSTAFFE

## BEGINNINGS

The name Wagstaffe first appears on the advertisement for the subdivision of land in 1904 when George Wagstaffe first attempted to sell his land (Appendix 1.9).

Captain George Wagstaffe (1853-1920) was an early settler who came into possession of Mulhall's land in 1890. George and his family are remembered by the naming of the suburb Wagstaffe, Wagstaffe Avenue, Wagstaffe Point and Wagstaffe Bar.

## HISTORY

George arrived in Australia from England in 1875 and spent some years as an agent for Burns Philp & Co. Ltd. in New Zealand and the Solomon Islands. He then moved around Queensland and NSW owning stores where he worked also as a draper. He married Christina Ogilvie and had eight children, some of whom died young.

Owing to the depression of the 1890s Wagstaffe was forced to sell his stores and so purchased the land at Brisbane Water with the proceeds. The land cost him £500 of which he had to put down £250 on signing the contract with the balance to be paid off over 5 years.

Although he is listed in the electoral rolls of the time as a farmer, he also became involved with shipping. He obtained a Master's Certificate (Coastal) in 1901 and became known as Captain George Wagstaffe. He also constructed a wooden vessel with his eldest son, George, which they used to convey produce to the markets at Hawkesbury and Sydney.

As he hadn't been able to pay the amount the mortgage required, George was required to sell his home and land. He then returned to Sydney and worked as a senior provider with Burns & Philp until his death in 1920.[480]

Wagstaffe's land failed to sell after an initial subdivision in 1904 was advertised, probably because the land had not been converted to Torrens Title. This

'Wagstaffe', 2009. Artist: Margaret Crane.

[ *Listing of Place and Street Names: R to Z*

*Kingfish, date unknown.* Photo: Bouddi Photos Past and Present, Flickr, CC BY 2.0.

*Swamp wallaby (Wallabia bicolor), 2019.* Photo: Myfanwy J. Webb.

*Carved Spirit Pole, 2013.* Artists: The Wagstaffe Carving Group, 2025. Photo: Myfanwy J. Webb.

*'Wagstaffe Wharf', 2014.* Artist: Margaret Crane.

*Listing of Place and Street Names: R to Z*

*George Wagstaffe, 1856-1920.* Photo: Courtesy of Central Coast Council.

1974.[482]

During the twentieth century the name began to be spelt as 'Wagstaff' without the 'e'. The Brisbane Water Historical Society argued that because George Wagstaffe had an 'e' and his descendants had retained the 'e' then it should be restored.[483] This was done and made official on 25th October 1991.[484] Residents affectionately shorten the word Wagstaffe to 'Waggie' or 'Waggy' especially when talking about 'Waggie (Waggy) Store' and 'Waggie (Waggy) Hall'.

# WAGSTAFFE AVENUE, WAGSTAFFE

## BEGINNINGS

Wagstaffe Avenue is named after the Wagstaffe family who lived here at the end of the 19th and beginning of 20th centuries. For further information about George Wagstaffe see the entry for WAGSTAFFE.

## HISTORY

Wagstaffe Avenue first appears on the 'Wagstaffe's Point Estate' subdivision advertised for sale from 22nd December 1906 (Appendix 1.8).

Two years earlier when the land was advertised in 1904, the emphasis had been on farming. Now the land had been divided into smaller lots and five roads added, Wagstaffe Avenue being the main road running parallel to the waterfront. Advertising was directed to buyers for recreational use.

Keen observers will notice that some of the waterfront blocks along Wagstaffe Avenue are quite narrow and this is explained on the developer's advertisement which states: 'Purchasers of lots not fronting water will be given one of the smaller water frontage allotments for Wharf and Boating facilities'. A few of these narrow blocks still remain but most have been joined together to make a larger block.

The Wagstaffe Wharf was the focus of the early settlement, bringing people and supplies to the area. This meant the Wagstaffe General Store (Nos.46-48) and

subdivision was called 'Wagstaffe's Subdivision, Mount Pleasant, Brisbane Water'. The original holding of 50 acres marked, was subdivided into 11 portions with no roads marked. All had water access.

In 1906, now converted to Torrens Title, it was resubdivided into smaller plots; renamed Wagstaffe's Point Estate Woy Woy and included roads, Wagstaffe Avenue being the main access. The advertising emphasis had changed from 'Rich Agricultural Land suitable for Orchards, Maize Growing, etc.' to 'The Manly of Brisbane Water', with the expectation that the land would be sold for holiday purposes. The blocks of land with no water frontage were given narrow blocks on the water 'for Wharf and Boating facilities' (Appendix 1.8). Water was still the principal way of reaching Wagstaffe as there was no road.

Before it was decided to build the Rip Bridge linking Booker Bay and Daleys Point, it was proposed to build a bridge from Ettalong Beach across to Wagstaffe. In 1939 the Coastal Scenic Road League pushed for a low-level traffic bridge with a lifting span to be built 'as a defence necessity'. Interestingly, the League also thought it important to construct roads to 'Capes First, Second and Third Point for transport of troops and guns'.[481] During the 1950s and 1960s there was an increasing push by the community to build a bridge or a punt between Ettalong and Wagstaffe and the issue was only resolved when the Rip Bridge was opened in

[ *Listing of Place and Street Names: R to Z*

*Manly Guesthouse Wagstaffe, date unknown.* Photo: Fred Paddison, Courtesy of Central Coast Council.

*St Peters Anglican Church Wagstaffe Avenue, 1996.* Photo: Bouddi Photos Past and Present, Flickr, CC BY 2.0.

*Manly House* guest house (where the Community Hall is now) became the first businesses. Other businesses followed along Wagstaffe Avenue. On the other corner to *Manly House* at No.44 was a mini golf course which was set up for the guests of *Manly House* as a holiday activity. Syd Osborne opened the Wonderland Greengrocer in 1936 which was on the opposite corner from Wagstaffe Store. The Kennedys lived at No.54 Wagstaffe Avenue and had a dairy farm; Kitty rounding up the stray cows sometimes as far as Box Head. Charles Hanscombe owned a dairy and had a house high up the hill. Customers bought his milk from a shed in No.38 Wagstaffe Avenue.

Ted Myer lived in a shed at the back of No.33 Wagstaffe Avenue and ran a sly grog trade. He stored the beer bottles in the outside dunny. Over time a few barbers lived in the Avenue. The first acted also as a local 'doctor' stitching up wounds when necessary. A second barber lived on the water side and later a third barber, Mr Polanski, lived at No.24 Wagstaffe Avenue.

In 1914 the Church of England bought land at No.12 and soon built a hall which initially was used for social events and occasional services. After World War I, a more substantial hall was built and dances, services, baptisms, weddings and funerals were held. The church closed in 1996 and the building is now a home.[485] The Murphy family ran a launch service to Wagstaffe before 1913 and built a house in the 1920s at No.45 where they moored their ferries. It became known as *'The Ferrymaster's Cottage'.* After some controversy about its listing as a heritage building it was demolished in 2001; the Norfolk Pines on the water's edge remain protected.[486]

## WAGSTAFFE BAR,

### BEGINNINGS

Wagstaffe Bar is often referred to as the Little Box Head Channel, Lobster Beach Channel and more recently as the Ettalong Channel. Wagstaffe Bar is an extensive mobile sand bar at the entrance to Brisbane Water. It is located between Half Tide Rocks and Little Box Head and restricts the area of navigable waterway to form a narrow channel. From the early days of the colony until the present-day, vessels have come to grief trying to avoid the sand bar at the entrance to Brisbane Water. In 1835 four convicted bushrangers stole a small boat from Sydney and headed north. They overturned on the bar and then went on a thieving spree by foot. In the 19th century there were at least five more ships wrecked on the bar.[487]

This bar was one of the key reasons which impeded any colonial settlement until the early 1820s and has always been and still remains an obstacle for large vessels In 2021 the New South Wales government issued a navigation warning for vessel operators advising that 'the depth of water has been decreased due to the ongoing movement of sand in the vicinity of Little Box Head to Lobster Beach, Brisbane Water potentially restricting navigation to some vessels'.[488]

The bar's official name is 'Wagstaffe Bar' and the Geographical Names Board of NSW lists 'Wagstaff Bar' (note spelling) and 'The Bar' as previous names. Contradicting this 'The Bar' is also listed as a variant of Wagstaffe Bar. It is described as 'a shoal on Brisbane Water off of Wagstaff [sic] Point'.[489]

For information about the name Wagstaffe see the entry for WAGSTAFFE.

*Woy Woy to the Bar Ferry ' Irene,' 1906.* Photo: via Gwen Dundon, Courtesy of Central Coast Council.

## HISTORY

In the nineteenth century sometimes people living around the bay from Rileys Bay to Wagstaffe were referred to as living at 'Brisbane Water Bar'. For example, in the 1891 NSW Census, Robert Hardy, John Murray, William Riley, Walter McDonnell and George Wagstaffe are all listed as living at Brisbane Water Bar.

Thomas W. Simpson built Manly House next to Wagstaffe wharf Walter McDonnell and George Wagstaffe are all listed as living at Brisbane Water Bar.[490]

Thomas W. Simpson built *Manly House* next to Wagstaffe wharf in 1907 and also began a launch service to bring not only customers to his new boarding house but also prospective purchasers of land at Wagstaffe. The launch became a daily return trip and would meet all trains at Woy Woy. Simpson's first launch was called *Irene* and had a board on top advertising the destination 'Woy Woy to the Bar'. It was known as the 'Red Ferry to the Bar'.[491]

For further information about the Wagstaffe family see the entry for WAGSTAFFE.

In 1887 a deputation was made to the Minister for Works pointing out the importance of dredging the bar as the steamers found it difficult to cross. Figures were given to show that 20,000 passengers and 6,000 tons of goods would travel annually across the bar. The Minister promised earnest consideration of the matter.[492] There are no further reports in the press indicating if dredging was carried out or not.

The bar remained a problem to shipping. One incident occurred in 1911 when the *SS Gosford* on a Sunday excursion, was bound for the Hawkesbury River but became fast in the sand. Some of the passengers were ferried across to Wagstaffe Point to picnic there and some remained on board and were entertained by the Gosford and Tamworth bandsmen. The *SS Gosford* lifted off with the high tide about 5pm.[493] This was not

*Wagstaffe and secondary sand bars.* Photo: Bouddi Photos Past and Present, Flickr, CC BY 2.0.

*'Florant' Lobster Beach, date unknown.* Photo: Bouddi Photos Past and Present, Flickr, CC BY 2.0.

an isolated case of vessels having problems negotiating The Bar. In 1913 the ketch *Florant* failed to negotiate the bar as it had silted up.[494] The vessel went onto the rocks just south of Lobster Beach and had to be towed to the Blackwall Shipyards for an overhaul.[495]

Council was approached to define the channel with marker buoys, a request which was turned down as 'there are no funds available for this work which cannot be considered as of an urgent nature'. In 1922 after three boating accidents in six months at the bar involving loss of life, Jack Murphy of Wagstaffe suggested that navigation marks be placed on the shore at Little Box Head, at the north point of Lobster Beach and on the end of Half-Tide rocks. He also suggested blasting the rocks away from the entrance to improve the navigation. This second request was denied, Council saying that that would not improve navigation.[496]

The New Bar Progress Association was active in the 1920s and is believed to have had 'a single intent… to have the channel [now mostly referred to as the Ettalong Channel] dredged, thus creating a 'new bar' meaning a sandbank'.[497]

Occasionally the bar has been dredged to make a safer channel for shipping. Dredging has been a controversial issue over the years, being opposed by environmentalists concerned that marine life on the bed would be affected. There were also disagreements between Gosford City Council and the NSW State Government as to which body should pay for work done.

The New Bar Progress Association was active in the 1920s and is believed to have had 'a single intent… to have the channel [now mostly referred to as the Ettalong Channel] dredged, thus creating a 'new bar' meaning a sandbank'.

Occasionally the bar has been dredged to make a safer channel for shipping. Dredging has been a controversial issue over the years, being opposed by environmentalists concerned that marine life on the bed would be affected. There were also disagreements between Gosford City Council and the NSW State Government as to which body should pay for work done.

In 1989 the NSW Public Works Department contracted with Patterson Britton & Partners P/L consulting engineers to prepare a report entitled 'Brisbane Water Entrance Options'. It was released in January 1990 and set out four options which could be taken to alleviate problems encountered at Wagstaffe Bar.[498] It is not certain what action if any was taken following this report.

In 2008 the need to dredge the channel off Lobster Beach was hotly debated. Gosford City Council and the NSW Department of Environment & Climate Change commissioned a 'Brisbane Water Estuary Processes Study' and found that sediment movement had 'led to a constriction of the navigation channel on the eastern side of the entrance. Water depths … are currently as shallow as 1-2m at low tide'.[499] Gosford Council pressured the State Government to provide the $500,000 needed and finally they shared the costs and the channel was dredged in 2009. Councillor Peter Freewater said at the time 'The maintenance dredging will not only make the channel safe again but will prove a boon for local businesses with a return of charter vessels and recreational boaters to Brisbane Water'.[500]

The debate about dredging continued. The Central Coast Council told the NSW Cabinet in 2017 that 'There is an urgent need to address the ongoing closing over and narrowing of the entrance bar at the Ettalong Channel so that it is safer and more navigable under all conditions'.[501] In reply the Department of Primary Industries stated that Brisbane Water does not include State owned maritime infrastructure and therefore does not qualify for dredging funded by the State Government. It does, however, fall into the category of the 'Rescuing our Waterways Program' which is funded by both State and Local Government.

Later in 2017 the Ettalong/Wagstaffe to Palm Beach ferry ran aground and the ferry service was diverted to Patonga for a few days. Emergency dredging helped initially but the effects were temporary.[502] During May 2018 commercial ferries ceased to run to Ettalong and Wagstaffe due to sand bar build up. Finally, after much community protest the State government agreed by September 2018 to supply $660,000 for emergency dredging at Ettalong Channel with the promise of further funds through the 'Rescuing our Waterways' program. The ongoing dredging program was to cost $2.45 million financed by a matching of funds from the State Government and Central Coast Council. The Peninsula Waterways Committee was formed representing the interests of both sides of the Brisbane Water to ensure the channel is maintained in perpetuity. The ferries resumed running in November 2018 after seven months absence bringing jubilation to the local community.

In December 2020 a new channel speed limit was imposed. This was as a result of 'the power of the people' which was concerned about the speeding of jet skis. By 2021 the NSW Transport Department, had issued a navigation warning and advice that there is a speed limit between Little Box Head and Lobster Beach of 4 knots and to navigate carefully.

Finally in March 2021 the State Government accepted responsibility for keeping the channel open and financing future dredging. In August 2023, Transport of NSW began dredging the channel after securing the necessary Environmental and Crown Lands license that allows them to remove up to 30,000 cubic meters of sand.

*Palm Beach Ferry & Wagstaffe Bar, 2025.* Photo: Myfanwy J. Webb.

# WAGSTAFFE POINT, WAGSTAFFE

## BEGINNINGS

Wagstaffe Point near Half Tide Rocks was originally called Mulhall's Point after the Mulhall family who took up the first land grant in 1841. The name continued for many years even after George Wagstaffe purchased the land in 1890. Charles Swancott said that it was then called Hall's Point when it was purchased by Mr Hall at the turn of the century.[508] No records have been found so far to substantiate this.

[ *Listing of Place and Street Names: R to Z*

*"Glenella" and wharf, Wagstaffe Point, 1941.* Photo: Courtesy of Central Coast Council.

*Wagstaffe Point, date unknown.* Photo: Courtesy of Central Coast Council.

*Wagstaffe Point Baths, date unknown.* Photo: Courtesy of Central Coast Council.

*Wagstaffe Point swimmers, 1920.* Photo: Photo: Bouddi Photos Past and Present, Flickr, CC BY 2.0.

For information about the name Wagstaffe see the entry for WAGSTAFFE.

## HISTORY

Newspapers of the time show that the first mention of Mulhall's Point appears in 1879 although locals probably called it this much earlier.[509] The name continued until Wagstaffe put it on the market in 1904 using the name 'Wagstaffe's Subdivision' (Appendix 1.9). Failing to sell he then put it on the market as 'Wagstaffe's Point Estate' in 1906 (Appendix 1.8). By 1907 we see the last reference to Mulhall's Point.[510] Wagstaffe Point now relates to the very point of theland and no longer to the full 50 acres which was granted to Patrick Mullhall in 1841. The name was formally recognised in 1991.[511]

Fishing has always been popular at Wagstaffe Point. In 1907 Mr Tucks caught a 56 pound (25 kilogram) jewfish and also landed a grey nurse shark measuring 8ft. 8in. (2.6 mtrs) on a number 30 schnapper line. The newspaper reported: 'This shark had been a terror to black breamers at The Rip, and there was in consequence great rejoicing at its capture'.[512]

For information about the name Wagstaffe see the entry for WAGSTAFFE.

# WAGSTAFFE SQUARE, WAGSTAFFE

## BEGINNINGS

Wagstaffe Square has been a central meeting place since the early 20th century and and remains so. Today it has

*Listing of Place and Street Names: R to Z*

# "MANLY HOUSE WAS BURNT DOWN IN 1939 AND WAS LATER REPLACED BY A MUCH-USED COMMUNITY HALL."

a garden bed in the centre with a central paperbark tree, a ferry wharf, a small park with carved poles, tables, benches and toilet facilities, a sandy beach, community hall, general store and post office.

For information about the name Wagstaffe see the entry for WAGSTAFFE.

## HISTORY

The building of the large guest house *Manly House*, right beside the main Wagstaffe Wharf in 1907 meant that the area outside the guest house was a popular place for people to gather. The guest house was built on the site of George Wagstaffe's original home.[513] Part

*Many House burns, 1939.* Photo: Photo: Bouddi Photos Past and Present, Flickr, CC BY 2.0.

of *Manly House* was two storied and part one storey. The long narrow one storey section had rooms opening on to the square and was used by fisherman who could leave their rooms at any time of the night when the tide was right, to go fishing and not disturb the other guests. A mini golf course was set up on the opposite corner (No.44) for entertainment. *Manly House* was burnt down in 1939 and was later replaced by a much-used Community Hall.[514]

The wharf has been integral to Wagstaffe from the very early days but became busier when launch services began to bring guests to *Manly House* and also to bring prospective buyers for land. A regular daily return trip met the trains at Woy Woy.[515] In 2020 there are regular ferry services which ply between Palm Beach, Ettalong and Wagstaffe and among their regular passengers they transport schoolchildren and tradesmen from the Bouddi Peninsula to Sydney's Northern Beaches.

Next to the ferry wharf there was a small area fenced for a swimming pool believed to have been put there for the guests of *Manly House*. The pool existed until the fences became dilapidated and were removed in the late 1970s or early 1980s.

The first Community Hall was financed by the community and built by local volunteers to fulfil the need for a communal meeting place. The local newspaper advertised its opening in 1954 stating: 'The atmosphere of the typical village green is being created for the fete which will mark the official opening of the Community Hall at Wagstaff [sic] on April 17.'[516] Picture shows were held outdoors to raise money for building the hall and once

[ *Listing of Place and Street Names: R to Z*

*Carved pole opening ceremony at Wagstaffe Square, 2013.* Photo: Photo: Bouddi Photos Past and Present, Flickr, CC BY 2.0.:

*Australia Day Wagstaffe Square, 2016.* Photo: Bouddi Photos Past and Present, Flickr, CC BY 2.0.

built, were so popular that there were two sessions each week. This meant the addition of a projection box to the end of the front wall was needed. Movies remained popular until televisions appeared in people's homes. The Hall was used initially for many other activities such as a Boys Club, Teenage Club, euchre, housie, dances, concerts, weddings and fetes. More recently, Yoga, Pilates, Playgroup, Bridge, Mah-jong, Dance and Ballet became available on a regular basis and of course many other local activities are held there. Robyn Warburton has included much more about the community and the Wagstaffe Community Hall in her book *People, place and 'progress'*.[517]

The Hall has always been heavily used for groups with special interests and by the late 1990s it needed a complete overhaul. One serious problem was structural, as the projection box had put stress on the front wall, and it was in danger of collapsing. Once again, with assistance from the Federal, State and Local government grants, it was the generous community support which brought about the complete restoration of the Wagstaffe Hall. This time, the opening in 1999 was celebrated with free afternoon tea, a barbecue and band recital, followed by a commemorative community dance the following Saturday night. With a newly equipped kitchen and a wide verandah opening onto a lawn, bookings were now encouraged for large groups such as weddings etc.[518]

A 'Trash and Treasure' event is held each Easter weekend in the Community Hall and money raised

*Wagstaffe Hall, 2025.* Photo: Myfanwy J. Webb

*Wagstaffe Store, 2025.* Photo: Myfanwy J. Webb.

helps the community. Each January, Australia Day is celebrated in the Square. After the flag-raising and formal ceremony, breakfast is served and the event is widely attended by the public. The Square remains an important meeting place for residents.

Integral to the Wagstaffe Square, has always been the Wagstaffe General Store and Post Office. It has been on the corner of Mulhall Street and Wagstaffe Avenue since the days of *Manly House*. Around the front and side was a wide verandah at a height which was comfortable for people to sit on the edge and rest their feet on the ground. The Post Office was at the end of the side verandah and in the early days the mail arrived by launch at 12 noon each weekday. It was then wheeled up to the Post Office by a local pushing a barrow, where it was sorted. By this time a crowd always gathered exchanging news while waiting. Only when the Post Mistress had finished the sorting was her window hatch opened and a queue then formed to collect mail. About the same time the baker from Pretty Beach would arrive with hot bread for the shop, so people received their mail, and went into the shop for fresh bread, newspapers etc.[519] At one time it also had a liquor license which was later transferred to Killcare.[520]

The Wagstaffe General Store remains important to

*Decorated bus shelter in Wagstaffe Square, 2020. Artist: Virginia Henderson, 2025.* Photo: Myfanwy J. Webb

locals. It still operates the Post Office and now provides hot and cold takeaway food and drinks. There are tables and chairs and umbrellas outside where locals often chat over meals and coffee. At one time on the corner opposite the store near the wharf there was the 'Wonderland Greengrocer' supplying fresh vegetables and fruit to residents and visitors.

No one is sure when the first tree was planted in the centre of Wagstaffe Square, but it appears to have been a coral tree, later replaced about 1960 with a Norfolk pine which grew to an impressive height. Christmas lights were hung from its branches with the use of Gosford Council's cherry-picker. However, by 2009 it was showing signs of ill health and was removed the following year and replaced by another one. The first one grew with a distinct lean to it and was nicknamed 'Eileen Dover', and then another one followed which did grow straight. This Norfolk pine was doomed however and died. The current tree happened accidentally. Ray Bass bought native plants to enhance the encircling garden bed and a small paperbark (*Melaleuca quinquenervia*) popped up unexpectedly right in the centre of the bed. It continues to grow well and so the decision about which type of tree to plant was made for us.[521]

A recent addition to the Square has been the 'carved poles'. In 2012 after a suggestion by local, Anne Jackson, some telegraph poles which were being replaced near the square were acquired. The Wagstaffe Carving Group was formed, and Terry Baker taught the members the art of wood carving. The carvings were done on the site in the small park and when completed were erected there. There are four poles. Terry Baker said, 'The poles are not, and were never meant to be 'Totem Poles' but we hope they illustrate our spiritual contact with this great place we live in'.[522]

Also in the park is a beautiful 'Whale' table and bench setting for picnickers, where the tabletop has been carved into the shape of a whale and the bench tops represent waves. Another longer table with benches was added in 2018. These were also carved by volunteers under the direction of Terry Baker.

In 2020 as COVID-19 corona virus restrictions eased and Wagstaffe Hall reopened community members undertook rejuvenation works around the Square. The garden in the centre was improved and local artist Virginia Henderson painted colourful murals inside and outside of the bus shelter near the corner of the Hall.[523]

*Smoking Ceremony, 2013.* Photo: Bouddi Photos Past and Present, Flickr, CC BY 2.0.

## WARD BEACH, BOUDDI NATIONAL PARK

### BEGINNINGS

The *Erina Shire Holiday and Touring Guide* of 1928 mentions Ward Beach as formerly Tallow Beach.[524] In November 1927 a motion was put to the Erina Shire Council 'That the first ocean beach north of Box Head be named Ward Beach'. In December the Council adopted the motion 'to name a beach north of Box Head, in memory of the late Manasseh Ward, at one time Shire President'.[525] Manasseh was also the son of William Ward, a very early settler of Hardys Bay.

For more about the Ward Family see the entry for WARDS HILL ROAD.

### HISTORY

It remains unclear whether it was Tallow Beach or Little Tallow Beach, which was intended to be named Ward Beach, although the map in the Tourist Guide mentioned above, places the name Ward Beach where today's Tallow Beach is. In any case the name does not appear to have lasted and neither beach is now called Ward Beach.

## WARDS BAY, BRISBANE WATER

### BEGINNINGS

William Ward was the first settler in what was initially known as Wards Bay. Later it became known as Hardys Bay.

### HISTORY

Robert Hardy himself stated he lived at Ward's Bay [*sic*] at an inquiry in 1868 into the drowning deaths of three people in the bay which he witnessed from the door of his house.[526]

For further information about Hardys Bay see the entry for HARDYS BAY. For information about the Ward family see the entry for WARDS HILL ROAD.

*Manasseh Ward and family, date unknown.* Photo: Courtesy of Central Coast Council.

[ *Listing of Place and Street Names: R to Z*

[IMAGE] (LEFT)

*William Ward, first settler in the area now known as Killcare Extension, Hardy's Bay, 1799-1876.* Photo: Courtesy of Central Coast Council

# WARDS HILL ROAD, KILLCARE HEIGHTS

## BEGINNINGS

Wards Hill Road is named after early settlers William Ward (c1799-1876) and Catherine (née Mitchell) Ward (1817-1898), whose land extended from the bay up to the ridgeline.

William arrived in Sydney in 1817 as a convict having stolen a shawl valued at 4 shillings and was immediately transferred to Tasmania. By 1825 he was living at Brisbane Water where he was timber felling and running shingles to Sydney by open boat. William took up 150 acres of land on what was later to be called 'Killcare Extension' in 1836 paying 5 shillings per acre. We assume he was living on the land well before this.

William married Catherine Mitchell, also a convict, in 1837 and built a small timber house, later replaced with stone where Noble Road and Araluen Drive meet. They had a large family of at least nine children and the schooling of these children was one of the reasons why William decided to move to Kincumber in 1854. He also wanted to expand his timber and shipping business and be close to the church for his family.

Catherine managed the timber business and also opened a general store selling the produce William would bring to her from Sydney in his boats.

When William died in 1878, Catherine gave the Killcare land to their son Manasseh (1851-1923). Manasseh trained and worked horse and bullock teams which were used for transporting timber to saw pits or to Kincumber Creek ready to be sent down river. Later he became interested in local government and became

*Mrs Catherine Ward wife of mariner and timber trader William, 1817-1898.* Photo: Courtesy of Central Coast Council.

Alderman and later Mayor. He was widely respected and his funeral in 1923 attracted an enormous crowd. In Gosford flags were flown at half mast, Christ Church bells tolled and most of the shops were shut.

Manasseh Ward sold the Killcare Extension land in 1913 to NSW Realty Co.[517]

## HISTORY

The earliest road linking Killcare to Empire Bay was a rough track from the Wards' property via Rileys Bay and was in use by the end of the 19th century. It was used by school children attending Empire Bay School which had opened in 1881. Later a track was built from Empire Bay up and over the top of Wards Hill and coming down through the Wards' property via what is now part of Fletchers Glen and ending up at Government Road now Fraser Road.[528]

Wards Hill Road remained a bush track until it was upgraded and reformed to meet at the junction of The Scenic Road during the 1930s Depression. In these early days the track was known as 'Humphreys Nightmare' (presumably after Councillor Thomas Humphreys who strongly supported local road improvements).[529] The Erina Shire Council officially named the road between Empire Bay and Killcare Heights, Ward Road in 1930, and in 1970 it was gazetted to become known as Wards Hill Road.[530]

It was a daunting task to build as it rose from sea level to 380 feet in half-a-mile making a variable grading of 1 in 9.[531] Rock was blasted out of the hill and it gave employment to a lucky few. The workers were paid with vouchers which could only be used to buy food from the local shops.[532] The road which was funded by the Government and the Erina Shire was completed in 1934 and the workers were praised for the quality of their workmanship.[533]

However, the surface of the road was rough and rocky and so was rarely used. It was upgraded by the 1960s and when the Rip Bridge was opened in 1974 it became more popular. Wards Hill Road offered easy access to Killcare and Wagstaffe from the Woy Woy Peninsula without going via East Gosford and Kincumber

*Wards Hill Road under construction, 1934.* Photo: Gosford News, Central Coast Council Library Service.

and so in the late 1970s the surface was sealed.

In 2001 the road was resurfaced with a non-slip (grooved) surface and a large rock was removed to improve vision.[534]

In 2019 a 'super' tower to improve mobile reception in the area was planned to be placed at No.37 Wards Hill Road on the same site as the Council's Water Reservoir.[535] Work had not commenced on the tower by early 2025.

# WARDS WALL,
## BOUDDI NATIONAL PARK

### KILLCARE

On the waterfront at the end of Stanley Street, hidden now by mangroves and shrubs is a sign which states: 'City of Gosford/ historic site/ please do not disturb'. It refers to what locals speak of as Wards Wall. It has always been believed by William Ward's descendants to be remains of his property either a boatshed or storage shed. Historian Gwen Dundon took a photo of Ethelean Ward (whose husband was the son of Manasseh Ward) and son Allan Ward at the wall. This was before 1984 and now in 2025 it has deteriorated and is filled with mud and is sprouting mangroves.

[ *Listing of Place and Street Names: R to Z*

# 1981 > 2025

*Listing of Place and Street Names: R to Z*

[IMAGE] (TOP LEFT)

*Ward's Wall, 1981.* Photo: Gwen Dundon, Courtesy of Central Coast Council.

[IMAGE] (BOTTOM LEFT)

*Ward's Wall, 2025.* Photo: Myfanwy J. Webb.

## HISTORY

The site, however, has been listed in the NSW Heritage database as 'Rickard's Wharf'. When the Killcare Extension Estate was developed in 1920 by Arthur Rickard & Co. there was a wharf at the end of Stanley Street drawn in on the street plan. The late Beryl Strom mentions in a letter, 'My research leads me to believe that NSW Re alty Co erected a structure with stone footings… between June 1916 and May 1918, in association with a jetty which they planned would service both their subdivisions'. Unfortunately, Beryl Strom's research has not been located to confirm this. Apparently, this jetty was abandoned in favour of two others in deeper water and still in use, at the foot of Killcare Road (Killcare) and on Hardys Bay Drive 'Killcare Extension.'[546]

The Heritage Officer at Central Coast Council recommends a professional archaeologist look at the site to determine its true origin. Unfortunately, the Council cannot afford to do this as of 2021. If the wall is considered historically significant then it needs a plan to ensure its preservation. The next step may be to apply for a Heritage Grant from the Central Coast Council.

For information about the Ward Family see the entry for WARDS HILL ROAD.

*Wards Wall, Killcare Waterfront Historic Site.* Photo: Bouddi Photos Past and Present, Flickr, CC BY 2.0.

*Allen and Ethelene Ward at Ward's Wall, 1981.* Photo: Gwen Dundon, Courtesy of Central Coast Council

# WHITINGS CORNER, WAGSTAFFE, PRETTY BEACH

## BEGINNINGS

Whitings Corner is an informal name for the junction of Pretty Beach Road and Wagstaffe Avenue and is named after the Whiting family.

## HISTORY

There was a small shop near the corner at No.48 Pretty Beach Road bought by Mr and Mrs Whiting. Their son Donald would accompany his father to the Haymarket in Sydney for stock. The *SS Erina* would bring the goods to Pretty Beach wharf and Don would deliver orders on his bicycle. Don and his wife Peg, who lived opposite, later took over the store and it was sold in 1957 to Mr and Mrs George F. Stewart who operated a general business until the

[ *Listing of Place and Street Names: R to Z*

*Whitings Corner, Wagstaffe Ave & Pretty Beach Rd, date unknown. Photo: Photo: Bouddi Photos Past and Present, Flickr, CC BY 2.0.*

late 1970s.

As traffic increased the corner became a dangerous one for pedestrians, with a narrow road and no footpath. Correspondence with the Council began in 1998 by locals Michael and Joyce Rasic and was taken up by the Community Association. Initially the road was widened but 'that only gave us less room to walk on'.

By 2005 the corner problem was still on the Community Association's agenda. 'Finally in 2008 the footpath along the property, approaching the corner, was cleared and a gravel footpath was constructed around Whitings Corner. Pedestrians could then easily and safely walk around the corner'.

# THE YUM YUM TREE, HARDYS BAY

## BEGINNINGS

At the end of the day a group of locals meet at the Yum Yum Tree. There are actually two trees, but locals refer to them in the singular. It is at the bottom of Killcare Road on the waterfront and is a shady spot under coral trees. With the 'bottle shop' just across the road locals can relax with a drink and the tradesmen in particular do some networking at the end of the working day.

Kel Gulliver puts forward these views on the origin of the name 'The Yum Yum Tree': 'In the mid-1970s the 'Firies' were enjoying a break and to satisfy their hunger, plates of sandwiches were obtained and devoured

*Killcare baths and Yum Yum Tree. Photo: Bouddi Photos Past and Present, Flickr, CC BY 2.0.*

*Listing of Place and Street Names: R to Z*

*Yum Yum, 2010s.* Photo: Barbara Morgan, Bouddi Photos Past and Present, Flickr, CC BY 2.0.

with relish. Neville Hazzard, a local Real Estate Agent and 'muso', was present and expressed his appreciation for the 'Yum Yum under the tree'. This probably struck a chord as 'Under the Yum Yum Tree' was the name of a Broadway play which opened in 1960 followed by a popular film in 1963. This is believed to be the most reasonable explanation for the naming of our 'Yum Yum Tree".[539]

## HISTORY

There are two plaques on the tree to remember locals who met their mates regularly under the Yum Yum Tree.

*Brian Burrows*
*Remembered by all your mates*
*The Yum Yum Tree*

\*\*\*

*Jack Morris*
*1913-2000*
*A true blue Balmain boy*
*Dedicated upholder and the keeper of the Yum Yum tradition*
*daily at 4pm*
*Friend of all – enemy of none*
*Remembered by his many friends under the "Yummy"*

*Wharf near Yum Yum, 2025.* Photo: Myfanwy J. Webb.

*Yum Yum Tree, 2009.*
*Photo: Barbara Morgan.*

APPENDIX

# APPENDIX

## 1-4

# APPENDIX 1: MAPS OF ESTATE SUBDIVISION

### 1.1 Kilcare [sic] Beach Estate

*"The Sun-Herald"* 8 January 1967

### 1.2 Killcare Estate, 1916

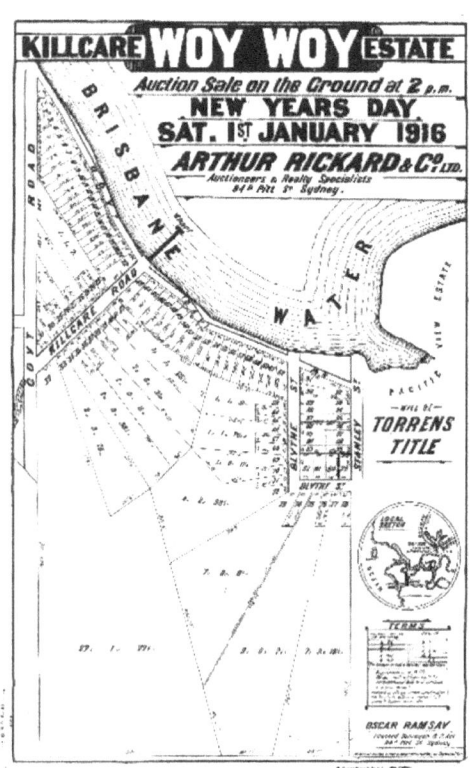

### 1.3 Killcare Extension Estate, 1920

# Maps of Estate Subivision

**1.4 Killcare Heights Estate, 1928.** Date for the auction was Easter Saturday 7th April 1928 but was postponed due to rain. It went to Auction on Saturday 21st April 1928.

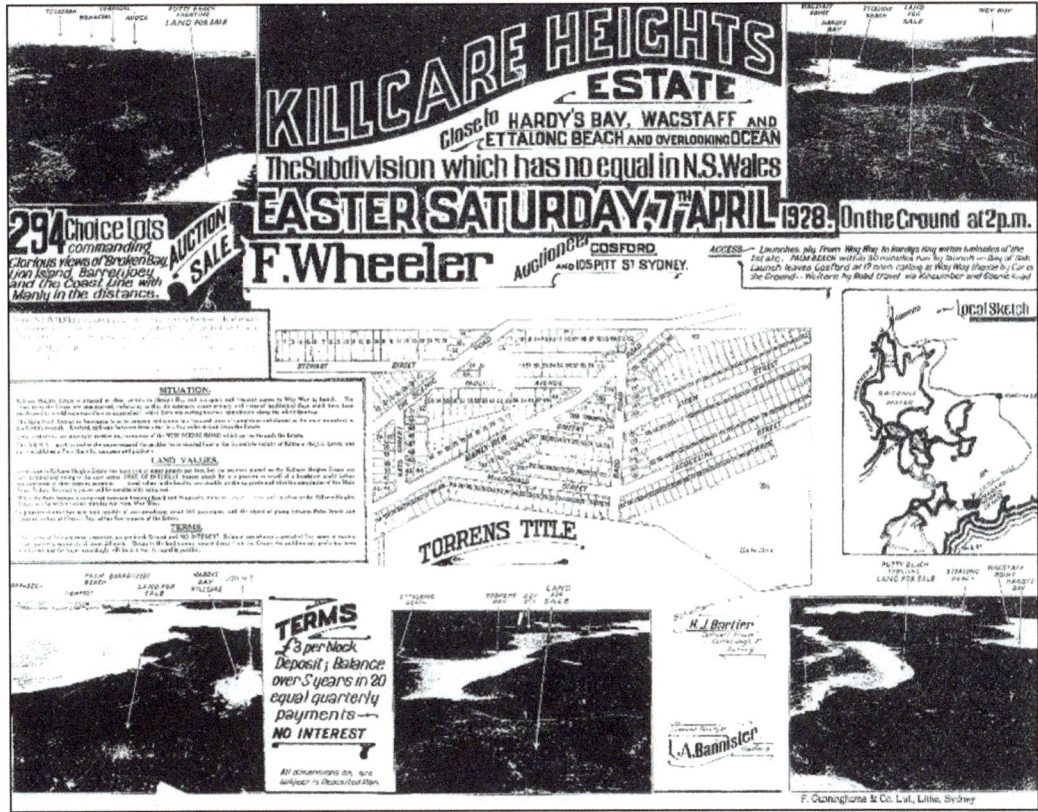

**1.5 Martins Killcare Beach Estate, 1930**

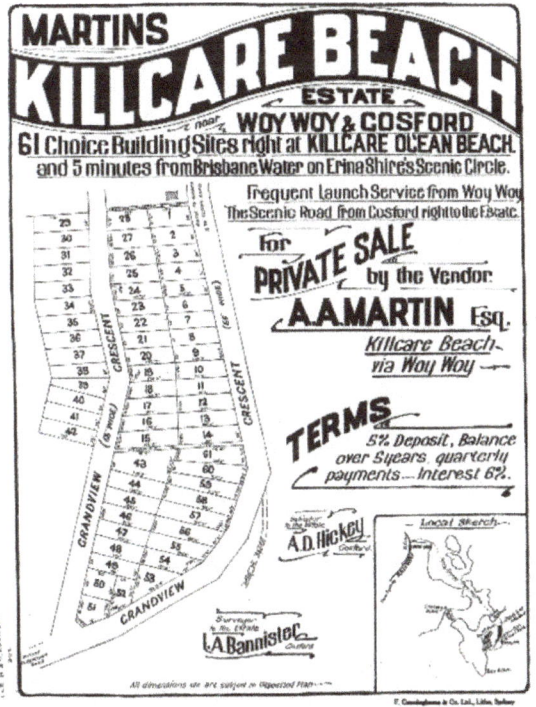

**1.6 Pretty Beach Estate, 1910**

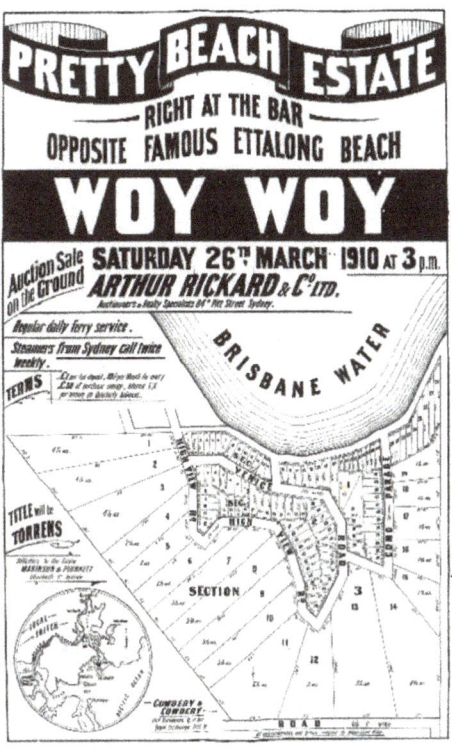

[ *Appendix*

1.7 Pretty Beach Extension Estate, 1912

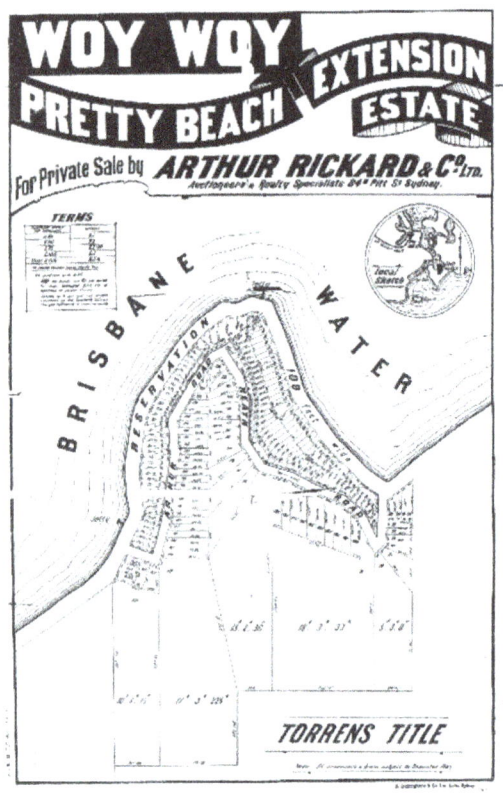

1.9 Wagstaffe's Subdivision, Mount Pleasant, 1904

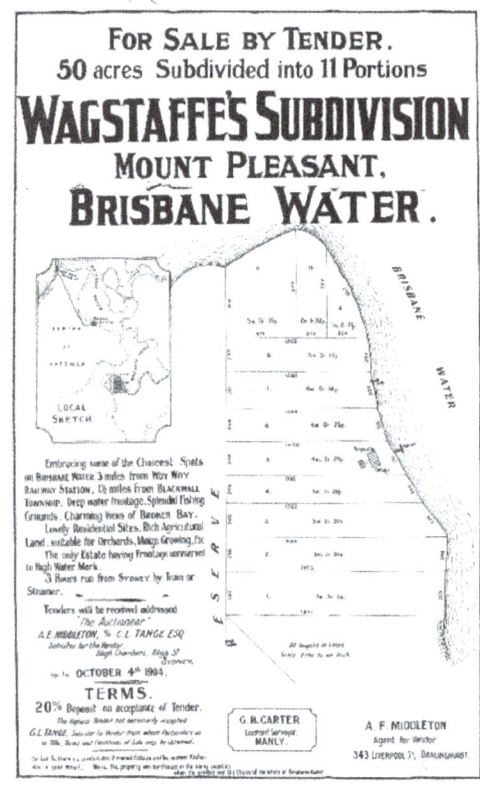

1.8 Wagstaffe's Point Estate, January 1906

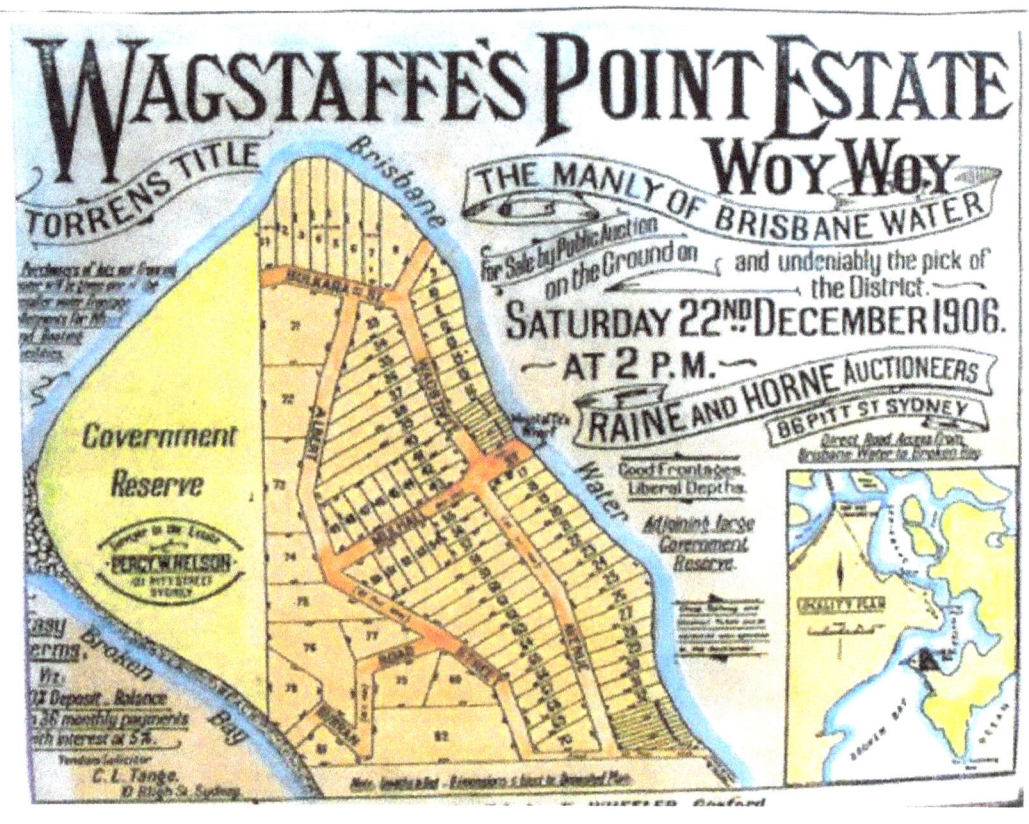

*Maps of Estate Subvivision*

1.10 The Rip Estate, Jan 1908.

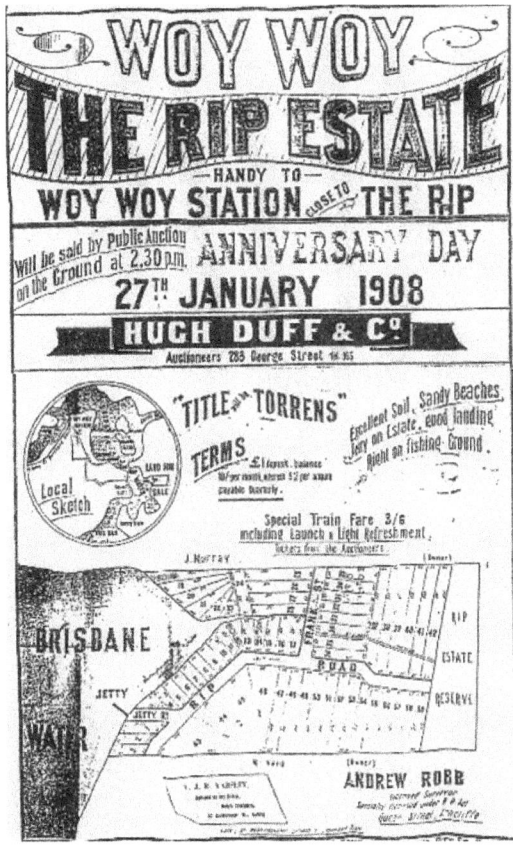

1.12 Daleys Point Estate

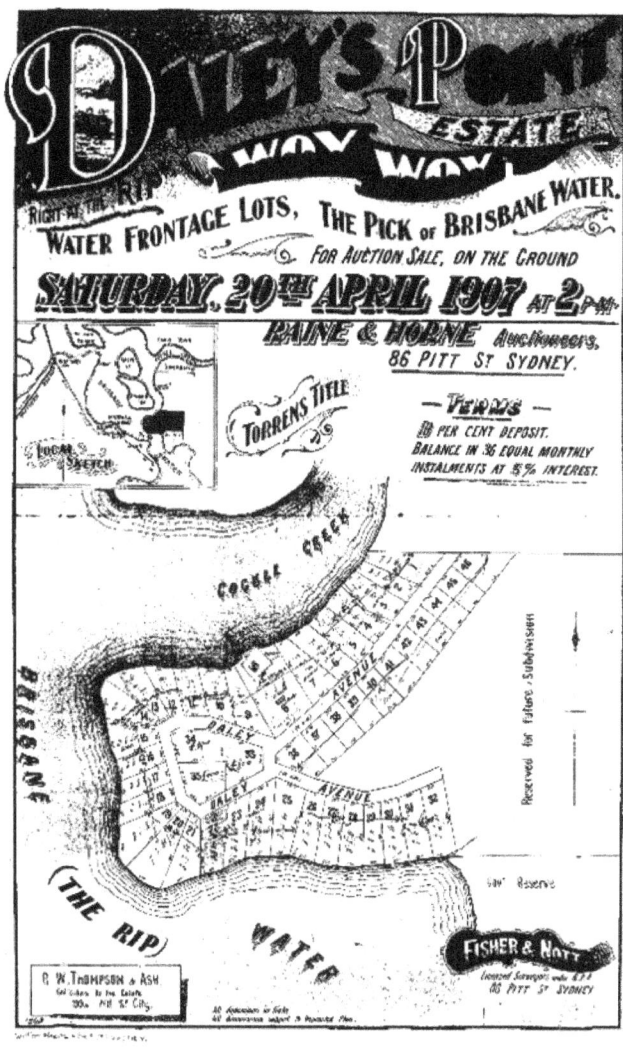

1.11 Holiday Land at Kilcare, March 1964

SIGNPOSTS TO THE PAST 195

# APPENDIX 2: ROAD TYPES OF BOUDDI PENINSULA

AVENUE: Broad roadway, usually planted on each side with trees

CRESCENT: Crescent-shaped thoroughfare, especially where both ends join the same thoroughfare.

DRIVE: Wide thoroughfare allowing a steady flow of traffic without many cross-streets.

LANE: Narrow way between walls, buildings or a narrow country or city roadway.

PARADE: Public promenade or roadway that has good pedestrian facilities along the side.

PLACE: Short, sometimes narrow, enclosed roadway.

ROAD: Open way or public passage primarily for vehicles.

STREET: Public roadway in a town, city or urban area, especially a paved thoroughfare with footpaths and buildings along one or both sides.

TRACK: Roadway with a single carriageway. A roadway through a natural bushland region. The interpretation for both Track and Trail is limited to roadways, whereas in many areas (e.g. Tasmania) these are often associated with walking rather than vehicular movement. [NPWS usually uses Trail when it has vehicular access and Track is confined to walking tracks]

For the full list of Road Types see the website of Geographical Names Board of NSW>NSW Address Policy and User Manual >6.10 Road Types, pp.106-108.

# APPENDIX 3: PLACE NAME TYPES OF BOUDDI PENINSULA

BAY: A well-marked indentation made by the sea or a lake into a coastline, whose penetration is in such proportion to the width of its mouth as to contain land locked waters and constitutes more than a mere curvature of the coast.

BEACH: The sloping shore along a body of water that is periodically washed by waves or tides and is usually covered with sand or gravel.

CAPE: A piece of land jutting into the sea; a projecting headland or promontory.

*Place Name Types of Bouddi Peninsula*

CREEK: A natural watercourse that is usually a tributary of a river or another creek. It may be perennial or non-perennial and in some areas its course may become indefinite or even peter out.

HEAD: A comparatively high promontory of land projecting into the sea with a steep face. An un-named head is usually described as a 'Headland' when a specific name is assigned, it becomes a 'Head'.

LOOKOUT: A natural scenic viewpoint on elevated ground. Works or structures within the immediate vicinity of the viewpoint improving the safety, amenities or view may be evident.

MOOR: A tract of unenclosed ground, usually covered with heather, coarse grass, bracken, and moss.

MOUNT: A natural elevation of the earth's surface rising more or less abruptly from the surrounding level, and attaining an altitude which, relative to adjacent elevations, is impressive or notable. In general, the elevation of a mountain is more than 300 metres from foot to summit, but this distinction is arbitrary. For reasons of euphony and local usage 'Mount' is usually used when the generic term precedes the specific term and 'Mountain' when it succeeds it.

PENINSULA: A piece of land almost surrounded by water, especially one connected with the mainland by only a narrow neck of land or isthmus.

PICNIC AREA: A location to which people bring food to be eaten in the open air.

POINT: A location, spot, or position. Point of land. A small promontory.

REEF: A ridge of rocks or coral lying near the surface of the sea which may be visible at low tide but is usually covered water.

RESERVE: An area proclaimed to be a public reserve by government legislation.

RIVER: A major natural stream in a large catchment basin, carrying water to another river, a lake or the sea. Usually perennial, but not necessarily so in arid areas.

ROCK: A prominent or isolated out crop of rock, even a single large stone. The designation includes 'boulder', 'crag', 'needle', 'pillar' and 'tor'.

SUBURB: A bounded area within the landscape that has an 'Urban' Character.

For the full list of designation values (place name types) see the website of Geographical Names Board of NSW >Place Name Policy>Appendix A. Glossary of designation values in the Geographical Names Register, p.14

# APPENDIX 4: MAPS OF BOUDDI PENINSULA

4.1 Box Head

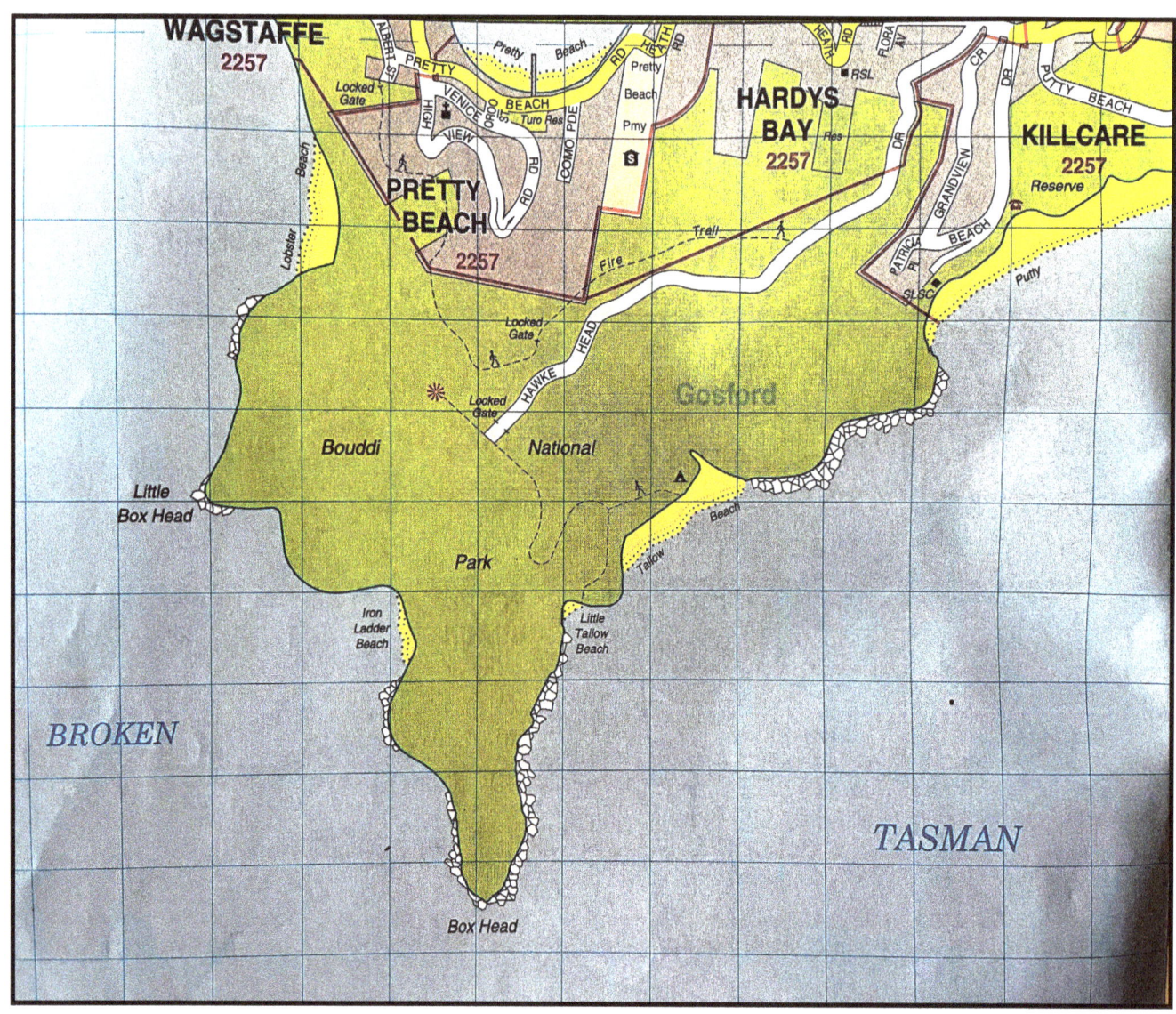

*Box Head, 1998.* Photo: Map Universal Press.

*Maps of Bouddi Peninsula*

## 4.2 Killcare Heights

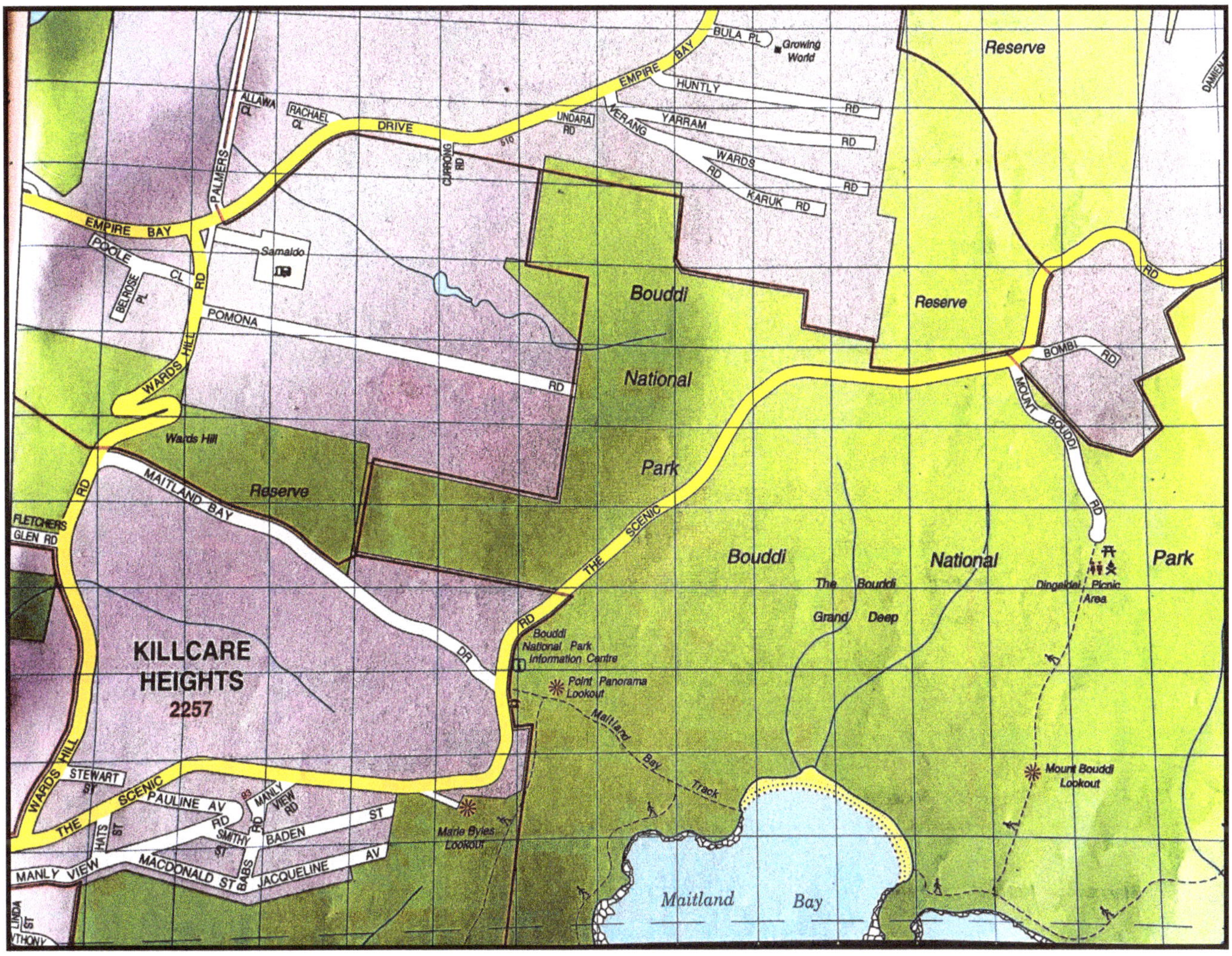

*Killcare Heights, 1998.* Photo: Map Universal Press.

## 4.3 Marine National Park

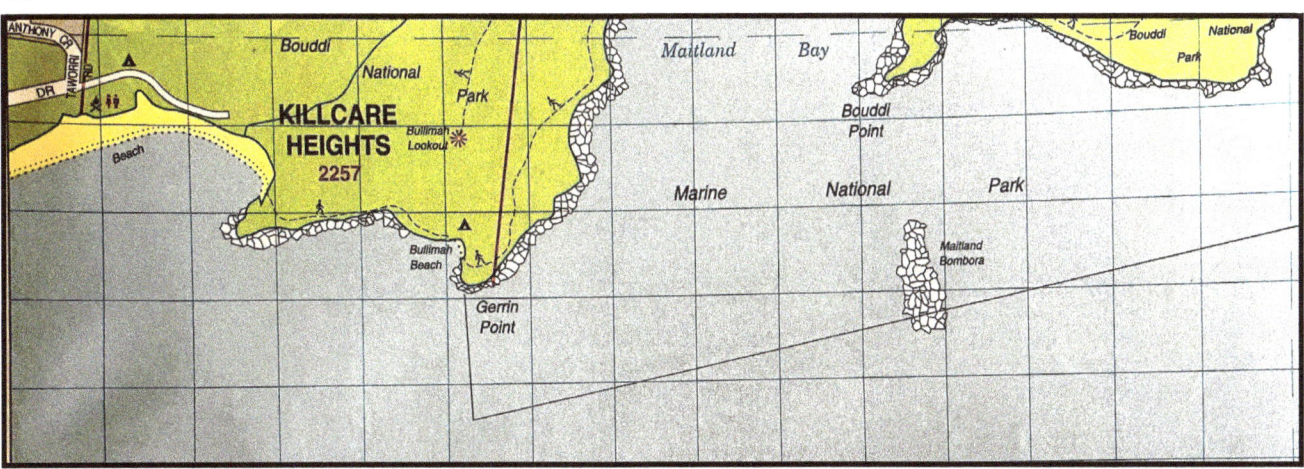

*Marine National Park, 1998.* Photo: Map Universal Press.

[ *Appendix*

### 4.5 Brisbane Water

*Brisbane Water Map, 1998.* Photo: Map Universal Press.

## 4.6 Copacabana and Macmasters Beach

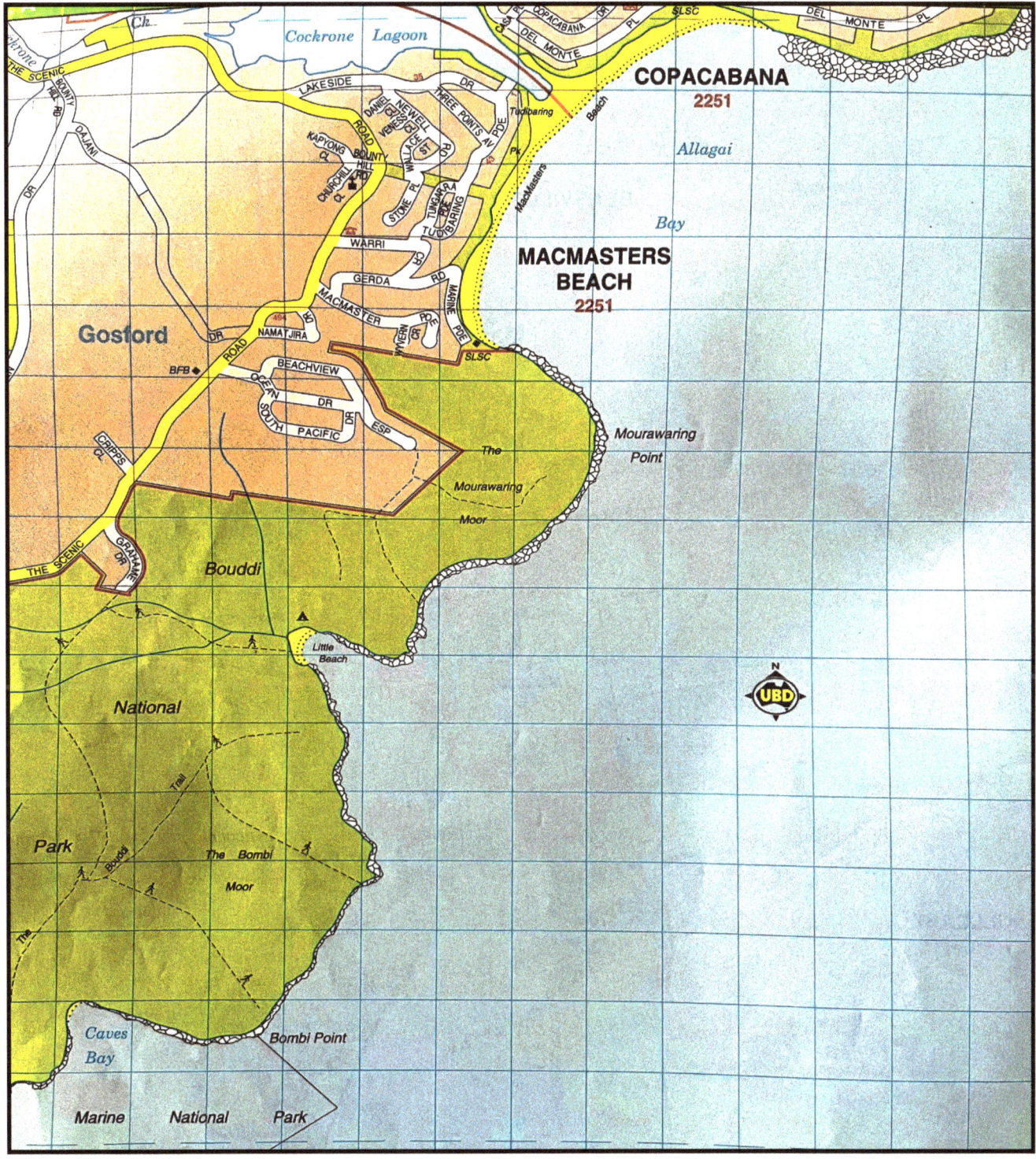

*Copacabana and MacMasters Beach, 1998.* Photo: Map Universal Press.

[ *Appendix*

## Maps of Bouddi Peninsula

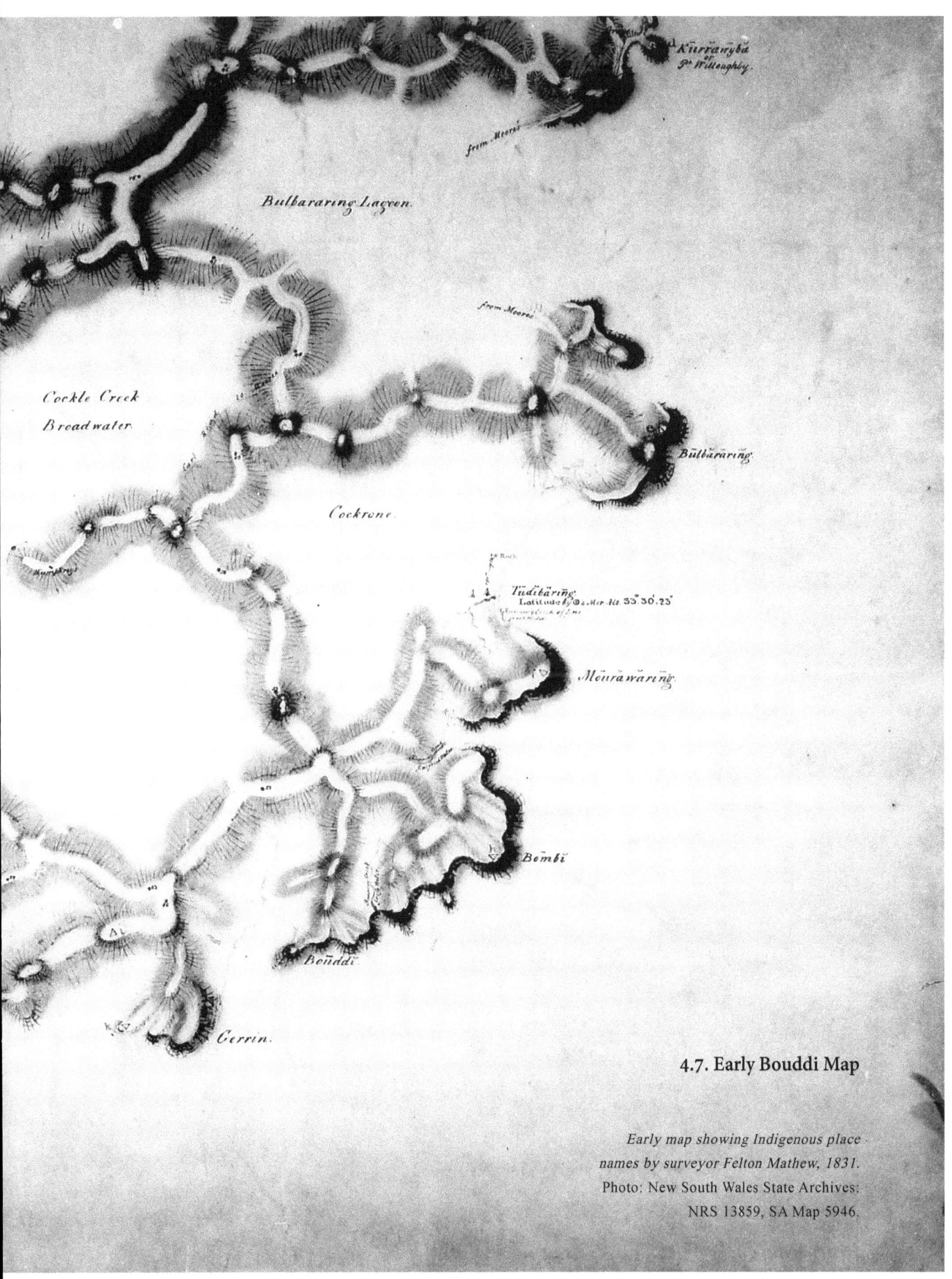

### 4.7. Early Bouddi Map

*Early map showing Indigenous place names by surveyor Felton Mathew, 1831. Photo: New South Wales State Archives: NRS 13859, SA Map 5946.*

# References

## CHAPTER 2 - THE BOUDDI PENINSULA: A BRIEF HISTORY

1. Attenbrow, Val (2010). Sydney's Aboriginal past: investigating the archaeological and historical records. 2nd ed. Sydney, NSW: UNSW Press, p.37-39, p.153.

2. New South Wales, Office of Environment and Heritage (2020). NPWS. Bouddi National Park, Plan of Management, p.2. Darkinjung Local Aboriginal Land Council. Culture & Heritage. Accessed online June 2021. Aboriginal Heritage Office (2015). Filling a void: a Review of the historical context for the word 'Guringai'. North Sydney, NSW: AHO. (Accessed online June 2021)

3. Bradley, William (1788). A Voyage to New South Wales, p.89.

4. Australian Institute of Aboriginal and Torres Strait Islander Studies (2019). Indigenous Australian Languages: Celebrating 2019 International Year of Indigenous Languages. Retrieved from AIATSIS website in October 2019.

5. The Bouddi Peninsula (2010). [CD-ROM]. Ch.6, Aboriginal Heritage, p.1.

6. Tunbridge, Dorothy (1987). *Aboriginal place names. Australian Aboriginal Studies,* No.2, pp.3, p.11.

7. Dundon, Gwen (2010). A history of ferries on the Central Coast of NSW: Gosford and Wyong areas, p.87.

8. Warburton, Robyn (2013). People, place and 'progress', p.23.

9. Warburton, Robyn (2013). People, place and 'progress', p.34, 67.

10. Elder, Bruce (1993). Day trips around Sydney: a daytripper's guide to 200km around Sydney. Port Melbourne, Vic: Lothian, p.110.

## CHAPTER 3 - NEED FOR STANDARDISATION OF PLACE & STREET NAMES

11. The Geographical Names Board of New South Wales. Road naming. Online at www.gnb.nsw.gov.au/road-naming

12. The Geographical Names Board of NSW. NSW Address Policy and User Manual. 2019, 6.10 Road Types, pp.106-108. Retrieved online.

## CHAPTER 4 - LISTING OF PLACE & STREET NAMES A-B

13. The Bouddi Peninsula [electronic resource]: Voices and images from a colourful past (2010). Disc 2. Bouddi stories, Bouddi bios, Bouddi artists: a CD-ROM of local history. Wagstaffe, NSW: The Bouddi Society, Ch.108, George Wagstaffe, p.3.

14. Who's Who in Australia (1947). Accessed on line via Ancestry.com. Communication between David Shaw and Beverley Runcie, July 2021.

15. NSW Dept. of Lands: LPI. Certificate of Title, vol.1757, Fol. 4. Primary Application 14376. Deposited Plan 4961.

16. *Sydney Morning Herald*, 2 April 1918, p.11.

17. Erina Shire Council (1941). Minutes of the Ordinary Meeting, 7 April 1941.

18. Warburton, Robyn (2013). People, place and 'progress': A history of the Association at Wagstaffe and Pretty Beach. Wagstaffe, NSW: Wagstaffe to Killcare Community Association, p.9-10.

19. Warburton, Robyn (2013). People, place and 'progress', p.33, 41, 55.

20. Reed, A.W. (1967). Aboriginal place names. Frenchs Forest, NSW: Reed New Holland, p.9.

21. Endacott, Sydney J. (1955). Australian Aboriginal words and place names and their meanings, p.7.

22. Cooper, H.M. (1949). Australian Aboriginal words and their meanings. [Adelaide]: South Australian Museum, p.5. James Baylis (1914). Aboriginal names and their meanings. Mitchell Library 1256. Accessed online from State Library of New South Wales.

23. *Government Gazette of the State of New South Wales*, No.77, 19 June 1970, p.2485.

24. Australia-Israel Chamber of Commerce. Retrieved from www.aicc.org.au/about.cfm. 23 Aug 2018.

25. *The Canberra Times,* 14 June 1980, p.11.

26. Endacott, Sydney J. (1955). Australian Aboriginal words and place names and their meanings, p.7. Reed, A.W. (1967). Aboriginal place names, p.9.

27. Swancott, C. (1955). The Brisbane Water Story: the rest of the story, Part 4. Booker Bay, NSW: C. Swancott, p.30.

28. *Government Gazette of NSW*, No.4, 10 January 1964, p.72.

29. *Government Gazette of NSW*, No.77, 19 June 1970, p.2485.

30. *Government Gazette of NSW*, No.10, 20 January 1978, p.241.

31. The Bouddi Peninsula (2010). [CD-ROM]. Ch.52, Bruce Dunlop, p.5.

32. Warburton, Robyn (2013). People, place and 'progress', p.24.

*References*

33. *Gosford Times and Wyong District Advocate*, 30 July 1954, p.3.

34. Warburton, Robyn (2013). People, place and 'progress', pp.71-73, 109-110.

35. Warburton, Robyn (2013). People, place and 'progress', p.45.

36. Warburton, Robyn (2013). People, place and 'progress', p.228. *Talking Turkey: monthly newsletter of The Wagstaffe to Killcare Community Association*, no.171, June 2017, pp.1-2.

37. *Peninsula News*, 23 December 2019, p.12.

38. *Gosford Times and Wyong District Advocate*, 16 June 1921, p.13.

39. The Bouddi Peninsula (2010). [CD-ROM]. Ch.15, Commerce and industry, pp.31-34.

40. *Gosford Times & Wyong District Advocate*, 5 April 1923, p.8, 21 October 1926, p.1. *Central Coast Express*, 13 March 1957, p.1. The Bouddi Peninsula (2010). [CD-ROM]. Ch.15, Commerce & Industry, p.34, Ch.38, The Churches, pp.9-13, Ch.35, Hardys Bay Returned & Services League of Australia, pp.12-13.

Robyn Warburton (2021). More than Bricks and Mortar: Bouddi houses and people. [Wagstaffe], NSW, Robyn Warburton, p.119.

41. The Bouddi Peninsula (2010). [CD-ROM]. Ch.35, Hardys Bay Returned & Services League of Australia, p.5.

42. New South Wales State Archives: Memorials to the Governor, 1810-25, NRS899, [4/1838App 573] No 611, Fiche 3098.

43. The Bouddi Peninsula (2010). [CD-ROM]. Ch.15. Commerce and industry, pp.31-34.

44. Erina Shire Development League (1928). Erina Shire holiday and touring guide: Woy Woy, Gosford, Wyong. Gosford: The League, p.116.

45. The Bouddi Peninsula (2010). [CD-ROM]. Ch.15, Commerce and industry, pp.41-43.

46. The Bouddi Peninsula (2010). [CD-ROM]. Ch.9, Early European settlers and their land, pp.18-19.

47. Spearritt, Peter (1988). Rickard, Sir Arthur (1868-1948). Australian Dictionary of Biography, National Centre of Biography. Australian National University. Retrieved from http://adb.anu.edu.au/biography/rickard-sir-arthur-8206/text14357, Aug 2018.

48. Laurie Hindmarsh (2002). Rickard, Arthur Lancelot (1895-1949). Australian Dictionary of Biography. Retrieved from http://adb.anu.edu.au/biography/rickard-arthur-lancelot-11520/text20549, August 2018.

49. *Gosford Times and Wyong District Advocate*, 2 April 1954, p.4.

50. *Government Gazette of NSW*, No.77, 19 June 1970, p.2485.

51. United States Marriages Transcription. Retrieved from Findmypast online.

52. *The Australasian* (Melb, Vic), 25 July 1942, p.24.

53. *The Australian Women's Weekly*, 8 May 1943, p.20.

54. United States, Genealogy Bank Obituaries, 1980-2014. United States Social Security Death Index database. FamilySearch online.

55. National Archives of Australia: A705, 166/43/765 and NAA: A9300, White, B.K. Retrieved from National Archives of Australia website http://recordsearch.naa.gov/SearchNRetriev/ in October 2016. Retrieved from

56. Commonwealth War Graves Commission. Retrieved online at http://www.cwgc.org/find/find-war-dead, July 2022.

57. North Sydney Council. North Sydney History walk: gem of the harbour: a walking tour of Kurraba Point. North Sydney Council, pp.8-9. Retrieved from Council website in September 2016.

58. Bouddi National Park Advisory Committee (1983/84). Minutes of meetings, 18 Sept 1983, 6 May 1984. Beryl Strom Collection, Central Coast Library Gosford.

59. Geographical Names Board of New South Wales. Register extract. Geographical Names Board of NSW http://gnb.nsw.gov.au/place_naming/placename_search. Retrieved online 2017.

60. *Gosford Times and Wyong District Advocate*, 1 October 1954, p.10.

61. *Government Gazette of NSW*, No.4, 10 January 1964, p.72.

62. *Gosford Times and Wyong District Advocate*, 9 January 1919, p.7.

63. The Bouddi Peninsula (2010). [CD-ROM]. Ch.15, Commerce and industry, p.61.

64. *Gosford Times and Wyong District Advocate*, 14 July 1927, p.20.

65. *Gosford Times and Wyong District Advocate*, 9 March 1934, p.6, 11 October 1934, p.16. Government Gazette of NSW, No.43, 2 April 1937, p.1459.

66. *Government Gazette of NSW*, No.121, 30 November 1962, p.3613.

67. The Bouddi Peninsula (2010). [CD-ROM]. Ch.40, The Surf Club.

68. Warburton, Robyn (2013). People, place and 'progress', p.45.

69. The Dream begins: residents of Brisbane Water in 1841. Vol.2. East Gosford, NSW: Central Coast Family History Research Society, 2008, p.315.

70. Swancott, C. (1961). The Brisbane Water Story, Part 3. Enchanted Waters. Woy Woy, NSW: Brisbane Water Historical Society, p.142. Historic sites [Local Studies]: John Menton's grave, Hardys Bay. Beryl Strom Collection. Central Coast Library, Gosford.

71. Warburton, Robyn (2021), More than Bricks and Mortar, p.164, 168.

72. Troy, Jakelin (1994). The Sydney Language. Canberra, ACT: J.Troy, p.69. Retrieved from www.williamdawes.org/docs/troy_sydney_language_publication.pdf. Book A p.7.

73. Historical Records of New South Wales (1893). Vol.2, Grose and Paterson, 1792-1795, ed. by F.M. Bladen. The

# References

Southwell Papers, 12 July 1788. Sydney: Government Printer, pp.699, 700. Facsimile reprint by Lansdown Slattery & Co., Mona Vale, NSW, 1978.

74. Smith, Keith Vincent (2008). Colebee. Dictionary of Sydney. Retrieved online 2019.

75. Newcastle City Council. History and Heritage, Heritage attractions, Bogey Hole. Retrieved online 2018.

76. *Gosford Times and Wyong District Advocate,* 22 March 1928, p.6.

77. *Gosford Times and Wyong District Advocate*, 6 January 1938, p.9.

78. Warburton, Robyn (Comp. & Ed.) (2014). Bouddi bites in words and images. Wagstaffe, NSW: Bouddi Society & Wagstaffe to Killcare Community Association, p.54.

79. Warburton, Robyn (2013). People, place and 'progress', p.83.

80. National Parks and Wildlife Service (1985). Plan of management. Sydney: NP&WS, pp.43-44. *Killcare Wagstaffe Trust Newsletter,* April 2015, p.2-3.

81. The Bouddi Peninsula (2010). [CD-ROM]. Ch.25, Bouddi National Park, p.2. New South Wales. NPWS (1985). Plan of management. Sydney: NP&WS, p.23.

82. Strom, Beryl (Ed.) (1986). Bouddi Peninsula study: 'coastwatch'. Killcare Heights, [N.S.W]: Association for Environmental Education (N.S.W.), Central Coast Region.

83. New South Wales State Archives: NRS 13859, SA Map 5946.

84. Bennett, F.C. (Ed.) (1968). The Story of the Aboriginal people of the Central Coast of New South Wales. [Wyong, NSW]: Brisbane Water Historical Society and The Entrance & District Historical Society, p.17.

85. McCarthy, F.D. (1952). New South Wales Aboriginal place names and euphonious words, with their meanings. Sydney: A.H. Pettifer, Govt. Printer, p.6.

86. Steele, Jeremy in personal correspondence with Beverley Runcie, 5 November, 2019.

87. Parkin, Ray (2003). H.M. Bark Endeavour: her place in history. 2nd ed. Carlton, Vic.: Miegunyah, p.206.

88. Geographical Names Board of NSW. Register Extract. Retrieved online.

89. Strom, Beryl (1985). MacMasters Beach: a history. [Gosford, NSW]: Gosford District Historical Research & Heritage Association, p.36.

90. The Bouddi Peninsula (2010). [CD-ROM]. Ch.20, The war years: Bombi radar station.

91. Geographical Names Board of NSW, Register extract. Retrieved online 2020.

92. Dixon, R.M.W. et al. (2006). Australian Aboriginal words in English: their origin and meaning. 2nd ed. Sth Melbourne, Vic.: Oxford University Press, p.190. Troy, Jakelin and Michael Walsh (2009). Reinstating Aboriginal placenames around Port Jackson and Botany Bay. In Aboriginal placenames: naming and re-naming the Australian landscape, ed. by Harold Koch and Luise Hercus. ANU EPress, pp.56-57. Retrieved online.

93. Bennett, F.C. (1968). The Story of the Aboriginal people of the Central Coast of NSW, p.17.

94. Geographical Names Board of NSW, Register extract. Retrieved online.

95. Stokes, J Lort (1852) Australia, East Coast. Sheet IV, Broken Bay to Sugarloaf Point [cartographic material] from a running survey. National Library Australia Bib ID 3791297. Royal Australian Navy (1955) [Map]. Broken Bay surveyed and published by the Hydrographic Service. 6th ed. with corrections, 1960.

96. Berry, Greig (1994). Shipwrecks of the New South Wales Central Coast: 1800-1899. Vol.1. Tacoma, NSW, Central Coast Shipwreck Research, p.87, p.95.

97. Potter, Geoffrey (2012). Wreck of the Maitland ... a scene to make the angels weep. Gosford, NSW, Gosford City Council, pp. 17, 22.

98. *Central Coast Express,* 22 August 1973, p.1.

99. *Sydney Gazette and NSW Advertiser*, 2 April 1809, p.1. Greig Berry (1994). Shipwrecks of the NSW Central Coast, p.14-15.

100. Warburton, Robyn (2021) More than bricks and mortar: Bouddi houses and people. [Wagstaffe, NSW]: Bouddi Society, p.213.

101. *Central Coast Express*, 9 March 1990, p.1.

102. New South Wales State Archives: NRS 13859, SA Map 5946.

103. Correspondence from Kevin Duncan to Beverley Runcie by email 16 September 2020.

104. Hunter, John (1793). An historical journal of the transactions at Port Jackson and Norfolk Island ... London. Australian Facsimile Editions no.148. Adelaide: Libraries Board of South Australia, 1968, p.407.

105. Steele, Jeremy Macdonald (2005). The Aboriginal language of Sydney. Thesis. Sydney, Macquarie University, p.271. Retrieved online.

106. Correspondence between Barry Corr and Beverley Runcie, 30 October 2019.

107. Stack, E (1906) Native names and meanings. Includes names and meanings 'taken from notes of surveyor Larmer in 1833'. Digitised copy from State Library of NSW, DLMS23

108. Illawarra Mercury, 24 March 1896, p.2. Royal Anthropological Society of Australasia records 1885-1914. State Library New South Wales, Mitchell Library SS 7603/Box 4 Folder 1: NSW place names, 1899-1903.

109. Bishop, W. (Comp.) (1928) Australian Aboriginal dictionary. Sydney, NSW, 1928. State Library New South Wales, Mitchell Library, MMS ID 991006049939702626

110. Jeremy Steele in personal communication with Beverley Runcie, 27 October 2019.

111. Bennett, F C. Place names of the Gosford area. Central Coast Library Gosford, Vertical File.

112. Geographical Names Board of NSW. Register extract. Retrieved online.

113. The Bouddi Peninsula (2010) [CD-ROM]. Ch.45, Bouddi Farm: Conversations at the table by Lee Casey. Klepac, Adriana (Ed.) (2017). Russell Drysdale: Bouddi. 9

Dec 2017-4 Feb 2018 at Gosford Regional Gallery. NSW: Gosford Regional Gallery.

114. Strom, Beryl (Ed.) (1986). Bouddi Peninsula Study: 'coastwatch'.

115. Bouddi Peninsula (2010) [CD-ROM]. Ch.17. Maitland Bay Centre, p.2.

116. Geographical Names Board of NSW. Register extract. Retrieved online.

117. Bouddi National Park (1985). Plan of management. Sydney, National Park and Wildlife Service, p.82.

118. Geographical Names Board of NSW. Register extract. Retrieved online.

119. Pratt, Eileen (1978). Place names of the Central Coast: origins and meanings. [Gosford, NSW]: Brisbane Water Historical Society, p.7. The Bouddi Peninsula (2010). [CD-ROM]. Ch25, Bouddi National Park.

120. $1.4 M makeover for Bouddi Coastal Walk. Adam Crouch [Newsletter], No.15, June 2020, p.1. Vicki Elliott ( NWPS) correspondence with Beverley Runcie. 31 August 2021.

121. The Bouddi Peninsula (2010) [CD-ROM], Ch28, Maitland Bay, p.1-2. Gladstone, W. (2001). Effects of a marine protected area on some Central Coast rocky reef fishes, in Making waves: exposing gaps and exploring solutions. Proceedings of the 11th NSW Coastal Conference, Newcastle, 13-16 November 2001.

122. Geographical Names Board of NSW. Register extract. Retrieved online.

123. Geographical Names Board of NSW. Register extract. Retrieved online.

124. Bradley, William. A Voyage to New South Wales: the Journal of Lieutenant William Bradley RN of HMS Sirius 1786-1792. Facsimile from the original manuscript. Sydney, Trustees of the Public Library of New South Wales in association with Ure Smith, 1969. Chart no.8. Broken Bay.

125. *Sydney Gazette & New South Wales Advertiser*, 26 March 1809, p.2, 2 April 1809, p.1.

126. New South Wales State Archives: NRS 13859, SA Map 5946.

127. *Government Gazette of NSW*, No.289, 16 August 1837, p.574.

128. Wells, William Henry, (Comp.) (1840). A Map of the County of Cumberland in the Colony of New South Wales. Sydney, engraved & printed by William Baker. (National Library Australia).

129. *The Gosford Times and Wyong District Advocate*, 9 March 1939, p.3.

130. Geographical Names Board of NSW. Register Extract. Retrieved online.

131. New South Wales State Archives: NRS899, James Webb, Fiche 3116; [4/1840A], No.1036, pp. 175-8.

132. NSW Land & Property Information: Grant Register, Ser.54, Fol.130.

133. The Bouddi Peninsula (2010). [CD-ROM]. Ch.9, Early European settlers and their land.

134. *Government Gazette of NSW*, No.119, 6 September 1911, p.4840.

135. Parkin, Ray (2003). H.M. Bark Endeavour: her place in history, p.205.

136. Flinders, Matthew (1814). A Voyage to Terra Australis ... Vol.2. London: G and W Nicol, p.8. Facsimile Edition 1966. (Retrieved online Gutenberg 2016).

137. Lipscombe, Trevor. Broken Bay- two bays or one? In Placenames Australia: News letter of the Australian National Placenames Survey, March 2019, pp.1-6.

138. Bradley, William (1788). A Voyage to New South Wales: the Journal of Lieutenant William Bradley, p.87, p.172, Chart no.8.

139. *Sydney Gazette and NSW Advertiser*, 8 May 1803, p.2, 29 May 1803, p.3. Greg Berry (1994). Shipwrecks of the NSW Central Coast:1800-1899. Vol.1.

140. *The Sydney Morning Herald*, 3 January 1865, p.5.

141. Bennett, F.C. (Ed.) (1968). The Story of the Aboriginal people of the Central Coast of New South Wales, p.17.

142. Parkin, Ray (2003). H.M. Bark Endeavour: her place in history, p.206.

143. New South Wales State Archives: NRS 13859, SA Map 5946.

144. Geographical Names Board of New South Wales. Register extract. Retrieved online.

145. Threlkeld, L. E. (1834). An Australian grammar: comprehending the principles and natural rules of the language as spoken by the Aborigines in the vicinity of Hunters River, Lake Macquarie etc., New South Wales. Sydney: Stephens and Stokes, p.82. Retrieved online from University of Newcastle. Also Maynard, John.ed. (2004). Awabakal Word Finder: an Aboriginal dictionary and dreaming stories companion. Southport, Qld: Keeaira Press, p.12.

146. McCarthy, F.D. (1952). NSW Aboriginal place names and euphonious words with their meanings, p.7.

147. Troy, Jakelin (1994). The Sydney Language, p.46.

148. Mathews, R.H. (1904). Language of the Kurnu people of New South Wales in Thomas, Martin (Ed.) (2007). Culture in translation: the anthropological legacy of R.H. Mathews. [Canberra, ACT]: ANU E Press and Aboriginal History Incorporated, p.184.

149. Warburton, Robyn (2013). People, place and 'progress', p.33.

150. Warburton, Robyn (2013.) People, place and 'progress', p.41.

151. Reed, A.W. (1965) Aboriginal words of Australia. Sydney: Reed New Holland, p.66. Parker, K. Langloh (1905). Euahlay Tribe. Glossary. Retrieved online 2016.

152. Bennett, F. C. (Ed.) (1968). The Story of the Aboriginal people of the Central Coast of NSW, p.17.

153. Two minute postcards: Charles D'Arcy Roberts: the story of a lost soldier' at www.twominutepostcards.com/2017/.../charles-darcy-roberts-the-story-of-a-lost-soldier. & https://www.youtube.com/watch?v=4CyN8n-GL-G4.

154. The Bouddi Peninsula (2010). [CD-ROM]. Ch.68,

# [ References

Marie Byles.

155. Byles, Marie B, Bouddi Natural Park. The Sydney Bushwalker, April 1971, p.13.

156. Geographical Names Board of NSW. Register Extract. Retrieved online.

157. Australian Aboriginal words. Grandpa Pencil online website, 2020.

158. Australian Government, Bureau of Meteorology, Indigenous Weather Knowledge. Retrieved online 2016.

159. Troy, Jakelin (1994). The Sydney Language, p.46, p.53, p.59. Baylis, James (1914). Aboriginal names and their meanings. Mitchell Library SS1256, accessed online at State Library of New South Wales. Karskens, Grace (2009). The Colony: a History of early Sydney. Crows Nest, NSW: Allen & Unwin, p.531, p.40.

160. *Gosford Times and Wyong District Advocate*, 21 November, 1939, p.2.

161. Correspondence from Central Coast Council to Beverley Runcie, 4 June, 2021. Correspondence from Helen Monks to Beverley Runcie, 18 April, 2017.

# CHAPTER 5 - LISTING OF PLACE & STREET NAMES C-P

162. Parkin, Ray (2003). H.M. Bark Endeavour: her place in history, p.206

163. Collier, Barry (2000). Discovering the Central Coast. Annandale, NSW: Envirobook, p.70. Fairley, Alan (1976). A Field guide to the Sydney bushland. Sydney: Rigby, p.220.

164. New South Wales State Archives: NRS 13859, Map 5946.

165. Geographical Names Board of NSW. Register Extract. Retrieved online.

166. Flemming, Claude (1936). [Film] Woy Woy: The Venice of Australia. https://www.youtube.com/watch?v=pwtc4poBDjo.

167. Warburton, Robyn (2021). More than bricks and mortar.

168. Warburton, Robyn (2013). People, place and 'progress', p38, p.41, p.55.

169. Geographical Names Board of NSW. Register extracts. Retrieved online.

170. The Bouddi Peninsula (2010). [CD-ROM]. Ch.9. The Early Settlers and their Land. P.9.

171. Sydney Herald, 23 July 1832, p.2.

172. The Maitland Mercury and Hunter River General Advertiser, 17 September, 1887, p.4.

173. Correspondence by email from Gwen Dundon to Beverley Runcie, 1 September, 2020.

174. Daleys Point Estate, Woy Woy. Central Coast Council Library. Rare Books Collection, Gosford.

175. Erina Shire Development League (1928). Erina Shire holiday and touring guide, p.103.

176. Parliament of New South Wales >Members. Retrieved online 2019. The Sydney Morning Herald, 17 July 1944, p.8.

177. Evening News, 28 February 1903, p.6.

178. Geographical Names Board of NSW. Register extracts. Retrieved online.

179. Byles, Marie B. Bouddi National Park. NPA Bulletin, NPA of the ACT, September 1979, vol.17, no.1, p.10.

180. The Bouddi Peninsula (2010). [CD-ROM]. Ch.25, Bouddi National Park, p.2. The Gosford Times, 12 November 1962, p.1.

181. Government Gazette of NSW, no.4, 10 January 1964, p.72.

182. The Bouddi Peninsula (2010). [CD-ROM]. Ch.14, Transport and communication, p.9.

183. Warburton, Robyn (2013). People, place and 'progress', pp.71-73, pp.108-111, p.193, p.215. Warburton, Robyn (2014). Bouddi bites in words and images, pp.28-29.

184. The Bouddi Peninsula (2010). [CD-ROM]. Ch.96, Gwen Perrie's Story by her daughter Alexandra Perrie.

185. *Talking Turkey, No.163*, September 2016, p.1.

186. Parkin, Ray (2003). H.M. Bark Endeavour: her place in history. P.206.

187. New South Wales State Archives: NRS 13859, SA Map 5946.

188. Geographical Names Board of NSW. Register extract. Retrieved online.

189. *Maitland Mercury and Hunter River General Advertiser*, 17 September 1887, p.4.

190. Daleys Point Estate, Woy Woy. Central Coast Council Library. Rare Books Collection, Gosford.

191. Geographical Names Board of NSW. Register extract. Retrieved online.

192. Warburton, Robyn (2013). People, place and 'progress', p.244.

193. *Government Gazette of NSW*, No.122, 17 August 1921, p.4846. The Bouddi Peninsula (2010). [CD-ROM]. Ch.26, Fletchers Glen, p.1.

194. *The Sydney Morning Herald*, 28 December 1936, p.5. The Gosford Times, 24 July 1935, Supplement p.2, 30 December, 1936, p.11.

195. The Bouddi Peninsula (2010). [CD-ROM]. Ch.90, Pamela Mainsbridge, p.3.

196. The Bouddi Peninsula (2010). [CD-ROM]. Ch.93, Bert and Jean Myer, p.1.

197. Baxter, Jill, (Comp.) (2000). Reflections from the beach and the bays: stories told by the Killcare, Hardys Bay, Pretty Beach and Wagstaffe community. Killcare: Hardys Bay, Killcare Progress Association, p.54.

198. *Government Gazette of NSW*, No.77, 19 June 1970, p.2485.

199. Correspondence by email from Vicki Elliott, Ranger

Central Coast Area, National Parks and Wildlife Service to Beverley Runcie, 27 August 2020.

200. *The Sun (Sydney)*, 12 October 1928, p.2.

201. The Bouddi Peninsula (2010). [CD-ROM]. Ch.78, The stories of James Burns Fraser (1878-1963 and his son James Wilson Fraser (1907-2008).

202. New South Wales State Archives: NRS 13859, SA Map 5946.

203. Bennett, F.C. (Ed.) (1968). The Story of the Aboriginal people of the Central Coast of NSW, P.17.

204. Troy, Jakelin (1994). The Sydney Language, P.64.

205. Steele, Jeremy. Communication with Beverley Runcie, 27 October, 2019.

206. Geographical Names Board of NSW. Register extract. Retrieved online.

207. *The Gosford Times and Wyong District Advocate*, 30 July 1954, p.3.

208. The Bouddi Peninsula (2010). [CD-ROM]. Ch.78, The stories of James Burns Fraser (1878-1963) and his son, James Wilson Fraser (1907-2008), p.7.

209. The Bouddi Peninsula (2010). [CD-ROM]. Ch.77. The Ford family of Killcare, p.4.

210. The Bouddi Peninsula (2010). [CD-ROM]. Ch.91, The Martinsyde story.

211. Warburton Robyn (2014). Bouddi bites in words and images, p.54.

212. Gosford (N.S.W.) Council. (1964). Shire of Gosford [cartographic material]: K14: Umina Wagstaff. Gosford Shire Council.

213. Baxter, Jill (2000). Reflections from the beach and bays, p.11, p.32. The Bouddi Peninsula (2010). [CD-ROM]. Ch.12, Marine activities, p.18.

214. *Sydney Mail and NSW Advertiser*, 7 October 1876, p.462.

215. *The Sydney Morning Herald,* 30 December 1885, p.10. The Maitland Mercury & Hunter River General Advertiser, 14 January 1886, p.4.

216. *The Gosford Times and Wyong District Advocate*, 4 May 1922, p.16, 6 July 1922, p.9.

217. The Bouddi Peninsula (2010). [CD-ROM]. Ch.11, Shipping and shipwrecks, p.4.

218. Bay News, Hardys Bay Residents Group. April 2014, p.5.

219. NSW. National Parks & Wildlife Service. Bouddi National Park, Plan of Management, 2020, p15. Accessed online. Talking Turkey, No.220, November 2021, p.2.

220. Geographical Names Board of NSW. Register extract. Retrieved online.

221. The Bouddi Peninsula (2010). [CD-ROM]. Ch.9, Early European settlers and their land, p.19.

222. *The Maitland Mercury & Hunter River General Advertiser*, 13 February 1868, p.4.

223. The Maitland Mercury & Hunter River General Advertiser, 9 August 1879, p.12.

224. The Bouddi Peninsula (2010). [CD-ROM]. Ch.9, Early European settlers and their land, p.14.

225. Swancott, C. (1961). The Brisbane Water story, Part 3, Enchanted waters, p.148.

226. *Sun*, 12 May 1912, p.23.

227. Daily Telegraph, 13 March 1915, p.4. The Bouddi Peninsula (2010). [CD-ROM]. Ch.61, Don Anderson, pp.7-8.

228. *Sun,* 2 November 1919, p.3.

229. Geographical Names Board of NSW. Guidelines for the determination of placenames. Fact sheet. Retrieved online.

230. Geographical Names Board of NSW. Register extract. Retrieved online.

231. The Bouddi Peninsula (2010). [CD-ROM]. Ch.115, The Woulfes of Killcare, p.1.

232. Warburton, Robyn (2013). People, place and 'progress', p.200.

233. Conversation between Penelope, Timothy and Jeremy Tyrrell and Beverley Runcie, 30 August, 2017.

234. Parkin, Ray (2003). H.M. Bark Endeavour, p.213. Placenames Australia, March 2014, p.11.

235. Powell, John P. (1994). Placenames of the Greater Hawkesbury region. Berowra Heights, NSW: Hawkesbury River Enterprises, p.55.

236. Bradley, William. A Voyage to NSW: 1786-1792. Chart No.8, Broken Bay. *Sydney Gazette & NSW Advertiser,* 26 March 1809, p.2, 2 April 1809, p.1.

237. Sparks, Jervis (1992). Tales from Barrenjoey. Palm Beach, NSW: J Sparks, front endpaper.

238. *Gosford Times and Wyong District Advocate*, 3 January 1929, p.10.

239. Geographical Names Board of NSW. Register extract. Retrieved online.

240. *Gosford Times and Wyong District Advocate,* 22 March 1928, p.6.

241. Gosford City Council (1991). Wetland management study: Brisbane Water area. Gosford, NSW: Gosford City Council, p.16.

242. *Peninsula News*, 9 December 2019, p.6.

243. *Government Gazette of NSW,* No.77, 19 June 1970, p.2485.

244. Powell, John P. (1994). Placenames of the Greater Hawkesbury region, p.55.

245. Collins, David (1798). An account of the English colony in New South Wales, vol.1. Edited by Brian H Fletcher. Sydney: A.H. & A.W. Reed in association with The Royal Australian Historical Society, 1975, p.357.

246. Smith, Jim (2009). New insights into Gundungurra place naming, p.87-114 in Aboriginal placenames: naming and re-naming the Australian landscape, edited by Harold Koch and Luise Hercus. Canberra, ACT: ANU E press, p.102. Grace Karskens (2020). People of the River: Lost worlds of early Australia. Crows Nest, NSW: Allen & Unwin, p.45.

# [ *References*

247. Collins, David (1798). An account of the English colony in NSW, vol.1, p.59.

248. Boon, Paul I (2017). The Hawkesbury River: a Social and Natural History. Clayton South, Vic: CSIRO, p.3, Ch.9 European Discovery and Early Exploration.

249. McGarvie, John. Rev. John McGarvie papers, 1825-1847. http://archival.sl.nsw.gov/Details/archive/110364940 Hawkesbury word list starts on last page of row 11. Digital copy.Grace Karskens, Exploring Dyarubbin. https://www.sl.nsw.gov.au/collection-items/hawkesbury-river-wordlist

250. Geographical Names Board of NSW. Register extract. Retrieved online.

251. Baxter, Jill (2000). Reflections from the beach and bays, p.53.

252. *Government Gazette of NSW,* No.77, 19 June 1970, p.2485.

253. Bouddi Peninsula (2010). [CD-ROM]. Ch.9, Early European settlers and their land.

254. Warburton, Robyn (2013). People, place and 'progress', pp.71-73, pp.108-111.

255. The Bouddi Peninsula (2010). [CD-ROM]. Ch.15, Commerce and industry, p.27.

256. Pretty Beach Community Preschool. Retrieved online at www.prettybeachpreschool.com.au/history.html

257. Warburton, Robyn (2013). People, place and 'progress', p.41, p.55.

258. *Gosford-Central Coast Star,* 30 August, 1985, p.3.

259. The Bouddi Peninsula (2010). [CD-ROM]. Ch.38, The churches, pp.6-7.

260. Holy Cross Catholic Parish, Kincumber. Email to Beverley Runcie, 23 January 2020.

261. Pretty Beach Community Preschool. Retrieved online.

262. *The Gosford Times and Wyong District Advocate.* 18 August 1921, p.4.

263. Geographical Names Board of NSW. Register extract. Retrieved online.

264. Royal Australian Air Force, World War II Nominal Roll. www.ww2roll.gov.au/. The Sydney Morning Herald, 29 May1946, p.22.

265. National Archives of Australia: B883, NX188. https://recordsearch.naa.gov.au/SearchNRetrieve/Interface/ Walter Astley Tyrrell.

266. Conversation with Penelope, Timothy and Jeremy Tyrrell and Beverley Runcie, 30 August, 2017.

267. *The Sydney Morning Herald,* 29 September, 1914, p.3.

268. *The Sunday Times*, 18 October 1914, p.14.

269. The Bouddi Peninsula (2010). [CD-ROM]. Ch.9, Early European settlers and their land, p.41.

270. Dundon, Gwen (2010). A history of ferries on the Central Coast of NSW: Gosford and Wyong areas. Berowra Heights, NSW: Deerubbin Press, p.70.

271. *Government Gazette of NSW*, No.122, 17 November, 1972, p.4603.

272. Geographical Names Board of NSW. Register extract. Retrieved online.

273. Geographical Names Board of NSW. Register extract. Retrieved online.

274. The Bouddi Peninsula (2010). [CD-ROM]. Ch.21, Sand mining.

275. *Peninsula News*, 12 February 2018, p.21.

276. *Daily Telegraph*, 23 October 1928, p.19.

277. *Sun*, 28 November 1928, p.2.

278. *Sydney Morning Herald*, 8 September 1948, p.10.

279. Geographical Names Board of NSW. Register extract. Retrieved online.

280. Geographical Names Board of NSW. Register extract. Retrieved online.

281. *Government Gazette of NSW*, No.77, 19 June 1970, p.2485.

282. Baxter, Jill (2000). Reflections from the beach and bays, p.28.

283. The Bouddi Peninsula (2010). [CD-ROM]. Ch.10, Real Estate, p.8.

284. The Bouddi Peninsula (2010). [CD-ROM]. Ch.15, Commerce and industry, p.52.

285. New South Wales State Archives: NRS 13859, SA Map 5946.

286. Bennett, F. C. (1968). The Story of the Aboriginal people of the Central Coast of NSW, p.18.

287. Troy, Jakelin (1994). The Sydney language, p.44, p.46, p.62.

288. Steele, Jeremy. Communication with Beverley Runcie, 27 October, 2019.

289. The Geographical Names Board of NSW. Register extract. Retrieved online.

290. The Bouddi Peninsula (2010). [CD-ROM]. Ch.9. Early European settlers and their land, p.27.

291. New South Wales State Archives: NRS 907, [2/7934] Reel 1166, 29/10/1841

292. New South Wales State Archives: NRS 13660, Probate Packets Series 1, 3003, 3004.

293. Communication between Beverley Runcie and Linda Newhouse. Messenger, 4 February 2020.

294. New South Wales State Archives: NRS 13859, SA Map 5946.

295. Strom, Beryl (1985). MacMasters Beach, pp.33-34.

296. *The Sydney Bush Walker Annual*, November 1935, p.36.

297. The Geographical Names Board of NSW. Register extract. Retrieved online.

298. The Geographical Names Board of NSW. Register extract. Retrieved online.

399. *The Sydney Morning Herald*, 13 February 1940, p.12.

*References*

300. The Geographical Names Board of NSW. Register extract. Retrieved online.

301. *The Australian,* 20 December 1826, p.4.

302. Swancott, Charles [1970?]. Good old Woy Woy. [Woy Woy, NSW: The Author], p62.

304. *Gosford Times and Wyong District Advocate,* 19 January 1922, p.7.

304. The Bouddi Peninsula (2010). [CD-ROM]. Ch.27, Lobster Beach, p.17.

305. The Bouddi Peninsula (2010). [CD-ROM]. Ch.8, Site of colonists' first landing: Lobster Beach. Alan M Dash (1990). Phillip's exploration of the Hawkesbury River in Jocelyn Powell, Lorraine Banks eds. Hawkesbury River History: Governor Phillip, Exploration and early settlement. Wisemans Ferry, NSW: Dharug and Lower Hawkesbury Historical Society, pp.13-14.

306. *The Maitland Mercury & Hunter River General Advertiser,* 17 September 1887, p.4.

307. *Gosford Times and Wyong District Advocate,* 14 May 1915, p.7.

308. The Bouddi Peninsula (2010). [CD-ROM]. Ch.27, Lobster Beach.

309. The Geographical Names Board of NSW. Register extract. Retrieved online.

310. *Gosford Times and Wyong District Advocate,* 19 March 1915, p.3.

311. *Gosford Star,* 25 September 1985, p.19.

312. Anderson, Graeme (2020). Correspondence between Beverley Runcie and Graeme Anderson, April 2020.

313. Riley, Marie (2004). MacMasters Beach: where waves pound like a heart beating and friendship abounds. [MacMasters Beach, N.S.W.]: Marie Riley, p.7.

314. Strom, Beryl (1985). MacMasters Beach, pp.6-12. Geographical Names Board of NSW. Register extract. Retrieved online.

315. Byles Marie B. (1971). Bouddi Natural Park in *The Sydney Bushwalker*, April, p.11.

316. Potter, Geoffrey on behalf of Gosford City Council (2012). Wreck of the Maitland: a scene to make the angels weep. Gosford, NSW: Gosford City Council.

317. The Bouddi Peninsula (2010). [CD-ROM]. Ch.17. Maitland Bay Information Centre, p.5.

318. Geographical Names Board of NSW. Register extract, Retrieved online.

319. The Bouddi Peninsula (2010). [CD-ROM]. Ch.25, Bouddi National Park, Ch.28, Maitland Bay.

320. The Bouddi Peninsula (2010). [CD-ROM]. Ch.15, Commerce and industry, p65-66, Ch.30, The Triangle, pp.8-9.

321. Potter, Geoffrey (2012). Wreck of the Maitland, p.122-124.

322. The Bouddi Peninsula (2010). [CD-ROM]. Ch.17, Maitland Bay Centre.

323. *Gosford Times and Wyong District Advocate,* 22 March 1928, p.6.

324. Byles, Marie B (1971). Bouddi Natural Park. *The Sydney Bushwalker*, April, p.10.

325. *NPA Bulletin* (1979). National Parks Association of the ACT Inc, vol.17, no1, September, p.8.

326. The Bouddi Peninsula (2010). [CD-ROM]. Ch.68, Marie Byles. McLeod, Anne (2016). The Summit of her ambition. [Katoomba, New South Wales]: Anne McLeod.

327. Warburton, Robyn (2014). Bouddi Bites, p.2.

328. The Bouddi Peninsula (2010). [CD-ROM]. Ch.79, The Frasers of Killcare Road.

329. Warburton, Robyn (2013). People, place & 'progress', p.189.

330. Crawley, Rhys (2014) Protecting the identity of ASIO agents: the case of Mercia Masson in David Murray Horner, The Spy catchers: The official history of ASIO, 1949-1963. Crows Nest, NSW, Allen and Unwin, pp.563-580.

331. Gosford City Council (2009). Minutes of meeting 3 November 2009, Naming of unnamed laneway, Killcare (IR 6463599).

332. Strom, Beryl (1986). Bouddi Peninsula Study 'Coastwatch'.

333. New South Wales State Archives: NRS 13859, SA Map 5946.

334. Bennett, F. C. (1968). The Story of the Aboriginal people of the Central Coast, p.18.

335. Parkin, Ray (2003). H.M. Bark Endeavour, p.206.

336. Geographical Names Board of NSW. Register extract. Retrieved online.

337. The Bouddi Peninsula (2010). [CD-ROM]. Ch.26, Fletchers Glen, p.3.

338. Webb, McKeowan & Associates Pty Ltd, Mudflat Creek Floodplain Risk Management Plan for Gosford City Council. Sydney, 2008.

339. *Bay News*. Hardys Bay Residents Group, April 2014, p.1, June 2015, p.6.

340. The Bouddi Peninsula (2010). [CD-ROM]. Ch.9, Early European settlers and their land, pp.26-29.

341. The Bouddi Peninsula (2010). [CD-ROM]. Ch.15, Commerce and transport, pp.14, 16-17. Warburton, Robyn (2021). Bouddi houses and people: More than bricks and mortar. Sydney: The author, p.44.

342. Warburton, Robyn (2013). People, place and 'progress', p.24, p.55.

343. *Government Gazette of NSW*, No.10, 20 January 1978, p.241.

344. *Bay News*. Hardys Bay Residents Group, June 2015, p.6.

345. Endacott, Sydney J. (1955). Australian Aboriginal words and place names, p.44.

346. Baxter, Jill (2000). Reflections from the beach and bays, p.52.

347. *Government Gazette of NSW*. No.77, 19 June 1970, p.2485.

# References

348. Endacott, Sydney J. (1955). Australian Aboriginal words and place names, p.45.

349. *Government Gazette of NSW*, No.77, 19 June 1970, p.2485.

350. Endacott, Sydney J. (1955). Australian Aboriginal words and place names, p.46.

351. *Government Gazette of NSW*, No.77, 19 June 1970, p.2485.

352. Endacott, Sydney J. (1955). Australian Aboriginal words and place names, p.46.

353. *Government Gazette of NSW*, No.77, 19 June 1970, p.2485.

354. Correspondence from Bert Myer to Beverley Runcie, 19 September 2010.

355. *Gosford Times & Wyong District Advocate*, 22 Oct 1915, p.12.

356. Conversation between Penelope, Jeremy and Timothy Tyrrell and Beverley Runcie, 30 August 2017.

357. White, Ernest Keith. Papers 1914-1980 [Manuscript]. National Library of Australia, MS 6455/9. Australian Dictionary of Biography (2012). Sir Ernest Keith White. Retrieved online. http://adb.anu.edu.au/biography/white--sir-ernest-keith-15803.

358. *The Sydney Morning Herald*, 5 March 1910, p.24.

359. Baxter, Jill (2000). Reflections from the beach and bays, p.17.

360. Troy, Jakelin (1994). The Sydney language, p.62.

361. Baxter, Jill (2000). Reflections from the beach and bays, p.16.

362. *The Sydney Morning Herald*, 28 March 1910, pp.2, 9.

363. *Sun*, 20 September 1912, p.12.

364. The Bouddi Peninsula (2010). [CD-ROM]. Ch.9, Early European settlers and their land, p.22.

365. The Bouddi Peninsula (2010).

366. Pratt, Eileen (1978). Placenames of the Central Coast, p.43.

367. Geographical Names Board of NSW. Register extract. Retrieved online.

368. The Bouddi Peninsula (2010). [CD-ROM]. Ch.15, Commerce and industry, p.19.

369. *Government Gazette of NSW*, No.44, 12 April 1957, p.1253. Central Coast Express, 6 March, 1957, p.6.

370. The Bouddi Peninsula [CD-ROM]. Ch.14, Transport and communication, p.11.

371. *Gosford Times & Wyong District Advocate*, 11 October 1934, p.16 & 29 November 1934, p.10.

372. *Gosford Times & Wyong District Advocate*, 16 May 1935, p.15.

373. Warburton, Robyn (2013). People, place & 'progress', p.45, p.126.

374. The Bouddi Peninsula (2010). [CD-ROM]. Ch. 15, Commerce and industry, pp.21-25.

375. The Bouddi Peninsula (2010). [CD-ROM]. Ch.15, Commerce and industry, p.27.

376. *Gosford Times & Wyong District Advocate*, 16 December 1926, p.2. The Bouddi Peninsula (2010). [CD-ROM]. Ch.18, Pretty Beach School, p.7. Erina Shire holiday and touring guide (1928), p.130. Warburton, Robyn (2014). Bouddi bites, pp.140-141.

377. Geographical Names Board of NSW. Register extract. Retrieved online.

378. Gems of coastal scenery revealed by the new scenic highway in the Shire of Erina, near Gosford, N.S.W., Australia: with illustrations, descriptive and historical data. [c1938], p.14. Available at Central Coast Library Gosford and online at issuu.

379. Baxter, Jill (2000). Reflections from the beach and bays, p.53.

380. Macqueen, Andy (2004). Somewhat perilous: the journeys of Singleton, Parr, Howe, Myles & Blaxland in the Northern Blue Mountains. Wentworth Falls, NSW: Andy Macqueen, p.162, p.20, p.130.

381. Prineas, Peter & Henry Gold (1997). Wild places: wilderness in Eastern New South Wales. 2nd ed. Sydney: The Colong Foundation for Wilderness, p.155-156.

382. Bigge, J.T. (1823) Report of the Commissioner of Inquiry on the State of Agriculture and Trade in the Colony of New South Wales, Report of State of Agriculture, and Regulations for granting Lands in New South Wales and Van Diemen's Land. No page numbers give. Accessed online Project Gutenberg Australia. MacLeod Morgan, H.A. (1958) The Bulga or Coal River: Australia's first North Road in *Royal Australian Historical Society Journal and Proceedings*, Vol.44, Part 4, p.188, p.200.

383. Putty Valley Online. http://putty.nsw.au/visitor-information

384. Kevin Duncan in personal correspondence with Beverley Runcie, 18 September 2020.

385. Macqueen, Andy (2004). Somewhat perilous, p.18.

386. Aboriginal names and words. Retrieved online at www.lowchensaustralia.com/names.htm

387. Jeremy Steele in personal correspondence with Beverley Runcie, 27 October 2019.

388. The Bouddi Peninsula (2010). [CD-ROM]. Ch.112, Marjorie Whiting, p.4.

389. *Gosford Times & Wyong District Advocate*, 20 November 1924, p.15.

390. *The Sydney Morning Herald*, 8 June 1850, p.4.

391. Baxter, Jill (2000). Reflections from the beach and bays, p.52. The Bouddi Peninsula (2010) [CD-ROM], Ch.13, Fishing. Ch.15, Commerce and industry, p.37.

392. The Bouddi Peninsula (2010). [CD-ROM]. Ch.21, Sand mining.

393. Warburton, Robyn (2014). Bouddi bites, pp.68-69.

394. Warburton, Robyn (2013). People, place & 'progress', p.215.

395. *Government Gazette of NSW*, No.77, 19 June 1970, p.2485.

396. Warburton, Robyn (2014). Bouddi Bites, p.69.

397. Argus (Melb.), 4 December 1956, p.11, 12 December 1956, p.14.

398. Warburton, Robyn (2013). People, place & 'progress', p.34.

399. The Bouddi Peninsula (2010). [CD-ROM] Ch.21, Sand mining. Ch.15, Commerce and industry, p.63.

400. *Coast Community News*, 11 December 2020, p.9. Correspondence from Kathryn Heinz, Central Coast Council to Beverley Runcie, 8 March 2022.

401. The Killcare Wagstaffe Trust website www.killcarewagstaffetrust.org.au and Community Environment Network, Friends of COSS website www.cen.org.au.

# CHAPTER 6 - LISTING OF PLACE & STREET NAMES R-Z

402. *The Maitland Mercury & Hunter River Genera Advertiser*, 17 September, 1887, p.4.

403. The Bouddi Peninsula (2010). [CD-ROM]. Ch.9, Early European settlers and their land, p.33-34. Ch.29, Rileys Bay.

404. The Bouddi Peninsula (2010). [CD-ROM]. Ch.15, Commerce and industry, p3, Ch.29, Rileys Bay.

405. Geographical Names Board of NSW. Register extract. Retrieved online.

406. *The Sydney Morning Herald*, 4 April 1900, p.2. Swancott, Charles (1966). Gosford and the Henry Kendall Country: Koolewong to Lisarow. Woy Woy, NSW: C. Swancott, p.VIII.

407. Bradley, William (1788). A Voyage to New South Wales, p.89.

408. Geographical Names Board of NSW. Register extract. Retrieved online.

409. Warburton, Robyn (2013). People, place and 'progresses, p.25 & The Bouddi Peninsula (2010). [CD-ROM]. Ch.14, Transport and communication, pp.19-20.

410. *Central Coast Friday Star*, 15 June 1984, p.6 &7.

411. Public Works Department of NSW (1990). Brisbane Water entrance improvement options, Patterson Britton & Partners Pty Ltd.

412. *Sydney Morning Herald*, 8 January 1908, p.15.

413. The Bouddi Peninsula (2010). [CD-ROM]. Ch.9, Early European Settlers and their Land, pp.35-37.

414. Geographical Names Board of NSW. Register extract. Retrieved online.

415. The Bouddi Peninsula (2010). [CD-ROM]. Ch.97, The Radfords of Wagstaffe Point.

416. Strom, Beryl (1986). Bouddi Peninsula study: coastwatch, p.13.

417. *Gosford Times & Wyong District Advocate*, 11 February 1926, p.15.

418. *Gosford Times & Wyong District Advocate*, 22 March 1928, p.6. Beryl Strom (1985). MacMasters Beach, p.34.

419. *Gosford Times & Wyong District Advocate*, 25 February 1926, p.6.

420. *Gosford Times & Wyong District Advocate*, 18 November 1926, p.14.

421. *Gosford Times & Wyong District Advocate*, 2 December 1926, p.8.

422. *Gosford Times and Wyong District Advocate*, 2 December 1926, p.8.

423. *The Sydney Morning Herald*, 22 November 1932, p.5.

424. *Gosford Times & Wyong District Advocate*, 3 August 1933, p.6.

425. *Gosford Times & Wyong District Advocate*, 2 July 1954, p.5. Beryl Strom (1985). MacMasters Beach, p.34.

426. The Bouddi Peninsula (2010). [CD-ROM]. Ch.14, Transport and communication, p.17.

427. New South Wales. National Parks and Wildlife Service (1985). Bouddi National Park: plan of management, p.22.

428. The Bouddi Peninsula (2010) [CD-ROM]. Ch.14, Transport and communication, p.15. & Strom, Beryl (1986). Bouddi Peninsula study, p.16.

429. New South Wales State Archives: NRS 13859, SA Map 5946.

430. Parkin, Ray (2003). H.M. Bark Endeavour, p.206.

431. Geographical Names Board of NSW. Register extract. Retrieved online.

432. Howard, Frederick (1983). Kingsford Smith, Sir Charles Edward (1897-1935). Australian Dictionary of Biography. Retrieved from http://adb.anu.edu.au/biography/kingsford-smith-sir-charles-edward-6964/text12095.

433. Discussion between Penelope, Jeremy and Timothy Tyrrell and Beverley Runcie. 30 August, 2017.

434. *Daily Commercial News and Shipping List*, 28 January 1935, p.3.

435. Correspondence from Vicki Elliott, NPWS and Beverley Runcie, 7 June 2021.

436. The Bouddi Peninsula (2010). [CD-ROM]. Ch.46, Oskar Speck.

437. Central Coast Express Advocate, 9 October 2002, p.9.

438. Gems of Coastal Scenery (c1938) p.1. Retrieved from https://issuu.com/gosfordcitylibrary/docs/gems-of-coastal-scenery-circa-1938.

439. *Gosford Times and Wyong District Advocate*, 19 August 1937, p.14, 15 September 1938, p.4, 10 January 1939, p.8, 9 March 1939, p.3, 21 March 1939, p.4.

440. Stanley Noble Rickard (1883-1976). Wikipedia online encyclopedia.

441. The Bouddi Peninsula (2010). [CD-ROM]. Ch.39, The Bush Fire Brigade and bushfires. *Gosford Times and Wyong District Advocate*, 23 April 1954, p.7.

442. *Daily Commercial News & Shipping List*, 18 February 1926, p.4.

# References

443. National Parks and Wildlife Service, NSW. Strom Centre (pamphlet) .n.d.

444. *National Parks Journal*, Vol.47, No.1, February 2003. Accessed online.

445. Central Coast Council, Office of the Mayor. Invitation for 5 June 2019.

446. *Peninsula News*, 2 September 2019, p.5.

447. The Bouddi Peninsula (2010). [CD-ROM]. Ch.103, Allen and Beryl Strom. Allan Fox (2016). Chief Guardian: The life and times of Allen Strom. Australian Association for Environmental Education (NSW). Pub. as an eBook.

448. Office of Environment and Heritage, NSW. Shipwrecks – Byron Bay. Retrieved online. www.environment.nsw.gov.au/resources/shipwrecksbyron.

449. Myer, Bert. Correspondence with Beverley Runcie, 19 September 2010.

450. *Gosford Times & Wyong District Advocate*, 20 November 1924, p.15. Gems of coastal scenery, p.14.

451. Loney, J.K. (1976). Wrecks on the N.S.W. North Coast. Portarlington, Vic., Marine History Publications, p.28.

452. Berry, Greig (1994). Shipwrecks of the New South Wales coast. Vol.1, 1800-1899. Tacoma, NSW: Central Coast Shipwreck Research, p.47.

453. Erina Shire Development League (1928). Erina Shire holiday and touring guide. p.136.

454. *Maitland Daily Mercury*, 2 January 1922, p.6.

455. *Gosford Times & Wyong District Advocate*, 23 October 1924, p.16.

456. *Gosford Times & Wyong District Advocate*, 27 November 1924, p.13.

457. Endacott, Sydney J. (1955). Australian Aboriginal words and place names and their meanings, p.50.

458. Webster's online dictionary. Retrieved online.

459. *Government Gazette of NSW*, No.77, 19 June 1970, p.2485.

460. The Bouddi Peninsula (2010). [CD-ROM]. Ch.30, The Triangle. Baxter, Jill (2000). Reflections from the beach and bays, p.46-48. Warburton, Robyn (2014) Bouddi bites in words and images, p.54.

461. *Talking Turkey*, No.196, September 2019, p.2.

462. Parkin Ray (2003). H.M. Bark Endeavour, p.206.

463. ASNSW: SA Item [5946] Mathew, 1831.

464. Geographical Names Board of NSW. Register Extract. Retrieved online.

465. Warburton, Robyn (2013). People, place and 'progress', pp.130-132.

466. Conversation with Fay Gunther, 10 July 2017.

467. The Bouddi Peninsula (2010). [CD-ROM]. Ch.73, Turo Downes. Baxter, Jill (2000). Reflections from the beach and the bays, pp.26-30.

468. *Gosford Times & Wyong District Advocate*, 6 April 1934, p.11.

469. The Bouddi Peninsula (2010). [CD-ROM]. Ch.73, Turo Downes.

470. Correspondence from Elizabeth Pope written in September 1986 and held by Gwen Dundon.

471. Warburton, Robyn (2013). People, place & 'progress', pp.68-70.

472. The Bouddi Peninsula (2010). [CD-ROM]. Ch.43, Other groups by bay and sea, p.20.

473. Geographical Names Board of NSW. Register extract. Retrieved online.

474. Warburton, Robyn (2013). People, place & 'progress', p.238.

475. *Coast Community News*, 14 February, 2022.

476. *Newcastle Sun*, 6 May 1936, p.9. Fleming, George (1936). [Film]. Woy Woy: The Venice of Australia. https://www.youtube.com/watch?v=pwtc4poBDjo.

477. Larwood, Jacob and John Camden Hotten (1875). The History of signboards: from the earliest times to the present day. 8th ed. London, Chatto & Windus, 1875, p.10. Retrieved online.

478. The Bouddi Peninsula (2010). [CD-ROM]. Ch.15, Commerce and industry, pp.19,26,28. Ch.19, The Great Depression.

479. Warburton, Robyn (2013). People, place & 'progress', p.38, p.41, 55.

480. The Bouddi Peninsula (2010) [CD-ROM]. Ch.108, George Wagstaffe.

481. *Gosford Times and Wyong District Advocate*, 9 March 1939, p.3, 21 March 1939, p.4.

482. Warburton, Robyn (2013). People, place and 'progress', p.11,21,24,25, 39.

483. The Bouddi Peninsula (2010). [CD-ROM]. Ch.108, George Wagstaffe, p.5. Warburton, Robyn (2013). People, place & 'progress', p.114.

484. Geographical Names Board of NSW. Register extract. Retrieved online.

485. The Bouddi Peninsula (2010). [CD-ROM]. Ch.15, Commerce and industry, pp. 26,28,11,15,18-19. Ch.38, The Churches, pp.1-5.

486. The Bouddi Peninsula (2010). [CD-ROM]. Ch.14, Transport and communication, p.4. Warburton, Robyn (2013). People, place and 'progress', p.191.

487. Berry, Greig (1994). Shipwrecks of the New South Central Coast, Volume 1, 1800-1899. Tacoma, NSW, Central Coast Shipwreck Research, pp.22, 47, 66, 67, 72, 78.

488. New South Wales Transport. nsw.gov.au/topics/using waterways/restrictions-and-closures/marine-notices/sy1816-little-box-head-to-lobster-beach-brisbane-water. Retrieved online

489. Geographical Names Board of NSW. Register extract. Retrieved online.

490. State Archives NSW: NRS683 Census 1891 Collectors' Notebooks, [2/8407], Gosford 25/E, Reel 2516, p.7. Copy also available online at Ancestry.com.au.

491. Dundon, Gwen (2010). A History of ferries on the

Central Coast of NSW, pp.87-89.

492. *The Sydney Morning Herald*, 8 October 1887, p.9.

493. *Gosford Times and Wyong District Advocate*, 13 October 1911, p.4.

494. *Daily Telegraph (Sydney)*, 1 November, 1913, p.17.

495. *Sydney Morning Herald*, 31 October 1913, p.13, 26 November 1913, p.14.

496. *Gosford Times and Wyong District Advocate*, 4 May 1922, p.16, 6 July 1922, p.9.

497. The Bouddi Peninsula (2010). [CD-ROM]. Ch.18, Pretty Beach School. Warburton, Robyn (2013), People, place &'progress', p.1.

498. New South Wales Public Works Department (1990). Brisbane Water entrance improvement options prepared by Patterson Britton & Partners Pty Ltd, consulting engineers. Retrieved online.

499. Gosford City Council and Department of Environment & Climate Change. Brisbane Water Estuary Processes Study, March 2008, p.34. Retrieved online.

500. *Peninsula News*, 13 July 2009, p.3.

501. *Peninsula News*, 20 February 2017, p.3.

502. *Peninsula News*, 3 April 2017, p.3, 21 August 2017, p.6.

503. *Peninsula News*, 24 September 2018, p.11.

504. *Talking Turkey*, No.187, November 2018, p.2.

505. *Central Coast News*, 3 December 2020, p.4.

506. NSW Dept of Transport, Roads & Maritime Services, Maritime, Maritime Services, Maritime Notices No.SY1816. http://roads.waterways.transport.nsw.gov.au

507. *Coast Community News*, 25 March 2021, p.5.

508. Swancott, C (1961). The Brisbane Water story: enchanted waters, Part 3, p.145.

509. *Maitland Mercury and Hunter River General Advertiser*, 9 August 1879, p.12.

510. *Gosford Times and Wyong District Advocate*, 18 October 1907, p.2.

511. Geographical Names Board of NSW. Register extract. Retrieved online.

512. *Referee*, 1 May 1907, p.6.

513. Warburton, Robyn (2013). People, place and 'progress', p.3.

514. Baxter, Jill comp. (2000). Reflections from the beach and bays, pp.18-19.

515. Dundon, Gwen (2010). A History of ferries on the Central Coast of NSW, p.87.

516. *Gosford Times & Wyong District Advocate*, 23 March 1954, p.2.

517. Warburton, Robyn (2013). People, place and 'progress', pp1-22, 162-171.

518. Warburton, Robyn (2013). People, place and 'progress', p.162, pp.164-171.

519. Baxter, Jill (2000). Reflections from the beach and the bays, pp.42-43.

520. The Bouddi Peninsula (2010). [CD-ROM]. Ch.15, Commerce and industry, p.15.

521. Warburton, Robyn (2014). Bouddi bites in words and images, pp.26-27.

522. Warburton, Robyn (2014). Bouddi bites in words and images, p.146.

523. *Coast Community News*, 10 July 2020, p.37.

524. Erina Shire Holiday and Touring Guide: Woy Woy, Gosford, Wyong [1928], p.136.

525. *Gosford Times & Wyong District Advocate*, 1 December 1927, p.1, 6.

526. The Sydney Morning Herald, 11 February 1868, p.5.

527. The Bouddi Peninsula (2010). [CD-ROM]. Ch.9, Early European settlers and their land, p.18-21.

528. The Bouddi Peninsula (2010). [CD-ROM]. Ch.15, Commerce and industry.

529. Baxter, Jillian (2000). Reflections from the beach and the bays, p.47.

530. *Gosford Times & Wyong District Advocate*, 12 June 1930, p.6, Government Gazette of NSW, No.77, 19 June 1970, p.2485.

531. *Gosford Times & Wyong District Advocate*, 11 October 1934, p.16.

532. The Bouddi Peninsula (2010). [CD-ROM]. Ch.19, The Great Depression, p.2.

533. *Gosford Times & Wyong District Advocate*, 6 April 1934, p.11.

534. Warburton, Robyn (2013). People, place and 'progress', p.189.

535. *Talking Turkey*, No.196, September 2019, p.2.

536. Letter from Beryl Strom to Gladys, 9 April, 1984 in Ward Family, Vertical File, CCL, Beryl Strom Collection.

537. The Bouddi Peninsula (2010). [CD-ROM]. Ch.15, Commerce and industry, p.23.

538. Warburton, Robyn (2013). People, place and 'progress', p.153, 219, 238.

539. Warburton, Robyn (2014). Bouddi bites in words and images, pp.14-15.

# Index

## A

Aboriginal i, iii, 4, 5, 8, 9, 12, 16, 21, 27, 37, 40, 42, 43, 48, 49, 52, 57, 58, 61, 64, 66, 71, 78, 87, 94, 96, 99, 110, 124, 127, 128, 129, 131, 135, 136, 143, 152, 162, 164, 165, 167,
Albert Street  20, 21, 61, 72, 108, 126
Allambie  12, 21
Allambie Road  21
Allen Strom Lookout  22, 23, 75, 145, 156
Anthony Crescent  21, 24, 25, 92, 97, 100, 139, 162, 163
Araluen Drive  26, 27, 28, 29, 33, 70, 78, 79, 82, 88, 93, 120, 127, 128, 142, 182
Arthur Road  27, 30, 31
Awabakal  5, 8, 43, 57, 78, 136

## B

Babs Road  31, 32, 92, 96, 131
Baden Street  31, 32, 92, 96, 131
Bay Road  27, 33, 79
Beach Drive  34, 35, 80, 121, 127, 148
Blythe Street  2, 36, 76, 78, 79
Bogey Hole  12, 34, 35, 36, 37, 38, 39, 94, 96, 129, 136, 157, 161, 165
Bogie  37 see Bogey
Bombi  12, 40, 41
Bombii Moor 40, 41
Bombi Radar Station  41
Bombi Road North  40
Bombi Road South  40, 41
Bombi Point  40, 41
Bombora  12, 42, 47, 113, 117
Bouddi Farm  46, 152
Bouddi Grand Deep  46, 114
Bouddi Lookout  47, 69, 122, 123
Bouddi National Park  2, 8, 21, 22, 39, 40, 43, 44, 46, 48-52, 55, 58, 60, 61, 64, 65, 66, 68, 69, 72, 74, 75, 78, 81, 84, 85, 91, 96, 100, 102, 104, 105, 108, 113, 114, 116, 119, 122-124, 136, 139, 142, 145, 152-155, 158, 160, 162, 163, 181, 183
Box Head  2, 21, 51-53, 55, 72, 84, 85, 87, 91, 111, 102, 104, 105, 118, 150, 155, 181, 198
Brisbane Water  2, 8-10, 22, 33, 36, 41, 46, 48, 54, 55, 67, 72, 81, 87, 94, 99, 102, 104, 105, 125, 132, 135, 142-145, 148, 149, 167, 169, 171-173, 175, 181, 182, 200
Broken Bay  2, 8, 10, 13, 42, 50-52, 54, 55, 60, 64, 72, 84, 87, 96, 109, 117-119, 136, 160, 161
Bulbararing  12, 57, 64, 71, 110, 111
Bulkara Street  5, 12, 21, 57, 81, 147, 148
Bullimah  5, 12, 44
Bullimah Beach  58-60, 78, 139
Bullimah Lookout (Outlook)  58, 60
Bullimah Spur  47, 58, 60
Burran Road  61

## C

Cape Three Points  40, 57, 64, 71, 113, 124, 152, 163
Como Parade  11, 65, 132, 135, 168
Copacabana  57, 64, 71, 110, 201 see also Bulbararing

## D

Dairy  28, 34, 36, 74, 79, 80, 142, 143, 168, 172
Daphnes Camp  68
Darkinjung  5, 8, 43, 61, 136, 202
Deerubin  8 see Hawksbury River
Dharuk  5, 8, 37, 42
Dingeldei Picnic Shelter  47, 69, 122, 123
Dog Track  2, 27, 70, 82, 88, 135, 142

## E

European Settlement  4, 9, 10

## F

First Point  64, 71 see Bulbararing

*Index*

Fish see Fishing

Fishermen see Fishing

Fishing 37, 50, 54, 61, 64, 65, 67, 71, 78, 91, 96, 100, 102, 104, 105, 114, 136, 138, 148, 160, 161, 164, 165, 167, 170, 176, 177

Flannel Flower Track 72, 85, 108

Fletchers Glen Reserve 74, 125, 162, 183

Fletchers Glen Road 75

Flora Avenue 76, 78, 127

Florant 174

Fraser Road 36, 74, 75, 76, 77, 79, 125, 127, 149, 183

## G

Garigal 5, 8

Geographical Names Board 5, 16, 33, 42, 52, 94, 119, 135, 143, 173

Gerrin Point 12, 50, 78, 79, 153

Government Road 29, 33, 76, 78, 79, 127, 183

Grandbeach Lane 80

Grandview Crescent 34, 36, 80

Guringai 5

## H

Half Tide Rocks 9, 81, 105, 106, 172, 175

Hardys Bay Parade 27, 83, 143

Hats Street 20, 83, 130

Hawke Head Drive 21, 52, 72, 84, 85, 108, 155, 161

Hawkesbury River 5, 8, 10, 55, 60, 84, 86, 87, 99, 173

Hawk Head see Hawke Head

Heath Road 26, 27, 30, 31, 70, 82, 88-90, 128, 135, 142, 165, 167

High View Road 65, 88, 90, 108, 168

## I

Indigenous 4, 5, 8, 9, 11, 12, 16, 20, 44, 45, 72, 87, 111, 112

## J

Jacqueline Avenue 92, 96, 97

Joy Street 92

## K

Killcare Heights 2, 24, 31, 32, 36, 46, 51, 75, 83, 92, 96-98, 110, 116-119, 125, 129-131, 148-152, 154, 156, 162, 182, 183, 193, 199

Killcare Road 27-29, 78, 98, 120, 127, 139, 185, 186

Kourung Gourung 4, 12, 99, 126, 131

## L

Linda Street 100, 139

Little Beach 39, 40, 45, 48, 64, 100, 101, 112, 123, 124, 139, 148, 163

Little Box Head 91, 102, 105, 172, 174, 175 see Box Head

Little Tallow 2, 102, 103, 160, 181

Lobster Beach 9, 61, 72, 81, 102, 104-109, 172, 172, 174, 175

Lobster Beach Track 61, 72, 108

## M

Macdonald Street 96, 97, 110

MacMasters Beach 2, 11, 40, 41, 44, 48, 51, 56, 100, 110, 112, 123, 124, 139, 148, 149, 201

Maitland Bay 42, 43, 46, 47, 50, 52, 58, 64, 68, 69, 74, 113-117, 119, 123, 139, 145, 149, 153, 157, 162, 163

Maitland Bay Drive 116, 162, 163

Manly 2, 60, 96, 110, 117, 118, 135, 148, 149, 171

Manly House 11, 20, 172, 173, 177, 179

Manly View Road 18, 97, 117, 118

Marie Byles Lookout 118, 119

Martha Jane Avenue 98, 120, 121

Masson Lane 121

Midden 8, 20, 48, 66, 112, 142, 143

Mourawaring 12, 39, 64, 110, 112, 124, 152

Mt Bouddi 2, 51, 123

Mt Bouddi Lookout 47, 122, 123

Mt Bouddi Road 122, 123

Mud Flat Creek 125, 127

Mulhall's Point 175, 176

Mulhall Street 21, 125, 126, 179 Murrays Bay 142

# Index

## N

Noble Road  27, 36, 76, 79, 83, 125, 127, 129, 182
Nukara Avenue  76, 78, 85, 127, 148

## O

Oroo Street  128, 132, 133, 135
Otella Avenue  28, 128, 129
Owanda Crescent  29, 129

## P

Palm Beach  2, 96, 108, 117-119, 136, 175, 177
Patricia Place  129
Pauline Avenue  96, 118, 130
Pittwater  2, 10, 42, 87, 117
Pretty Beach  2, 11, 21, 30, 31, 51, 65, 70, 90, 93, 108, 126, 128, 131-135, 142, 143, 144, 150, 154, 161, 164, 165, 168, 179, 185, 193, 194
Pretty Beach Road  ii, 65, 70, 128, 132, 133, 135, 142, 168, 185, 186
Pretty Beach School  27, 31, 70, 88, 135, 150, 164
Putty Beach  2, 11, 34, 42, 44, 48, 58, 62, 64, 94, 96, 110, 121, 123, 129, 135-139, 160
Putty Beach Drive  21, 24, 96, 98, 121, 135, 139, 162

## R

Radar Station  41
Rileys Bay  51, 90, 142, 143, 145, 173, 183
Rip Bridge  11, 29, 66, 143, 144, 152, 171, 183
Rock Engraving  6-8, 48, 66, 72

## S

San Toy  20, 57, 140, 146-148
Second Point  110, 124, 152 see Mourawaring
Ship  31, 42, 54
  Argument  42, 52
  Attunga  42
  Brothers 81
  Chicago  31
  Elizabeth Cohen  161
  Florant  174
  General Gordon  86
  Hazard  52
  Heath  42
  Hope  55
  Irene  33, 173
  Island Girl  42
  John  55
  Kilcare Star  94
  Maggie Riley  142
  Palm Beach Ferry  72, 81, 175
  Rebecca  42
  Regent Bird  94
  Rose of Eden  161
  Scud  136
  SS Gosford  173
  SS Maitland  113, 115, 116
  Volunteer  160
Smithy Street  32, 96, 152, 153
Specks Lane  153, 154
Spooners Lookout  150, 155
SS Maitland  113, 115, 116
Stanley Street  27, 29, 36, 76, 78, 79, 129, 155, 156, 183, 185
Stewart Street  125, 156
Strom Centre  158

## T

Tallow Beach  48, 72, 118, 102, 160, 161, 181
Taworri Road  5, 12, 21, 96, 139, 162
The Reserve  27, 36, 142, 167
The Rip  10, 11, 29, 54, 66, 67, 71, 90, 99, 143-145, 152, 165, 171, 176, 183
The Scenic Road  11, 34, 40, 41, 46, 52, 96, 98, 100, 116, 118, 121, 125, 144, 148-153, 155, 171, 183
The Triangle  F116, 162, 163
Third Point  163, 164, 171 see Bombi Point
Tudibaring  57, 71, 110
Turo Reserve  128, 164, 165, 167

## V

Venice Road  11, 65, 108, 128, 132, 168

## W

Wagstaff Bar (The Bar) 33, 105, 172-175
Wagstaffe Avenue  21, 57, 90, 126, 132, 135, 147, 169, 171, 172, 179, 185
Wards Hill Road  11, 22, 66, 74, 75, 79, 116, 125, 129, 144, 145, 152, 153, 156, 162, 163, 182, 183
Wards Wall  29, 183-185

## Y

Yum Yum Tree  2, 186-188

www.ingramcontent.com/pod-product-compliance
Lightning Source LLC
Chambersburg PA
CBHW041710290426
44109CB00028B/2834